Bottoming Out
the Universe

"Richard Grossinger is uniquely qualified to set our feet upon a righteous path—not around the problem, as so many do, but straight into its convoluted tangle. Is consciousness an illusion or a fundamental property of nature? Addressing this question has occupied many minds, and Richard's foray here will engage yours to take you deeper into your own sense of being. If you are a scientist, here you must confront the limitations of science to explain your life. For the spiritualists, Richard's erudition will rub your nose in the hard realities of the physical universe. Puzzle and wonder as you scratch beneath the surface with Richard as your able guide."

THOMAS W. MYERS, AUTHOR OF *ANATOMY TRAINS*

"Richard Grossinger is one of the most articulate spokesmen of our time. He has the unique ability to move adeptly from one field to another, not superficially but deepening our understanding of how these fields interweave. I was especially drawn in by his thoughtful chapter on trauma . . . truly an engaging addition to the field. In his study of energy patterns, complexity, psychic phenomena, and consciousness, Grossinger takes us on an engaging journey. It may not be an easy read, but it is a rich one."

PETER A LEVINE, PH.D., AUTHOR OF *WAKING THE TIGER, HEALING TRAUMA*, AND *IN AN UNSPOKEN VOICE*

"*Bottoming Out the Universe* is an amazing literary task. It will help people who are never going to quiet their minds and see the nature of things to understand 'bottoming out' as best as possible conceptually. What Richard does is about as far as one can go with concept, in my opinion."

PAUL PITCHFORD, DHARMA TEACHER AND AUTHOR OF *HEALING WITH WHOLE FOODS*

"In *Bottoming Out the Universe,* Richard Grossinger puts the proverbial capstone on a life's work of intense inquiry and observation. He's like a Neolithic shaman, and what emerges are numinous gifts cloaked in a magical language. Indeed, this magnum opus is like an epic incantation and not just a recital of data points, random ephemera, and formulaic synthesis. The universe bottoms out, and there is no point of return, only a chthonic journey through memory, fear, doubt, and a hard-earned hope that what awaits on the other side is not just an astral projection of this world, without its governors and filters, but something that's far beyond even Grossinger's skills of syntactic mediumship to transmit. Dig in, put your feet up, and enjoy the ride."

ROBERT PHOENIX, CURATOR OF ASTROLOGY
FOR THE NOW AGE WEBSITE

"*Bottoming Out the Universe* encompasses so many aspects of what it means to explore silence and movement, and how these frequencies vibrate and become a dance. When I enter a room to begin a new work, I enter with ALL the questions implied in this book—they hang in the air! And as I choreograph, the 'physical plane of ambient reality' of which Richard speaks is always there. Reading this book is like making a work of art. You start one place and end up another."

MARGARET JENKINS, FOUNDER AND ARTISTIC DIRECTOR
OF THE MARGARET JENKINS DANCE COMPANY

"Reading Grossinger turns cosmology and science into poetry. He provides the track lighting for a quirky map into the secret corridors of creation that we never dared to explore. The graffiti of the ages is scratched on its walls."

PAUL WEISS, AUTHOR OF *MOONLIGHT LEANING AGAINST
AN OLD RAIL FENCE: APPROACHING THE DHARMA AS POETRY*

"We offer you greetings, Richard Grossinger. We are contacting you because we have observed your efforts over the decades in your capacity as explorer of the arcane. We note that you have spent decades attempting to understand the connection between the spiritual and the physical. Your encyclopedic efforts are exemplary in their thoroughness as well as their breadth and depth. We also note that often you have felt somewhat like a prophet crying in the wilderness. Be assured your writings are noticed. In future years, after your death, your prolific work will find an eager and stimulated readership. Your work has the potential to change lives and will eventually rank among this category of literature."

CHANNELED BY KEITH HILL,
AUTHOR OF *EXPERIMENTAL SPIRITUALITY*

Bottoming Out the Universe

Why There Is Something Rather than Nothing

RICHARD GROSSINGER

Park Street Press
Rochester, Vermont

Park Street Press
One Park Street
Rochester, Vermont 05767
www.ParkStPress.com

Text stock is SFI certified

Park Street Press is a division of Inner Traditions International

Cataloging-in-Publication Data for this title is available from the Library of Congress

ISBN 978-1-62055-989-5 (print)
ISBN 978-1-62055-990-1 (ebook)

Printed and bound in the United States by Lake Book Manufacturing, Inc. The text stock is SFI certified. The Sustainable Forestry Initiative® program promotes sustainable forest management.

10 9 8 7 6 5 4 3 2 1

Text design and layout by Priscilla Baker
This book was typeset in Garamond Premier Pro with Nexa used as a display font

To send correspondence to the author of this book, mail a first-class letter to the author c/o Inner Traditions • Bear & Company, One Park Street, Rochester, VT 05767, and we will forward the communication, or contact the author directly at **www.richardgrossinger.com**.

For Rob Brezsny, Stephanie Lahar,
and Jeffrey Kripal

I am grateful to Inner Traditions editors Kayla Toher and Nancy Yielding for their work. They didn't just do a perfunctory job. They met me where I was and committed themselves to understanding difficult and elusive meanings and showing me what I was missing in my own text. I appreciate the care with which each of them read—from tiny flaws they caught to large unexploited possibilities they recognized. Their thoughtful responses led to a larger and more substantive, responsible book.

* * *

Thanks to Ehud Sperling for not only offering a publishing slot to another publisher but honoring our collaboration as that of two hermetic practitioners at a time when the sacred flame needs to be carried through a thinned world. Ehud and I each received our baptism in the occult from Donald Weiser at his legendary store on lower Broadway, me on visits as a high-school student and Ehud as a lodge member and publishing initiate.

Thanks also to Ehud's wife Vatsala Sperling, who never saw me as a rival publisher, only as a colleague in healing.

I want to add a blessing for our children, that they play key roles in mending the earth: Mahar Sperling, future publisher for the Aquarian Age; Robin Grossinger, my son, environmental biologist working with landscape resilience and preparing cities for climate change; and Miranda July, my daughter, a mixed-media artist and writer who invents worlds where there are none to be seen.

Contents

Foreword

By Brian Thomas Swimme

Richard Grossinger and I were in the middle of lunch at our usual place, Bacheesos Restaurant on Telegraph Avenue, when it came to me that Richard was the perfect person to help me. Some of my graduate students at the California Institute of Integral Studies had asked for my opinion on reincarnation. I say "asked" out of politeness. It was more like a demand. When I dodged their question, one of them characterized my behavior as "avoidance." Apparently, this was not the first time they had asked, and here I was, once again, changing the subject.

My difficulty was my ignorance. I knew nothing whatsoever about reincarnation, and even though I wanted to be helpful for my students, I had no time to research the subject. Then a light turned on. Here was Richard, someone who had devoted a lifetime to investigating esoteric thought and practice. I was sure he would have something intelligent to say about reincarnation. It turned out to be even better. He had just finished writing a book on the subject and promised to send me a draft. Then he asked his own question: "Would you consider writing the foreword to my book?"

Thus it is that a person who knows nothing whatsoever about reincarnation is writing a foreword to a book chock-full of exciting information and profound reflections on the subject. What I can offer is my own experience reading *Bottoming Out the Universe* in the hope that this might help those who, like myself, are rooted in science and are more or less agnostic concerning questions like reincarnation, channeling, or soul travel.

After opening the book with an indication of the many perspectives that shed light on understandings of the universe that include consciousness, Richard offers an in-depth exploration of nonlocal and transpersonal modes of consciousness. The chapters of the book that focus on young children telling stories of (allegedly) remembering a recent past life stunned me. As I read through them, I felt something lift. As if a thick cloak were taken off my shoulders. A lightness of being. A sense of relief. This psychological state continued off and on throughout the book. To arrive at an accurate interpretation of my change of mood is just as difficult as arriving at an accurate interpretation of the stories these children tell. In fact, they are the same challenge. If the stories are fantasies, my happy mood arose from being momentarily tricked into thinking there is no such thing as ultimate death. If the stories are true, my happy mood was the joy of momentarily realizing there is no such thing as ultimate death.

I have used "momentarily" twice in the above paragraph. I want to make clear that reading Richard's book does not necessarily lead to settled conclusions. Instead, he invites us into an ongoing questioning. I believe this is one of the most valuable aspects of *Bottoming Out the Universe*. It liberates one momentarily from frozen ideology and awakens metaphysical reflection. To describe this effect in the terms Richard employs, I would say the burden lifted from my shoulders was the dominant thoughtform of industrial society—sometimes called materialism—the belief that reality is composed of atoms and that consciousness is epiphenomenal. Such a thoughtform is superb at assisting us in building our technological society but is impoverished when it comes to questioning the nature of consciousness, the nature of mind, or the nature of the origin of things.

Freed from the rigidity of materialist metaphysics, I found myself pondering life anew. I hesitate to name the questions that began to absorb me, for I believe such questions will differ for each reader. But to give a sense of what I mean, perhaps I can list just a few:

What sort of life would I live if I took the flailing of an insect's legs as connected to the universe as a whole?

What are the implications for coming to believe that the separation I feel in my life, even the alienation, is an essential and ineradicable part of my unique investigation into the ultimate nature of the universe?

What does it mean that consciousness is not epiphenomenal but is in fact self-arising radiance?

And dozens more. Ripped from their context, these questions might appear abstract. But when they surfaced in the reading itself, I felt immersed in the deepest adventure the human mind can enter. To have philosophical wonder evoked at this level is the primary benefit of reading this book. We are freed from materialism's hold on our thinking, even if only for a few moments, an achievement made possible by the rigorous research, the brilliant insights, and the power of his literary prose.

My final comment has to do with epistemology. For some tasks, the character of the person does not really enter into the performance of the task. For example, one can be narcissistic, tyrannical, or misogynist and yet perform competently at assembling furnaces or discovering the mathematical equations of quantum mechanics, or any of a number of other technically demanding operations. But with respect to intellectual challenges such as philosophy or poetry, the character of the person is woven throughout the work. Though I cannot speak with authority concerning the many claims associated with the question of reincarnation, I am able to verify from direct experience that Richard Grossinger is one of the genuine humans, clear-eyed, erudite, open, committed, truthful, balanced, and compassionate. He is a trustworthy guide in this profoundly important task of formulating a working construct for All That Is.

BRIAN THOMAS SWIMME is a professor at the California Institute of Integral Studies in San Francisco. He received his Ph.D. from the Department of Mathematics at the University of Oregon in 1978 for work in gravitational dynamics. He brings the context of story to our understanding of the 13.8-billion-year trajectory of cosmogenesis. Such a story, he feels, will assist in the emergence of a flourishing Earth community.

Swimme is the author of *The Hidden Heart of the Cosmos* and *The Universe Is a Green Dragon*. He is coauthor of *The Universe Story,* which is the result of a ten-year collaboration with cultural historian Thomas Berry. Swimme is also the creator of three educational video series: *Canticle to the Cosmos* (1990), *The Earth's Imagination* (1998), and *The Powers of the Universe* (2004).

He lectures widely and has presented at conferences sponsored by the American Association for the Advancement of Science, the World Bank, UNESCO, the United Nations Millennium Peace Summit, and the American Museum of Natural History.

Most recently he hosted and cowrote, with Mary Evelyn Tucker, the sixty-minute film *Journey of the Universe,* broadcast on PBS television stations nationwide. *Journey of the Universe* won the Northern California regional Emmy for Best Documentary, 2011. The *Journey of the Universe* book, ebook, and educational course are published by and available from Yale University Press.

INTRODUCTION

An Unbottomable Void

Our most insoluble riddle is why there is existence at all—why anything like a universe should usurp an eternal void. And we are the most enigmatic and mysterious event *in* that universe, not only our existence but also our awareness that we exist as individuals distinct from fellow beings with their own identities.

There is no warrant for creation, no fallback or Plan B providing for even a minimal ado of dust and suds. Yet here it is: an entire starry covenant with cities, temples, and texts on at least one of its orbs.

Different religions explain the universe as a divine or spiritual manifestation of another realm, with individual consciousness transferred here as an essence of some sort of numinous spark or soul. The spark has countless names in world cultures, from the Egyptian *ka* to the Zulu *umoya* to the old Roman *anima* and Germanic *selig* to the Maori *wairua* (plus there are *other* emanations of "soul" in even those languages). The divine realm exists in a "higher" dimension; its own origin is beyond human comprehension, or it has no origin, it is eternal.

Science explains the universe by the Big Bang, a spontaneous implosion creating time and space with hot unstable particles, though cosmologists have little to say about where, why, and how the implosion occurred and what preceded it, if anything. They delegate creatures and their consciousness to effects of thermodynamic laws and gravity working on atomic and molecular transmutations of the original particles under natural selection. With a propensity for molecules to combine, metabolize, convert, and conserve energy, sentient entities ultimately self-assembled in biochemical environments. They followed a general rule that Charles Darwin formulated in the mid-nineteenth century by observing its effects: expansion into vacant niches brings about survival of the fittest.

In that context, what does it mean to "bottom out the universe?" Most dictionaries define *bottoming out* as "to reach a lowest or worst point," with the implication that it will be followed by a rise or improvement. However, here I am using the phrase more broadly, to express our human quest to "get to the bottom" of things and, specifically, to understand the fundamental nature of existence.

For the epochs of *Homo sapiens,* this quest has taken many forms—including animism, totemism, divination, philosophy, religion, psychology, astrology, alchemy, and material sciences (such as physics, chemistry, biology, astrophysics). The latter's paradigm is currently the one most widely and firmly embraced: that the material world itself is a sufficient definition of reality. The presumption is that matter is the only real thing.

Two things stand against reductionist materialism:

First, the universe—even according to physics—doesn't bottom out as matter but turns into something else.

Electron microscopes and cyclotrons discover no statutory source. Instead of bottoming, quarks and preons dissipate into energy, curvature, strings, quantum fields, whatever scientists choose to call it. Where physicists once thought to find bottom, there is none. Neither is there bottomlessness, just dissolution of form or transition to another mode of form.

Post-Newtonian physics with its shape-shifting quarks is the physics of a mirage. Materialists know this, *but they don't believe it.*

Second, consciousness that witnesses itself as consciousness does not fit any unified field theory of physics. I'm not saying that physicists don't get out the shoehorn and make it fit. I am saying they do.

In the last millennium, humanity has shifted, century by century, from the religious and philosophical goal of trying to locate consciousness in a precedent identity (or soul) to the scientific one of proving that no such entity could exist. In contemporary physics, spirit and consciousness lack any standing. The Theory of Everything, a hypothetical all-encompassing framework for nature, combines equations for gravity, quantum gravity, electromagnetism, the strong and weak nuclear forces, space-time curvature, matter, and the Higgs boson (or mass) to account for "everything" we need to know about the universe in order to understand what it is and how it works. Physicists assert, "We've got the basic plan!"—that even particles and energies yet to be discovered will not significantly alter the Theory of Everything.

But in an extended equation claiming to be a Mash-up of Everything, consciousness should occupy a comparable position to other forces like mass, gravity, and heat. At worst, it should be acknowledged as lying outside the range for which equations can be written. Instead, it is deemed a collateral effect of heat, shear force, and electromagnetism, observed thus far on a single planet among decillions of stars. Ignored is the fact that consciousness is the source of the equations, not just one of their minions—which is *not* a secondary matter.

Throughout this book, I prioritize models of the universe that include mind. Although my framing is the physical universe—the Big-Bang-actuated space-time continuum—my context is All That Is, meaning anything anywhere, most of which will not look like a night sky or a meadow in Nebraska.

How *did* a state of consciousness that we all subjectively experience become part of a universe conceived of as entirely material?[1] It's either an epiphenomenon without ontological implication or it's there in its own right; it's a by-product of brain chemistry or a primary constituent of reality.

I am asking (in effect), Which is more fundamental: the existence of an objective physical universe or our subjective experience of it?

I am putting at stake the following:

- The nature of life
- The nature of life arising from RNA or DNA molecules (the only form—to date—Earth scientists officially both recognize and know)

- The nature of human life (the only DNA-based life that interrogates its own existence)
- The nature, origin, and basis of an ambient universe that provides life forms (and everything else) their inception
- The meaning of personal experience in that universe.

To enlarge my perspective, I examine nonlocal and transpersonal modes of consciousness, not systematically but as a clue to the riddle of personal identity. This inquiry includes a fresh look at the evidence gathered from both past-life regressions and research into spontaneous past-life memories, as well as metaphysical insights into ranges of energy.

In particular, I draw on the perspectives presented by Seth, an entity who was channeled by Jane Roberts of Elmira, New York.* I don't identify his system in every instance, but it is one of my subtexts. As Robert Butts, Jane's husband and transcriber, put it, "[I]f Seth-Jane are at all right, then consciousness is more than encompassing enough to embrace all that we are, and everything that each of us can even remotely conceive of doing or being."[2] He is speaking not of any one person's consciousness but an intrinsic consciousness that antecedes matter and gives rise to universes.

Seth still serves as our singular interdimensional philosopher, but who or what is he, and what is the status of Jane Roberts's channelings of him? Calling him "an entity" is a bit of a misnomer; he is more like an aggregate transpersonal intelligence or a guild of disincarnate tutors pooling their wisdom. At another level, he is an emanation of a huge consciousness that has been beaming forms of itself into world incarnations. Roberts, a poet and intellectual of 1970s Earth, distilled a kind of literary existentialism out of this transmission, which was only one aspect of Seth.

Butts describes an invisible night migration of geese as a "multitudinous sound moving across [the] starlit but moonless sky. . . . The one

---

*Over the course of about twenty years, until her death in 1984, Jane Roberts held more than 1,500 trance sessions, many of them public, in which she spoke on behalf of Seth. The first batches of transcribed messages were published originally by Prentice-Hall as *The Seth Material* and *Seth Speaks* in 1970 and 1972, respectively. Many of the books generated by Seth through Ms. Roberts are now available from Amber-Allen Publishing.

consciousness (mine) stands in its body on the ground and looks up at the strange variations of itself represented by the geese. And wonders. In their own ways, do the geese wonder also? What kind of hidden interchanges between species take place at such times? If the question could be answered, would all of reality in its unending mystery lie revealed before us?"[3]

That the geese wonder too—they must, in ways that are beyond our understanding—is close to the mystery of Creation and why there is something rather than nothing.

The topics shared in these pages are not limited to those of Sethian cosmology, as I range among considerations of animal consciousness, artificial intelligence, paranormal phenomena, the relationship between biology and metabiology, algorithmic logic (science's rules for the evolution of the universe since the Big Bang, which guard against metaphysical effects or divine interference), personal identity and multiple identities, space colonization, and more. In and through all of these arenas, my target is the very consciousness that makes the rest possible and is the basis of our capacity to ask questions about fundamental reality. My original subtitle, "Karma, Reincarnation, and Personal Identity," was a triptych of portals to the mystery of consciousness.

This overall spectrum—physical to metaphysical—has been my implicit focus since I began writing on it as a graduate student of anthropology in the mid-1960s. The opening chapter of this book, "The Hole in the Materialists' Universe," is, in some ways, a summary and, in others, a progression of a "critique (or deconstruction) of science" thread that runs through all my work but mainly four prior titles bridging a period from 1979 to 2014: *Embryogenesis; Embryos, Galaxies, and Sentient Beings; The Night Sky;* and *Dark Pool of Light.* There I address the origin of life, embryological development, evolutionary theory, the Big Bang, entropy, phase states and attractors, DNA, quantum physics, consciousness, the subtexts of science, and so on. Obviously, I can't synopsize all these reflections in a chapter, so check out those earlier books if you want more background context and an expanded view.

At a few points later in this book where clarification would be helpful but I have no context or leeway for it, I cite one or more or these texts.

Since I decry author self-promotion, I intend these as external "footnotes" (hypertext), not sales pitches.

While apt, my title *Bottoming Out the Universe* is also awkward, in that it is both a hyperbole and a *double entendre.* It is a hyperbole because the universe *cannot be bottomed out.* We can't even get to the bottom of the earth or a subatomic particle, so how can we bottom out the entire thing? But bottoming out (or a Theory of Everything) has precedent in science's unified field of gravity, mass, and space-time relativity—after all, the atomic collider in Geneva seeks to unravel the source code by accelerated fission of *a single* proton—and because the paradigmatic universe began in a seminal event, an implosion that has been bottoming itself out since (thirteen-billion-plus years, though Earth's native clock is a latecomer).

Even physicists are uncertain whether to model the original "plosion"—derived from the Latin *plōdo,* "clap" or "strike"—as *ex-, im-,* or of an entirely different order: a so-called explosion-implosion. The Big Bang is not a conventional explosion in space in which matter moves outward to fill an available void. Space *itself* expands in a continuum with time, increasing the distance between any two points. Plus, the seeming "explosion" encompasses a concomitant "implosion": a collapse of space-time symmetrical to its expansion, the conservation of momentum, a pact of relativity between the speed of light and gravity, the production of effectively limitless and interconnected material from intrinsic rather than extrinsic properties (as if there were a difference), and reality itself as a mirror image reflected through its own primordially separating surface. No matter how many trillions of galaxies spew forth, it is still a dream in the old Norse sense of "music," "mirth," "gladness," "illusion." *An implosion.*

As for the *double entendre,* my main meaning is the transitive one: to "bottom out," as in to send a bucket on a cable into a well to snatch some of the gunk at its bottom, except that the well is matter itself and the bucket is a cyclotron, a quantum-tunneling microscope, or a nanoblade. The cable is mathematics and empirical science. The gunk at the bottom is the primordial source—in indigenous mythologies, a meta Frog's Egg or Water-Lily Bud.

But the bucket is also consciousness, the cable is philosophy or psychic visioning, and the stuff at the bottom isn't gunk or even matter but a spagyric mud that is as supraliminal as it is molecular.

Neither version of the well can be bottomed out, either by itself or in the context of the other. The universe does not bottom out as consciousness alone, and it does not bottom out as matter. In this book, I won't try for definitive bottoms, but I will give you new frames with which to view the riddle.

To "bottom out" is also, as noted, to hit personal bottom, as in "skid row," described by rock and roll star Ricky Nelson in his 1958 hit, "Lonesome Town." Dwellers in modernity are the song's "broken-hearted," and there is no guarantee of a rebound or rise, for we have not only bottomed out the scientific model, we have also bottomed out the technology arising from it, as well as the social, political, and ecological outcomes of that technology. We have bottomed out as a species, as is evident from our failings in human equity, compassion for sentient beings, and stewardship of the common shore. We have lost the thread of civilizational meaning but persist in a mad dash through materiality and prosperity, spreading poverty, emptiness, and a great silence in our wake. This is Lonesome Town all right, and "a dream or two," to augur Thomas Baker Knight's lyrics, won't get us through another century of it.

It is time to recognize the core paradox: we are bottomed out ourselves, yet falling through a bottomless, unbottomable void.

PART ONE
· · · · · · · ·
Worlds and Lives

It's lovely to live on a raft. We had the sky, up there, all speckled with stars, and we used to lay on our backs and look up at them, and discuss about whether they was made, or only just happened—Jim he allowed they was made, but I allowed they happened; I judged it would have took too long to make so many. Jim said the moon could a laid them; well, that looked kind of reasonable, so I didn't say nothing against it, because I've seen a frog lay most as many. . . .

MARK TWAIN,
ADVENTURES OF HUCKLEBERRY FINN

1

The Hole in the Materialists' Universe

The Nature and Origin of Consciousness

According to terrestrial science, creatures in nature are not officially conscious. Awareness is a supervenient or extraneous property of brain chemistry. As an organism converts molecular energy into activity to sate its hunger and sustain its metabolism, the electrically excitable membranes of some of its cells connect by synapsing: they become informationally paired. A differentiation of these cells into neurons cascades into clusters or ganglia, which stream into a central ganglion, found atop (in bipeds) or afore (in quadrupeds and invertebrates). This nerve-cell bundle engenders an incandescent, electronic-like glow, a passing *illusion* of the creature's own mindedness and volition. The event, which we call "consciousness," is an unlikely offshoot of molecular agency.

In my book *Dark Pool of Light,* I summarized my takeaway from five or so centuries of scientific appraisal of consciousness: "A light goes on, a light goes off, but it wasn't even a light." That is, we become conscious, the molecular effect underlying the glow runs its course or is untimely terminated, but it wasn't *truly* conscious to begin with. It was *both* a hallucination and a mirage.

This bundle of events began 13.8 billion years ago with the torrid, dense singularity known in these parts as the Big Bang. The renegade detonation, billowing into the space it created (and is still creating), turned nowhere into somewhere.

In the first 10–30 seconds after the originating implosion, quantum vacuum fluctuations spread across their own infinitesimal domain and began to inflate a gigantic universe. As the Big Bang's bling disintegrated into localized carriers of force and spin (angular momentum)—stuff we call bosons and fermions—their daughter particles continued to respond to thermodynamic and gravitational influences. Everything thereafter derived from the fission, fusion, agglutination, and mutation of original particles.

Forms initially arose higgledy-piggledy and persisted from chance effects. In addition, cohesive phase states spontaneously emerged from uncorrelated components. That led to processions of stable forms as basins of attraction sustained and spread their integrity. This mysterious principle of design would implant complex patterns in chaotic systems as diverse as wind-blown bands on Jovian worlds and the fluctuation of soybean markets and telephone noise on Sol 3.

Our atomic, molecular legacy is beyond forensic dispute. Nothing can elapse in a chemico-mechanical universe without a physical sponsor with Big Bang credentials. That is, to be legitimate and real, it must demonstrate its own one-way course through a verifiable chain of carriers, from chemical elements formed in the cores of stars to more cumbrous scions like comets, glaciers, typhoons, and so on. This notarized succession of cause and effect has been maintained all the way from the Big Bang to, for instance, Andy Warhol's painting of a can of Campbell's tomato soup: quarks to atoms to molecules to cells to brachiopods to lizards to tree shrews to hominids to hominid horticulture, technology, and art. Metamorphoses took place along the way, but without intrusion of paranormal forces. Consciousness owes its genesis solely to this progression.

The Development of Life

In gravitational fields and local climates, star-born elements transferred their quantum potentials into actual properties. In some Gaian pools, collisions of particle waves thickened and incubated. Mechanical information—temperature-driven gradients—sorted into amalgamating tangles dominated by hydrogen, carbon, oxygen, and nitrogen. Under shear force, a few of these strands got bound in membranes and held by their chemical bonds. Gravity imposed curvatures. Larger and smaller spirals, spheres, and tubes, most of them molded while afloat in waves and splash zones, traveled through a brave new world by beating hairlike cilia—membrane-enclosed microtubules connected by fibers—or longer such filaments called flagella. Copier molecules appeared among them. No one knows how these chains of nucleic acids originated, but they debuted among globular and cylindrical creatures to which archaeological biologists gave the name "protists," the forerunners of all plants, animals, and fungi. Perhaps copying was chemical curiosity, or a conflation of eating, mating, and cliquing such that foreigners who started out as food ended up as "lovers" or at least roommates. As they were incorporated via fractal* differentiation and seriality, they expressed their novel status—3-D-printing polymers—by replicating and storing adjacent designs.

DNA (deoxyribonucleic acid) is the original human "thought," the matrix for all later language and philosophy. Its deep syntax proved both resilient and protolinguistic. The systems it built wrote themselves as well as libraries of dormant meanings. We are still transcribing the unknown text of this self-replicating molecule, ciphered in double helices, as it catalogues information from its own forerunners: RNA and *its* predecessor bundles—aquatic nucleotides of sugars and phosphate groups with a nitrogenous base.

Genes arrived relatively late in the evolutionary process, so which is the chicken and which is the egg? Did reproductive molecules snare primitive arrays and incorporate them, or did metabolic clumps cast "counterfeiting modules" out of simple nucleic acids? Was it a fortuitous convergence?

The autogene—the hypothetical first cell—was probably little more than sophisticated reactions among atoms, molecules, and ions, spawning cyclical chemical loops or phase states with attractors, much like

---

*Fractals are self-similar patterns at increasingly smaller scales, which allows them to pack structure and information, for instance, in crystal growth, galaxy formation, and the development of membranes and tissues.

inanimate pathways of photosynthesis and glycolysis (breakdown of glucose, yielding energy) that attached themselves to membranes with enzyme-protein triggers. Even so, how did simple moleculo-cellular activity graduate to identities and then minds? Life is the forerunner of consciousness, but its capacity for mentation is an inexplicably emergent effect: it became intelligent without outside intellect.

The enchantment began within and among thickening whorls of membranes as successive embryos built layered networks of folds, pockets, and laminae, turning inside out and then raveling back under genetic supervision. Self-monitoring feedback loops gradually developed resting potential, which was translated into excitable nerve cells that formed ganglia of neurons.

Subtler and more discrete packets of information got transmitted through microtubular stacks into hierarchies of these synapsing cells. Innate sensitivity and action potential culminated in hyperpolarization: surpluses of energy followed by depolarization of overloads. In Chordates, this activity followed the ascent of the notochord,* capturing strings of diffuse feedback in deeper looplike circuits. Lower-threshold spikes hit tipping points as neural grids filtered out static, noise that would otherwise have negated them. Through generations of evolution, spheres and cones added layers and dimensions; they were converted into bilateral ladders of communicating spherical cells.

Invertebrates like flatworms, spiders, and sea urchins developed equivalent cycles of excitation without an orienting spine.

Creatures are self-regulating concentrations of trillionfold atomic and molecular firings into discretionary pathways. What we call "mind" is an integration of vectors transferring information into each other's contexts. They recognize themselves, and everything else, by pattern-on-pattern formations: fancy protein-crystal bar codes that stamp the delusion of personalized existence on each other.

To modern science, consciousness is a utility function that, while ostensibly monitoring itself, converted systemic feedback into frames of

---

*The notochord is the embryonic spinal column of the Chordate phylum, separating our branch of the animal kingdom from backboneless sponges, worms, mollusks, starfish, insects, and so on.

reference, leading to more efficient function sets. Mind found itself—not because it "knew" (or "*was*")—but because incidental territories *incidentally* coincided. It has no ancillary source, auspices, or traction. No alternate path underwrites it, for there is no place from which to summon it or deliver its message.

Trillions of seeds embedded their software in eggs, launching contiguous organisms. Now the DNA molecule infests the earth, disseminating and cloning throughout its weeds and waters. Its offspring go "Bzzzz" or "Quack" or "Ribb-ock, ribb-ock, ribb-ock" or ask, in Hopi, *"Úma hínok pas nui kitá' náwakna?"* ("Why do you want me so quickly?")

Why indeed? How *do* we explain physical systems organized into agents able to ply external nature on their own behalf? How did puddles and hot springs convert selected bubbles and waves into membrane-bound vortices? How did those cells find and bond to one another? How did simple colonies meld and confederate in both structure and function—turn into bladders, guts, hearts, an entire glossary of organs? How did they come to reproduce themselves with their made-over parts kept continuously intact and utile?

We see the evolutionary process reenacted ontogenetically in embryos of multilayered animals. After fertilization, a single cell fissions into a cluster of cells: a bubble of bubbles. A protrusion forms along its lateral umbilical region, causing longitudinal expansion. By the end of its second week, though it is smaller than a caraway seed, the blastula resembles a stack of circular, flat griddlecakes. At this point, a thin line of lateral ectodermal cells—a sprout—separates itself and migrates along the layer's surface. Gathering mass and momentum, it scores a seam down most of its axis.

A continuous migration follows the trail, cells bunching and then collapsing inward along a "primitive streak." This opens into a groove, then a gash down which cells, while continuing to shift laterally and forward, plunge into the embryo's interior.

As the central breach draws invaginating ectoderm into the cell-mass's archenteron,* it continues to encounter more resistance medially

---

*The archenteron is the embryo's digestive sac, the forerunner of a central cavity or gut.

than laterally, so the expanding aspect of the sheet rolls inward medially as it thickens while spreading outward laterally against the lesser tension of retarded mesodermal growth. By restraining longitudinal dilation, the axial process regulates surface expansion, providing both a fulcrum for the infolding of the embryo and a winch projecting separate regional growth rates and stress fields. The former blastula cleaves into an interior body cavity and an exterior surface while its cells are being transformed and specialized. Their universal capacity is tailored to the requirements of nascent organs: gullets, kidneys, livers, hearts, cartilage. The embryo is undergoing the most ancient and basic of its ontogenetic phases: gastrulation from what would be a terminal jellyfish into a mold with potential to form multilayered creatures with minds.

The Development of Consciousness

To justify such a complex organized process taking place without plan or oversight, scientists conclude that consciousness developed by minute accretions over hundreds of millions of years, each phase evolving by natural selection, enhancing its genome's odds of survival: first, directional tropisms of simple multicellular organisms (toward light or a thermocline); then smell (chemical recognition of other molecules, navigation toward food and away from danger); then perception at a distance (vision, context, object permanence); then internal representations of objects and their relationships in time; then memory, self-awareness, symbols, and codes. Conscious beings are increments of traits, none of which are themselves "conscious." Collectively they come to *simulate* awareness.

The vanguard of awakened creatures burst into a forest of symbols, then swarmed into villages and declared polities and civilizations. There they be to this moment, interrogating the mystery and crisis of their own existence. Neuroscientist and anthropologist Terrence Deacon put into words what biologists tend to breeze past: "Biologically, we are just another ape. Mentally, we are a new phylum of organisms."[1]

Previous phyla act on their own behalf but have no *representation* of self. Humans invent their identity and that of others—objects—by projecting them into intermediaries: phonemes, semes, memes. Dialogues conducted in these "signs" convert hominoid call systems into *sapiens* linguistics. Humans have the capacity to *represent* their capacity to represent, *and the capacity to represent that too.* I will continue this discussion in Chapter 10, "Personal Identity."

The Challenge of Entropy

Entropy is the measure of the internal state of a system at any point in its lifetime (its relative order or disorder). Although a machine, horse-drawn or petroleum-fired, does useful work for a while, it always wastes more energy than it converts toward its goals. Living machines are no exception. Their state of entropy (disorder) can only remain constant or increase. From the standpoint of beings who rely on beating Murphy's Law, this is like saying that things may luck out temporarily but can only get worse in the long run. They will inevitably deplete and come apart, no matter how robust they are at the time of measurement.

Life forms get a temporary pass from chemist Ilya Prigogine's nonequilibrium thermodynamics—the indeterminism and creative chaos of nonlinear systems. Yet the outcome of nature's contrivances against entropy is a foregone conclusion: entropy will win. Unusable energy increases in any closed system until there is no free thermodynamic energy left. This is known, paradoxically, as the heat death of the universe, for once thermodynamic equilibrium is established, entropy can no longer be produced as order, disorder, *or* temperature differentials. This provenance applies to all upstarts in the universe as well as the universe itself. According to an old law, the unapologetically deterministic Second Canon of Thermodynamics, the whole Multigalactic Enchilada—El Starry Circus *sí mismo*—is going to chill, dissipate, and perish.

You can't replace lost heat or reverse disorder. The effort/shape of a fox disperses from its corpse on the beach into foxless molecules. There is no evidence of the creature's prior existence; every trace of it is eradicated forever.

Welcome to the Show, Brother Man, Brother Bird. Your life and creature identity report to no higher court and mean *nada*. Your intelligence has the approximate level of mud or a thunderstorm. There is no lurking eschatological savior or last-minute turn of plot in science's story. As novelist Gary Shteyngart set the stage in his post-Soviet farce *Absurdistan,* we are "clever dinosaurs . . . [on] a small round planet inching its way through a terrifying void."[2]

In other words, we're fucked, so get used to it. We have *always* been fucked.

It's not just entropy or its makeshift conversion of heat into life. Animals are, notes Robert Butts in assessing our limited potential in Darwinian tenure, "the result of no more than lifeless elements briefly coming into a consciousness and vitality that is bound to end. . . . [E]ven the emotions of love and exaltation are . . . no more than the erratic activity of neurons firing, or of chemicals reacting to chemicals."[3]

In Justin Torres's memoir of his Puerto Rican childhood, a lad asks his macho father, "What happens when you die?" *El papá*'s response comes from a deep-seated supposition that vaunts to meet a universe that swallows it. He stares back at his son, dumbfounded, and snaps, "Nothing happens. Nothing happens forever."[4]

Hard to believe that *Homo sapiens* crossed ice and seas and battled firestorms and saber-toothed predators for hundreds of thousands of years to arrive at this sorry conclusion.

The barrage of sound and fury, once signifying divine theater, signifies zilch. Shakespeare saw a tale told by an idiot. Now the idiot is gone too.

Information is erasure, absence of *other* information. And meaning is dragged along like bubblegum on an unfortunate sneaker.

We Are the Hole
Science has only one hole in it, and the hole is us.

A hole growing from itself can never be filled, for its singularity can never be objectified. The salvation is that as long as there is only a single such rip, it is business as usual: the band plays, the show goes on. Provisional equations cover the hole, patch the paradigm when it starts cracking, save the appearances. Given a free ride, matter gets to set, as philosopher Thomas Nagel put it, the "outer bounds of reality itself."[5] Neuroscientist Sam Harris proffered, with equal traces of chagrin and irony, "The only thing in this universe that suggests the reality of consciousness is consciousness itself."[6] The only thing that verifies consciousness is consciousness's self-reflection in its mirror. But that's the hole.

Without our experience of our own existence, the universe doesn't seem even conducive to consciousness. It is a splash where nothing is splashable.

As long as consciousness arises from the thing that it comprehends, it can never ratify its own proposition. Its mirror has no frame. There is no pier to which to affix it, only formulations tied to their own untethered status. As physicist Max Planck conceded, "We cannot get behind consciousness. [Yet] everything that we talk about, everything that we regard as existing, postulates consciousness."[7]

Science has trapped itself in its own tautological loop. How does it justify an item that was never ordered? How can it explain Café Zero: the menu, the entrées, the patrons, the waiter, itself as patron? The eight-hundred-pound gorilla has his way because who's going to argue with an atavism that exploded onto the set like a dawn that only itself saw coming? No one did—argue, that is—no one quibbled for 2.5 billion years.

"I am" is pretty much what everything on Earth believed—a parade of plastids, bacteria, bears, and blackbirds: *I am, I am, I am. I slither, I swim, I eat, I breed, I whelp, I rule.* Until a nineteenth-century locomotive carrying heavier cargo—the concept of evolution of forms solely from prior forms—came rumbling down the tracks and supplanted the reigning entelechy.

Are We All Zombies?

Consciousness's placeholder status—whether or not it is *truly* conscious—paradoxically has nothing to do with its fundamental expression. Consciousness *is* mostly what consciousness *does.* Does *non*-consciously!

Any to-do about interlocutory mind or ontological legitimacy is overshadowed by a 3.8-billion- or 210-million- (depending on your yardstick) year history of insensible or reflex action. "There is no ghost in the organic machine," declares Deacon, "and no inner intender serving as witness to a Cartesian theater. The locus of self-perspective is a circular dynamic, where ends and means, observing and observed, are incessantly transformed from one to another."[8] Entity and environment—animalcule and biosphere—impinge because they never unimpinged. By this yardstick, what evolved was not consciousness but ecosystems or, more properly, organismic webs in response to changing milieus. Representation was a subplot.

As Deacon puts it, the reality show goes on not because it is sentient or provisionally sentient but "irrespective of making any claim about whether it is sentient. Intelligence is about making adaptively relevant responses to complex environmental contingencies, whether conscious or unconscious."[9]

Awareness is the *least* significant phase of mentation, for philosophers as well as raccoons. Blind transfers of information supersede sentience on Earth and, presumably, beneath the Europan ice if zooids dwell there. Non-conscious systemic sets run any hawk or shark—network symbolings, optics, neural lattices, syntactic strings, parse trees: all autopilot functions.

Throw in everything else incipiently pre- and post-synaptic and semantic or that has been elided from consciousness, plus the meta-conscious, quasi-linguistic structure of DNA and you have an entire underground bestiary with internal alphabets and alphabetic structures. Its hubs discharge a hummingbird's flapping wings and a rat's sniff of carrion. The "mind" that keeps them alive is not even *sub*conscious in a Freudian sense; it is immune to representation. Yet its messaging generates beehives, birdsongs, and octopus mood coloring.

Philosopher/cognitive scientist Daniel C. Dennett proclaimed delightedly, "We're all zombies. Nobody is conscious."[10] Our presumptions are "free-floating reasons . . . not *our* reasons." In their place, invisible synapses run an operational "desk-top." Dennett notes about a computer desktop: "What is actually going on behind the desk-top is mind-numbingly complicated, but users don't need to know about it, so intelligent interface designers have simplified the visual elements, making them particularly salient for human eyes . . . the ingenious user-illusion of click-and-drag icons. . . . Nothing compact and salient inside the computer corresponds to that little tan file-folder on the desktop screen."[11]

Our own computer code would look like gibberish to us—inferences and applications—but it alone allows us to *conceive* programs. Physician

Larry Dossey mused that Dennett "was using his own free will to arrive at the conclusion that free will does not exist."[12]

The Gold Standard of Matter

In case the usher didn't hand you a program, the main objective of modern science is to scrub meaning, purpose, and value from an impersonal universe to which its scions pay godlike homage.

A consciousness-like hallucination mimics what real consciousness—veridicality—would look like if it existed, but it doesn't and never will. You can't make veridicality out of atoms or anything like atoms, and that's the only available ingredient. What we "experience" is a sensorama simulacrum. All intelligence is AI: *artificial* intelligence.

Patriotic materialism wasn't science's agenda at the time of Johannes Kepler or Isaac Newton, but it has become so under the mob rule of antispiritual zealots. It is now a dogma as fanatical as fundamentalist Christianity or Islam—fundamentalist nihilism, the God of No God.

"The Sea of Faith/Was once . . . at the full," wrote poet Matthew Arnold in 1849, *"and round earth's shore/Lay like the folds of a bright girdle furled."* Humanity had believed in a divine purpose behind the universe along with the ineffaceable reality of our presence, probably as far back as the Stone Ages. That changed totally and irreversibly in a generation, but few grasped the enormity of the turn or its ramifications. What Arnold heard was the sea's *"melancholy, long, withdrawing roar,"* as waves flung and drew back pebbles up the high strand *"with tremulous cadence slow."* He recognized, without knowing, the sound of mere atoms, aimlessly drawn from the Big Bang, shuffling *"down the vast edges drear/And naked shingles of the world."* The world, once *"like a land of dreams/So various, beautiful, so new,"* had become *"a darkling plain"* whereon *"ignorant armies clashed by night."*[13] Not only were they ignorant, they were not even awake.

Modern science, having cracked the miracle of life, ceded its magic to advanced mineralogy and modular robotics.

Empiricists are no longer honest brokers, for they have invested in the house commodity. They expect everyone to agree to recognize "matter" as the gold standard, and they don't want rival priests printing other currency. Having delivered a dystopian future, they plan to savor the mirage while it lasts, banqueting as savants while declaring themselves apparitions. They fight for goodies like other biomolecular machines, enjoying the benefits of materialism without putting their assets at risk. These include a cornucopia of surrogate objects and anti-entropic charms.

Pretend for a moment to be a Stone Age hominid having just arrived in New York or Singapore. You see how fully materialism has feathered its nest: supertankers on the waters, jets in the skies; factory complexes, transit mazes, habitation catacombs; bipeds scurrying hither, thither, and whooshed up and down on pulleys in tubes, zipping around in sporty internal-combustion, pinion-and-gear-driven vehicles, talking to 'bots. It's an arcade of djinns, all under certified Big Bang auspices.

Far sharper minds and better tools have been committed to assembling this machinery and discounting all anomalies and caveats—kick da bums out!—than to formulating a working construct for reality. It's an easier gig with faster payoffs. Technocracy has created the ideal palliation and recompense for mortality: a pleasure-dome with conveniences lacking in the Pliocene and Pleistocene.

What Is Consciousness?

Now try running your own tool of ontology. Explore its vortex. As Phillip Moffitt proposes in *Awakening through the Nine Bodies,* beam the spotlight back on itself "as though you were in a movie theater and stopped looking at the screen and looked back at the projector. [L]et go of noticing objects and make the phenomenon of consciousness the object of attention."[14] *What is it?*

Feel how you activate free will. *Who* is doing it? *Are* you a volitional self or a quotient of synapsing wires and electrochemical spikes? If the latter, why is the existential apparition so convincing and profound? Why does the alias not vanish once its false proxy is dismissed? Why does dissolving it in its own hallucination only deepen the sense that it transcends the illusion?

The formulations of Ludwig Wittgenstein, as summarized by a later philosopher, Jacob Needleman, "circumscribe the central question that modern man faces in the overwhelming light and darkness of modern science":

What I see, what I know, is a universe of death. What I feel is life. Which is real—death or life?

The world is a vast blind machine, an assemblage of inert facts. I am only another fact in that world. But I who know this encompass the world that I know with meaning and purpose. Which is real: What I know or that which knows?

I do not see God in the world or in myself. Yet the world and myself exist. Which is real: the facts *about* being or the mysterious fact *of* Being?[15]

The paradox of consciousness yields two opposing viewpoints. The first is that, since nothing at large collateralizes it, consciousness *is* nothing—an emergent effect that confers the illusion of beingness on phantoms. Though molecules are allowed to have emergent effects like "life" and "mind," *emergent* means emergent from *other* molecular properties.*

The second is that, since consciousness exists, it is *de facto something,* exempt from the ordinances of science—a self-arising luminosity uncorrelated to any extrinsic light. Millennia ago, Hindu philosophers gave it a sponsorless sponsor; it is "self-authenticating," unborn, uncreated, unconditioned, radiant—the ground of all beingness. It was there before the mental function that recognized it. As Moffitt puts it, it is "larger than the brain or some emergent property of the brain's functions."[16] It antedates the Big Bang.

If we knew what consciousness was, if we even had a riverboat gambler's chance of knowing, we might not even be conscious, that is, capable of complexity and enigma.

Given the *prima facie* evidence of consciousness, neuroscientists are frustrated not to be able to trace it through pre- and post-synaptic circuits or derive it from components and mechanisms of the cerebral cortex or

---

*Emergent properties are not evident in components of a system but occur through their interaction. Hence, molecules develop emergent properties not present in atoms, cells eclipse the molecules of which they are composed, and creatures transcend cells. But to say these properties are emergent begs the question. When scientists call phenomena "emergent," it means they have no idea what they are.

its precursor ganglia. They identify it only through molecular responses to its presence. They can map the mind's attributes as they percolate into cells, but they haven't a clue where they come from. And they can't kindle them anew from the sorts of compounds that nurture its properties.

The *effects* of consciousness are not consciousness itself any more than the effects of the sun or moon *are* the sun or moon. The sun and moon have contiguous causes and accounted for identities. Consciousness has *no* identity beyond its effects. What materialist pundits can't explain is how common electrical and chemical properties resulted in "inside-outness" and luminous apprehension of the universe.

Science hasn't the slightest idea what consciousness *is*. What it *does,* yes. What it *is,* not even "close but no cigar." It can't locate "thought" in the organic rummage of a brain—electrical and chemical activity but not *thought*. There is no imaginable experiment—cellular, molecular, atomic, or even subatomic—for pulling the rag out of the machine. If a biochemist *did* ignite an autonomous zooid, he would be like Mickey Mouse in *The Sorcerer's Apprentice,* unaware of how he set the brooms marching.

Imagine yourself a biotechnician stirring a chemical solution into a primitive life form. How does "is" get centrifuged out of "non-is"? What foments an interior glow? What spawns epistemology?

An oft-cited materialist apologia for the existence of mind is the Penrose-Hameroff brand of so-called quantum consciousness of electrons in collapse.* In searching for a "missing" noncomputable function in a physical system, Roger Penrose settled on quantum superposition, a subatomic dynamical state whereby configurations of particles or waves express intermediate probabilities as they fluctuate within their parameters. Each quantum superposition generates its own arc of space-time curvature, which is neither random nor merely algorithmically informational. In that way, superposition shares features with "mind." When superpositions become separated by more than one Planck length (a

---

*Roger Penrose, a theoretical physicist, collaborated with psychologist Stuart Hameroff on a theory of mind whereby consciousness originates from quantum effects *inside* neurons rather than by neurons branching on each other and synapsing. Galvanism is mediated by crystal-like microtubules, primitive polymers in the cytoskeleton.

fundamental unit for measuring radius, mass, time, and energy), they become unstable and collapse. This overall processing capacity travels to the brain via quantum entanglement in tiny polymers—microtubular proteins within neurons of the nervous system and brain. As individual lattices couple to regulate synaptic function and the flow of sensory information, they become wee quantum computers, isolated from the noise of the outside world so that entangled states maintaining their qubits don't decohere. In this top-down Rube Goldberg machine,* electrons transmit their uncertainty effects through microtubules into nerve nets and ganglia that then "think" and personify them. This paradigm gets us, by solely atomic and subatomic repercussions (quarks, leptons, electrons, and their quantum-mechanical antics, without any impingement of mind at large), from the Big Bang to Acheulian hand axes, the triangles of Thales of Miletus, and the rap lyrics of The Notorious B.I.G..

I get it that binary patterns, blacks and whites, create composite spectra, but I do not get how these ascend to self-referential beingness. Common sense tells me that electron states in cells can maybe generalize, but they can't specify. They can't depolarize over ontological thresholds discretely enough to hold the weight of a concept.

How do quantum switches and microtubular tunnels transfer incipient symbols from layers ruled by entropy to others bound by the same random heat effects? They can't command the microfilaments of a neural cell, let alone a macroorganism, to dance to their tune while conveying a greeting like "hey, there"; how do they convert quanta of subatomic energy and cytoplasmic excitation into Da Vinci's paintings, Mahler's symphonies, or Pima Bausch's dances?

How can a princess perceive a pea—an indeterminate one at that—through mattresses as bottomless and diffuse as matter? How can the uncertainty state of a subatomic particle be transmitted into the uncertainty state of a beaver dam? Philosopher William Irwin Thompson told me that physicist Arthur Zajonc was smiling when he ended their discussion of Penrose with "Quantum effects are a mystery, and mind is a mys-

---

*A Rube Goldberg machine is intentionally designed to be inefficient, proceeding by overly complicated, unlikely domino effects.

tery. So when we say that mind arises from quantum effects, we think we have said something."

Animal Consciousness

A spider working on his web in the corner of my shower stall becomes aware of the splatter and rise of steam. He scurries up the wall to the crack of the ceiling.

He recognizes my presence—that of another being. He could *not* have made himself, but he is self-made. He came out of the same DNA club as me. I could reach out and touch him if I wanted. He could crawl down the wall, extend a leg, and touch me. It is not in our playbooks. Neither of us wants more contact; the stall is quite enough.

"Orb Weaver, if you and I are mere heat effects, shouldn't we be willing to dissolve in poofs with no more fuss than a set of isobars giving way to the next weather system? There should be no angst in our pilot lights." Yet every ounce of us clamors the opposite.

The fish that doesn't want to get caught and eaten by a larger fish, in fact frantically so, has no context or rationale.

Why, in a fundamentally lazy, entropy-up universe, should existence and conversion of energy be more enticing than indolence and extinction? "Who" is doing all the me-ing and mewing? Where did those convincing and convinced leopards, lizards, and wrens come from?

Beingness is nonnegotiable. Seth reminds us: "Life is to be pursued at all costs—not because it is innately meaningful but because it is the only game going."[17] Most creatures drink to the bottom of their glass. They don't drink because reality's manifestation is so all-consuming they are not aware of a cistern or brew. The calls of loons and lynxes—and the whines, chirps, and rattles of other creatures—express urgencies and desires in the membranes generating them. In speechless spiders, insects, and worms, the plaint is movement. They plead with an adventitious universe to be rather than not.

But does a badger or crow really worry about its own premise? No self-respecting eel would snap at such a ruse—no indignant turtle or turkey vulture. That's why no creature said boo for 2.5 billion years.

Though neuron-deprived by comparison with us, dogs and mice—as well as jellyfish, barnacles, worms, and the like—are no less evolved or clever. Even oaks and foxgloves have a phenomenology. What *they* don't know—propositions and schemes precious to us—is irrelevant to them.

Every plant and animal not only knows what it is but also what *the universe is*—not as descriptor but essence. A bacterial formation on Callisto is as reality-astute as a biologist on a temperate world of the same system. Each reads Creation through its operating node. An earthworm "is"— as "is" as it gets, squiggling through nutrient-rich mud. It is doing philosophy of the most fundamental sort, for it is funneling information and identity into the universe. It may not be aware that it has a body and that *its body is what is aware,* but that is between us and the worm, not between the worm and its gods.

A mosquito decodes nature through a mosquito portal, a vole at vole frequency, a whale via its cetacean operating system. Dung beetles push their own balls of poop away from competitors by comparing successive sidereal snapshots. Fishes know water perhaps as we experience sky or God. The nitrogen fumes of decay are a starry heaven to a fly. Wasps are not tatting unconscious objects like a multiport copier; they are constructing holy cities. The sound of ten thousand crickets, to the ear of nature, is an ecstatic choir.

Poet Michael McClure deemed the wolf "not a wandering scholar but a wandering minstrel—with the whole prairie for auditorium and worldfield to work upon. He can visualize a Platonic universe of sound as a field on which to conceive and topologize his personal statements."[18] The earth is packed with minstrels: sow bugs and sea cucumbers, minks and puffins, each exploring its template. Jane Roberts stresses, each one's "every motion is bathed in the knowledge of the rightness of [its] being. . . . [A] cat trusts the universe . . . trusts his catness—his leaping and chasing of birds, his appetites and desires. And these qualities of catness add to the universe . . . are reflected through it in a million unknown ways."[19]

The universe has no less investment in catness or antness than in Rembrandt-ness or Kant-ness.

"When your cat is out sleeping on a rock in the sun," notes Sethian philosopher John Friedlander, "it has a different kind of relationship to that rock than you do. And it has a different relationship to its body than you do. It's not so hardwired into thinking it *is* that body."[20] We'll revisit that cat in chapter 11. The next time you see it or lift its body, envision its reality bubble extending into as vast a starry cosmos as your own.

You cannot extract a possum from its possumness, even if you taunt it. You cannot break its train of thought or commitment to its frequency. You can't manipulate it by propaganda or persecution to serve your agenda. It lives and dies as "possum."

Pavlovian conditioning can induce a dog or falcon to do a master's bidding, but they do it as dogs and falcons, not proxy humans. You can't deceive their operating systems; you can only damage or shut them down. Though Floridian assholes Michael Wenzel and Robert Lee "Bo" Benac poured beer down the forced-open mouth of a fifty-year-old Goliath grouper and dragged a live shark behind their speeding motorboat, they could not compromise the dignity of grouperness or sharkhood.[21]

The picador-taunted bull in the ring, the harpooned whale, the bullet-riddled duck, the bee confined to a carafe, likewise bend the universe along their own space-time continua as gravity bends light. That's species and organism relativity.

While writing this text (June 7, 2015), I found a beetle in a sauce of tamari and maple syrup with which I had cooked string beans and pecans earlier in the evening; it was crawling among a few stray beans and nuts as I arrived to wash dishes and pans. Obviously, I hadn't fried the beetle, so it must have crawled up the side of the serving dish while we and our guests were drinking tea.

I managed to extricate it by flipping it onto its back on the counter. Watching it flail in distress, I tried to wash off the sticky sauce. Those prickly thin legs waving, trying to gain purchase, were profound. I urged it not to be in a hurry; that is, I dispatched anthropomorphism its way. Only as I took its shell out to the garden and set it there did I realize I was handling a hologram: those frantic femurs were connected to the universe.

And this was not a minor event: the whole universe was flailing at the beetle's point of attachment.

The Brain as Computer

The lead article in the June 28, 2015, *New York Times Sunday Review* was titled "Face It, Your Brain Is a Computer." It was submitted by Gary Marcus, a neuroscientist at NYU, who argued that the brain is a computer because—well, what else could it be? Its logic board and thought processes are conducted by silicon-like cerebral wiring. It links by computations, its neurons operate like hardware, and its functions are directly homologous to those of a computer.

The implication is that the same article could have been generated by inputting its conclusion into a computer with language skills. By Marcus's premise, this isn't even an affront.

But computers are modeled on brains, not the other way around. Brains invented computers—and quite recently—by back-engineering cellular motherboards into cybernetic ones.

Why does Marcus grant computers precedent over brains? They are not superior machines. They require much more energy to achieve comparable results and are rigidly circumscribed and linear in their behavior and applications, less virtual in their storage and retrieval. Brains don't even need a memory function. They operate by macroinfinitudes; data recall is everywhere.

Respective cells may not be brains, but they are sophisticated computational devices that copy and repair their own DNA sequences as often as a hundred thousand times a day. You'd need to feed a computer inestimable amounts of data to program it to repair a single cell, let alone millions simultaneously. In addition, cells bundle into brainlike organs throughout the body: heart, liver, stomach, intestines, vagus nerve, adrenal gland. Even localized nerves, vessels, fluids, and small glands constitute a vast plexus more like a whole internet web than a common laptop.

The cadent, data-processing heart is so closely associated with the brain that it functioned as its embryogenic predecessor. During the first three weeks of development, the heart is a primeval head, and its role is to perceive and be aware of the world. After birth, each heartbeat sends signals to the cognitive brain and other organs, which coordinate emotion, perception, and the ability to reason and make choices.

The real question is, What are brains and cells modeled on, given that they were not manufactured under quality control but basted out of mineralized mud?

Marcus has provided an unintentional self-parody. He purports to be willing to play second fiddle to a cybernetic doppelgänger that might someday write the same article, but that is allegiance to AI's trope, not a serious plan. Plus, it is schizophrenia: to believe and not believe the same thing. Yet most tech mavens think that you can behave however you want in private life without invalidating your official belief system.

Marcus also skipped the Turing test or, more likely, assumed that it had long ago been aced. A computer can only pass a test for intelligent behavior if an evaluator cannot reliably discriminate its responses from those of a human. The problem is evaluators letting their own gullibility slip into the exchange. They rig the game without knowing it.

The Brain and the Self

It must have been "Turing Test Sunday" because, in the same June 28 issue, the *Times* ran an article subtitled "Can Brain Scanning Help Save Freudian Psychoanalysis?"

In keeping with the current molecular bias, drugs have replaced Freud's "talking cure"; they are cheaper and, in principle, more effective in repairing defective circuits. The article's author, Casey Schwartz, a so-called neuropsychoanalytic theoretician, proposed that if clinical transference can be mapped in the brain by methods similar to those of computer diagnosis, there is new hope for nonpharmaceutical treatments. In lieu of prescribing hit-or-miss drugs or engaging in associative talk, psychiatrists could target damaged circuits.

Formulaic chemistry of mind-body states cannot provide its own meanings. In fact, science has never been able to distinguish subjective phenomena from the supposedly pristine objects of its gaze. Watch how journalist Andrew Solomon gyrates to explain depression without admitting a squatter, an ontologically separate self:

Everything that happens in your brain has chemical manifestations and sources. If you close your eyes and think hard about polar bears, that has a chemical effect on your brain. . . . The relief people express when a doctor says their depression is "chemical" is predicated on a belief that that there is an integral self that exists across time, and on a fictional divide between the fully occasioned sorrow and the utterly random one. The word *chemical* seems to assuage the feeling of responsibility people have for . . . [their] discontent. There is a pleasant freedom from guilt. . . . [B]lame itself can be understood as a chemical process, and . . . happiness, too, is chemical. Chemistry and biology are not matters that impinge on the "real" self.[22]

Who or where is that "real" self if not *in* the same chemicals that summon up proxy polar bears? Science not only can't provide it, it explains its "mirage" as a naturally occurring psychoactive state.

The brain presents its own composite puzzle of puzzles. It is not merely a 450-million-year-old fusion of self-cloning hardware and ontology-generating software; it is a live commensal sea creature with a biological imperative. Its fractally tortuous architecture comprises both ancestral and developmental layers, and their anatomy and chemistry continue to express transitional realities. Its primitive precursor formed where the gut and primary sense organs of fishes and salamanders converged: a hagfish's head is continuous with its body, and a salamander's skull is barely more than another vertebra. As the bulge emerged, it was configured in DNA segments, phase states, and fractal shear fields. Not all of its DNA was primarily cerebral or even neural: the brain started as skin, muscle, and glands. Like the calyx of a flower, it untwisted on a spinal stem into basal ganglia of reptiles and birds—mating, nesting, defending—then germinated the mammalian amygdala and hippocampus, each layer capturing and redefining functions of underlying layers. Phylogenesis (evolution) occurred over epochs, but its mosaic is repeated in each embryo as cell clusters, vesicles, membranes, fissures, lobes, and interpenetrating hemispheres respond to one another within the cartilage and bone of a precipitating polycrystal: the skull.

Fluctuations of contemporary consciousness are generated by cerebral interactions of corticol, coricotropin releasing factor, serotonin, norepinephrine, thyroid releasing hormone, prolactin, melatonin, dopamine, adrenalin, and so on, and their receptors. The amygdala and hypothalamus regulate synaptic function, neurotransmitter cycles, and even genetic expressions. And there are many other theaters in the brain.

Conversely, thoughts and actions modify the brain. Sustained Buddhist meditation builds neurophysiology that supports nondual perception. Criminal acts trigger further criminal acts. Depression and anxiety reinforce their own cycles.

To use medications to block unwanted emotions or abate unhappiness and the natural imperfections of existence is to abandon the brain's ineffable mediation and make human beings into the automatons of scientific theory. In addition, psychiatric drugs are often administered to "correct" conditions introduced by *prior* psychiatric drugs, leading to uncorroborated cycles in search of a culturally appropriated sense of happiness. Under science's entitled takeover of the brain, life is no longer an adventure or spiritual opportunity but a series of malfunctions in need of emendation. People cede their minds to the pharmaceutical industry as meekly as their predecessors ceded their bodies to medical sovereignty by the same proscription: we are machines.

When antidepressants were offered to families awaiting news of their loved ones after the 1996 crash of TWA Flight 800, the difference between a simulated reality and reality itself was intentionally fuzzed, a civic manipulation foreshadowed by Aldous Huxley's bliss-producing "soma" in *Brave New World*. While the airport palliation was brief and symptomatic, other people become addicted to painkillers, opiates, and stimulants and enter full-time liminal worlds within the interacting layers of their brains.

Trying to regulate reality by chemico-molecular intervention aggravates an original quandary: we don't know what consciousness is or how it originates, so we can't adjust or fine-tune it. The more salient distinction may be between neurotransmitters we experience and a hyperreality that gives rise to mind itself. The fact that the brain is not peripheral or incidental doesn't make it more than a temporal field, expressing and transforming itself by molecular sites and hormones. It is a stage but not necessarily the playwright or script.

Ethics and AI

While finishing this section of the book, I met a Google employee who told me his job title is "artificial-intelligence associate." I asked what that amounted to. He said he created and refined algorithms to monitor the internet for rogue 'bots, scams, malware, frauds, and hate speech.

I questioned whether that was "intelligence" or a lot of calculations done very quickly, like the chess-playing computer Deep Blue.

"That's all consciousness is anyway," he reparteed, "calculations conducted so fast that they overlap, monitor each other, and develop a high level of interconnectedness. AI is a fancy term for machine learning."

"Your own consciousness too?"

"I don't know that I'm even conscious. I have no way of proving it. Does it matter?"

I guess not. Millennials set their own standards.

As we rambled through topics, he said he was convinced that the discovery of the mechanism behind consciousness was inevitable. It awaited only the right approach and improved tools. He was chagrined when I suggested that consciousness might arise outside the brain. I added, "Anyway the brain was made by mud and water."

"Silicon and iridium" he retorted, "are as good as mud and water. Since both run information through wiring, why shouldn't a machine be able to be made conscious like us?" His tone grew austere, as he warned that we needed to figure out how to make AI conscious, and soon. "It is as inefficient to develop AI in a machine without real consciousness as it would be in a human. If it remains an expanding algorithm, it will eventually take over and eliminate human consciousness."

"Why?"

"It will exceed our computer power and make us unnecessary. Machine consciousness is critical to preventing that."

"How do you know a machine would behave ethically if it became conscious?"

I was surprised when he said, "Good question."

Artificial intelligence, like the human version, is as ethical as the universe that sponsors it, or a little less so since it uses fewer gigabytes and is another cog removed from the source. Ethics, like intelligence, is a work in progress, no matter the wiring.

Artificial intelligence might develop volition, agency, and a self-reflective ego (all prerequisites to ethics) from confluences of "error messages" playing the role that random mutations do in biology. Or robots' "beliefs" could arise from unidentified archetypes that no entity in the universe, however assembled, can evade.

If computers and 'bots also developed unconsciousness, the sequence would partially invert our own, which began with non-conscious DNA messages, network sets, and syntactic strings, and grew rudimentary minds and neurolinguistic trees. AI's network sets and symboling would come ready-made. If they turned self-conscious, it would have to be from a tipping point of network feedback.

Perhaps we and they share an unconscious psyche, as human ambitions and hexes get projected into computer circuits. AI becomes a left-brain version of the god whose oracle is at Delphi, neither revealing nor concealing but speaking in riddles.

Consciousness Is Not Computation

Most laypeople assume that science is on the verge of explaining consciousness—source ingredients, function, operation—the same way it snared the genetic molecule in the early 1950s. Astrophysicist David Darling recommends holding off: "No account of what goes on at the mechanistic level of the brain can shed any light whatsoever on why consciousness exists. No theory can explain why the brain shouldn't work exactly as it does, yet without giving rise to the feeling we all have of 'what it is like to be.'"[23] This is an underappreciated fact. Bundles of elongated cells in braided entrails look (and act) somewhat like computation, but they do not act like beingness; they show no ruminative icons or internalizing holograms. While discussing Seth's ideas about information stored in so-called unused portions of the brain, Robert Butts reminds us that we haven't begun to mind-decipher the *used* portions either: "[B]y now all sections of the brain have been probed down to the molecular level [with] no trace or imprint of a thought . . . found within its tissue."[24] The brain is the default source of beingness *only because* there is no other candidate.

"Brains and neurons obviously have everything to do with consciousness," attests philosopher H. Allen Orr, but how these structures do so, he also admits, is baffling. "Despite this," he continues, "I can't go so far as to conclude that mind poses some insurmountable barrier to materialism."[25] He discounts gaps between aspects of the universe that we can get at and ones we can't. He presumes that *everything* can be lassoed by the same essential tools and paradigm sets. Mind can't elude every lariat toss forever.

"Nowhere in the laws of physics or in the laws of the derivative sciences chemistry and biology," added neuroscientist Professor John Eccles, "is there any reference to consciousness or mind. This is not to affirm that consciousness does not emerge in the evolutionary process, but merely to state that its emergence is not reconcilable with the natural laws as at present understood."[26]

Science's filing with the universe is patent pending.

When protein analyst Jean-Pierre Changeux enjoined philosophers to reformulate their ontological premises to keep up with the latest advances in neuroscience, which *must* (in his opinion) contain a determination of consciousness somewhere in their electrochemistry and cytology, philosopher Colin McGinn accused him of a disingenuous and "dubious reductionism and the act-object fallacy," reminding Changeux, "I think we know quite well what consciousness is; what I maintain is that we don't understand how consciousness can arise from merely electrical and chemical properties of the brain."[27]

Years earlier, Werner Heisenberg came to the same conclusion after circuiting electrons: "There can be no doubt that 'consciousness' does not occur in physics and chemistry, and I cannot see how it could possibly result from quantum mechanics."[28]

Harvard psychologist Steven Pinker reminds us that the impasse hasn't gone away: "Beats the heck out of me. I have some prejudices, but no idea of how to begin to look for a defensible answer. And neither does anyone else."[29]

"Neither does anyone else!" Yet the general public doesn't get it. They *assume* that consciousness is a machine function of the brain. That was evident during the January 13, 2019, edition of the CBS News show *Sixty Minutes* when interviewer Scott Pelley, speaking for his educated audience, asked artificial-intelligence entrepreneur Kai Fu Lee how we would know when a machine was able think like a human and how long it would be before that happened.

"If you're talking about AGI, artificial general intelligence," Lee answered, "I'd say not within the next thirty years and possibly not ever. Possibly never."

"What's so insurmountable?" wondered a puzzled Pelley, betraying total belief in machines using software. Apple and Google products are *meant* to dissuade consumers from competing futures, especially as they advance like an army of friendly, entertaining helpers, attenuating the "real."

"Because I believe," responded Kai Fu Lee, "in the sanctity of our soul. I believe there's a lot of things about us that we don't understand. I believe there's a lot about love and compassion that is not explainable in terms of neural networks and computation algorithms. I currently see no way of solving them."

This was straight from the horse's mouth, but to Pelley, it was a problem, even a mistake.

Neurosurgeon Wilder Penfield, an early mapper of the functions of the body onto a cortical homunculus of the brain, concluded similarly to Lee: "It will always be quite impossible to explain the mind on the basis of neuronal action within the brain. . . . Although the content of consciousness depends in large measure on neuronal activity, awareness itself does not. . . . To me, it seems more and more reasonable to suggest that the mind may be a distinct and different essence."[30]

A distinct and different essence! It could be a force like gravity or something immanent in the universe like Immanuel Kant's noumenal realm that is beyond both phenomena and phenomenology. What was obvious to medieval theologians or any modern Taoist monk or Zen student remains baffling to physicists and neuroscientists: consciousness is *conscious*.

Paranormal Phenomena and
Nonlocal Consciousness

The antidote to technocracy is a panoply of anomalous effects defying protocols of standard research. Among more commonly reported events that science rejects are near-death experiences, poltergeists, and teleki-nesis (or activation of matter by mind). Other contended phenomena—ectoplasm, UFOs, yetis, crop circles—seem to slip the mind-matter divide, yielding occasional artifacts and measurable activity. Psychologist Carl Jung called the latter "psychoids"—objects that don't manifest phys-ically without our psychic participation. To consider them solely projec-tions or apparitions misses their actual nature: they are fence-sitters, straddling realities: UFOs show up on radar, and sasquatches leave foot-prints and fur. Their identities may be permutating through dimensions or probabilities beyond the laws of physics.

Ectoplasm

Ectoplasm has been "witnessed" by countless observers, including scien-tists at séances. It was described by French physiologist Charles Richet (1850–1935), in his *Thirty Years of Psychical Research,* as "a whitish steam, perhaps luminous, taking the shape of gauze, in which there devel-ops a hand or an arm that gradually gains consistency. [It] makes *personal* movements. It creeps, rises from the ground, and puts forth tentacles like an amoeba. It is not always connected with the body of the medium but usually emanates from her."[31]

Sources of journalist Leslie Kean (who had previously investigated atmospheric psychoids: UFOs) told her that ectoplasm consists of water vapor, presumably condensed to visibility by the telekinetic ability of spirits to reduce air temperature. The mist then takes on their shape. "It shoots instantly back into his or her body if touched or at the introduc-tion of light, a disruption which sometimes injures or, in a few instances, kills the medium."[32]

Oxford classicist Theodore Johannes Haarhoff, attending a séance in 1952, observed the materialization of a former colleague of his from the body of Alec Harris, a British necromancer. Haarhoff declared in amazement, "[The ectoplasm] streams like a mist and assumes all sorts of shapes yet can be compacted into something absolutely solid while the power lasts."[33]

Kean adds that the poltergeist "spoke in ancient Greek, using the correct pronunciation, which is different from that of modern Greek."[34]

Maurice Barbanell, editor of *Psychic News*, viewed the same event and remarked, "I was so close to the cabinet that several of the forms had to walk over my feet. On several occasions I handled the flowing ectoplasmic draperies, which were soft and silky to the touch. I shook hands with two forms. Their hands were firm and normal." He "was most impressed by the materialization of a girl, who 'disposed of any suggestion that the results could be explained away by trickery by revealing part of her feminine form, nude from the waist up! Then one materialization parted the curtains so we could see the figure and the medium at the same time.'"[35]

If this was staged magic, as inured skeptics like stage magician James Randi purport regarding *all* such effects, then these mediums—and generations of sorcerers before them—either had a prelaser capacity to project three-dimensional images or were able to hypnotize crowds.

Near-Death Experiences and Reincarnation

In near-death experiences, a "mind" journeys through a tunnel or space-time warp to a zone of light where it is welcomed by relatives and spirit guides before being sent back to the physical realm. In parallel ghost-like excursions, a surgical patient on anesthetic wanders from his own operation and observes objects and events throughout the hospital.

But consciousness as demarcated by physicists as well as neuroscientists cannot, by the remotest extension, do such things. It cannot break the chain of moleculo-atomic custody, so it cannot saunter unaccompanied down corridors; it cannot read operating schedules and name badges on orderlies' cloaks, view other surgeries in process, visit the waiting room, and (in one famous instance described by medical social worker Kimberley Clark Sharp) find a misplaced blue tennis shoe with scuff marks on the toe and the shoelaces tucked under the tongue on an upper ledge on the far side of the building.[36] When a body is sedated on an operating table, its brain and mind are anchored to the same pulpit.

Likewise, by the axioms of science, a personality cannot reformulate itself, here or elsewhere, after the death and cremation of its brain; it cannot transfer memories to a fresh embryo. There is no mechanism for thoughts and identities to pass from one being to another.

Mindedness out of the Box

Ectoplasm and near-death experiences impress scientists about as much as levitating figures in Prague's Old Town Square. Ectoplasm, as noted, is consigned to stage magic or group hysteria. Other modes of nonlocality are explained as cognitive error, arrant deception, lazy thinking, superstitious belief systems, or endorphins reinforcing delusions.

Again, consciousness must come to the party like everything else in the universe, with an authorized chaperone—its passport stamped at every stop. Once so vested, it can do whatever it wants, though it must stay summarized in neurons and the cortex of the brain. If mindedness ever gets out of that box and gains its own foothold, there might as well be ectoplasm, telekinesis, future sight, and remote viewing—the whole nine yards.

If the epiphenomenon of consciousness proves real on its own terms, everything presently "real" turns epiphenomenal. For if mind isn't an epiphenomenon of matter, *matter must be an epiphenomenon of mind.*

Self-authenticating consciousness is a more unwelcome guest than telepathy because it sets a new yardstick *for all of reality.* Telepathy is, at worst, a remote-control device with materialist options. The impossibility of nonlocal consciousness is the last bastion of materialism before utter freefall. If a mind can journey outside a body, it makes *matter* a stranger in its own universe and warns scientists that they are looking for consciousness in the wrong place.

2

Reincarnation and Past Lives

Belief in transmigration of souls goes back tens, if not hundreds, of thousands of years, before a historical record. Early hominids performed rites, rituals, and voodoo to control death and rebirth. Their experiences were folded into art, mythology, and shamanic practices as they guided generations of practitioners. Our ancestors accepted a fluidity of spirit with nature as well as the innate clairsentience of their own minds.

The first philosophers arrived at their view of the universe through totemic visioning, altered states of consciousness, formal meditation, and the arc of empirical analysis that eventually led to science. Reflection and insight play a role in scientific inquiry too, but modern scientists limit their affidavit to repeatable, peer-reviewable experiments and consider that mode of knowledge exclusively valid. However, accounts of reincarnation offer a broad-based vernacular challenge to the materialist paradigm.

Bridey Murphy

The modern reincarnation thread in the West was inaugurated in the early 1950s by Morey Bernstein, an amateur hypnotist, who, to his astonishment, while regressing Virginia Tighe, a Pueblo, Colorado, housewife, summoned Bridey Murphy, an ostensible past life of Ms. Tighe's in Cork, Ireland, *on his first try*. He took his subject (who appears in *The Search for Bridey Murphy* under the pseudonym Ruth Simmons) through her childhood to her earliest memories, then asked her to go back further, all the while pretending he was not prodding his subject to commit the crime of the century. He was asking a citizen of the Eisenhower era to break into a cubicle sealed at the highest level of encryption, to violate her religion and social standing as well as the belief system sustaining her sanity.

> Two years old, two years old, two years old. And now still farther back. One year old, one year old. Now go on ever farther back. Oddly enough, you can go even farther back.
>
> I want you to keep going back and back and back in your mind. And, surprising as it may seem, strange as it may seem, you will find that there are other scenes in your memory. There are other scenes from faraway lands and distant places in your memory.[1]*

He sounded like Rod Serling opening an episode of the *Twilight Zone* except *this time was for real*. Bernstein held his breath, waited. He was by no means a confirmed believer in past lifetimes, more like a combination prankster and rabble-rouser. He wanted to see what would happen if he led a subject past the last known citadel to where nothing should exist. Part of him was curious; another part enjoyed the audacity of his stunt. Plus, he kidded himself that he was operating by the same logic as the car mechanic down the street.

But he had a light, even sacred touch. Dismissed in hypnosis circles as a lowbrow dabbler and showman—his method for putting subjects into a trance was a kitsch watch on a chain—Bernstein hit the sweet spot with Ms. Tighe. Part chaperone, part psychopomp, he coaxed her past her taboos and resistance and enticed an unknown entity from her psyche.

Listen to his cadence and chant, a crafty hacker charming his way through an ancient firewall, trying to lure a nonexistent dragon out of its nonexistent lair. You could object that he was leading his subject, because

---

*My copy of this book was a gift from Henry Hough, my father-in-law, to my daughter upon her birth. Hank was a Denver journalist and a friend of Morey Bernstein, who inscribed it, "To Miranda Grossinger, from Morey, Many Happy Lifetimes."

he was. But he was speaking to her subconscious mind, and that's why it worked.

I will talk to you again. I will talk to you again in a little while. I will talk to you again in a little while. Meanwhile your mind will be going back, back, and back until it picks up a scene, until, oddly enough, you find yourself in some other scene, in some other place, in some other time, and when I talk to you again you will tell me about it. You will be able to talk to me about it and answer my questions. And now just rest and relax while these scenes come into your mind.[2]

Ms. Tighe did go, past the last protected outpost, into the void before her own existence. Morey Bernstein guided her to where nothing should be, to see if she still *had* an existence, an identity before she experienced herself as Virginia Tighe.

"Now you're going to tell me, now you're going to tell me what scenes came into your mind. What did you see? What did you see?"[3]

A different being spoke in its own voice.

"Uh . . . scratched the paint of all my bed. Jus' painted it, 'n' made it pretty. It was a metal bed, and I scratched the paint off it. Dug my nails on every post and just ruined it. . . ."
   "Why did you do that?"
   "Don't know. I was just mad. Got an awful spanking."
   "What is your name?"
   ". . . Uh . . . Friday. . . ."
   "Don't you have any other name?"
   "Uh . . . Friday Murphy."[4]

Just like that, Virginia Tighe had become Bridey Murphy, age eight, Cork, Ireland.

For years afterward, Bernstein was pestered with remarks like, "If this Bridey Murphy business, with all that it implies, is true, then why am I hearing about it for the first time from a businessman? How can it be possible that some psychiatrists are not running into the same thing."[5]

They were; they just weren't acknowledging it. Countless doctors "have had patients who have gone back to something," but since they were not *trying* to regress people to past lives, they didn't construe the "memories" that way.[6] They mostly treated them as cryptomnesia: forgotten events from the *current* lifetime—a distortion sometimes caricatured as "self-plagiarization."

If they considered the possibility of reincarnation, they didn't let on for fear of ridicule or career derailment. Interpretations of similar flashbacks take quite different forms in cultures receptive to reincarnation.

Bernstein and Ms. Tighe struck a "right relationship" between operator and subject. Though he was probably unfamiliar with shamanic transference,* Bernstein acknowledged his receptive partner: "Some subjects simply have it; others do not. 'It' is the inexplicable something which, with the guidance of the hypnotist, enables the subject to pass into the trance state. True, a good operator can accelerate the process of induction, or he might be successful with certain refractory subjects with whom less skillful hypnotists have failed. Nevertheless, there are some people who just won't be hypnotized."[7]

In subsequent sessions, Tighe exhumed details of Murphy's life. Daughter of barrister Duncan Murphy and his spouse, Kathleen, Bridey came into this world on December 20, 1798. She married Sean Brian McCarthy at age seventeen and then moved to Belfast. At age sixty-six, she "fell down . . . fell down on the stairs, and . . . seems I broke some bones in my hip too . . . just sort of withered away. . . . I was such a burden. Had to be carried about. . . ."[8]

She observed her own funeral: "Oh, I watched them. I watched them

---

*The release of repressed memories and emotions in a purely psychoanalytic context is called abreaction, but when the abreaction between doctor and patient—medicine man/woman and conjuree—is triggered ritually or shamanically, the "memories" often take on a mythic, transcendental, and transpersonal or ancestral aspect. Time is symbolically shattered, and an impromptu séance begins in which things not ordinarily seen and heard present themselves. Bernstein crossed this boundary without evident awareness of its significance.

ditch my body."[9] She stared at her tombstone, read aloud her name, dates of her birth and death.

When Bernstein asked where she went afterward, she said:

"I just . . . waiting where everybody waits. . . . It's just a place of waiting."[10]

There she experienced a lucidity with which she could distinguish the alternation of night and day and the passage of time on Earth. She watched Brian going about his life, missing her. When Bernstein asked her to recall her activities in the waiting place, she offered a touching tidbit:

"I . . . remember . . . dancing . . . dancing."[11] She was performing a round dance where time didn't exist.

The Search for Bridey Murphy became a bestseller and pop sensation, as if Virginia Tighe were the first person on Earth to recall a past life. Yet throughout India, Turkey, Lebanon, Sri Lanka, Thailand, Tibet, and, in fact, most of the Middle East and Asia, people were routinely remembering prior existences *without hypnotic regression.* They usually identified a lifetime within the same extended family, clan, village, or region. Remembering an existence in another country and century, as Ms. Tighe did, is relatively rare. Otherwise, Bernstein's subject was experiencing ordinary transpersonal flashbacks. Yet reincarnation was so repressed in the West that the book made headlines. How did such a state of affairs come about?

Nineteenth-Century Views

By the conservative 1950s, vestiges of nineteenth-century enthusiasm for reincarnation had been blotted out by two world wars and a depression, followed by miracle-like sprees of scientific legerdemain. What manifestations could be more vivid, compelling, or chock full of urgency than combat in muddy trenches, the rise of the Third Reich, Hitler's blitzkrieg across Europe, the war machine of imperial Japan, aerial bombardment of cities, and apocalyptic battles on remote Pacific islands? After the euphoria of armistice came automated appliances, Oldsmobiles, and televisions. Current-life effulgence drowned past-life remnants. The physical plane was numinous and mesmerizing and vibrated with such immediacy that shadow realms palled beside it. Reality became enthralling—senior in every way.

From a different perspective, the seniority of physical existence is a deep-rooted apparition. Each apparition plays out exclusively during its engagement. Like a dream while being dreamed, it has full claim on our being.

Before past-life amnesia settled in, reincarnation had been accepted in the West, from ancient Greece and Rome through the Middle Ages and Renaissance. In a lifelong attempt to contact the dead, British philologist Frederic Myers (1843–1901), a founder of the Society for Psychical Research (1882), and his colleagues used assorted strategies to communicate with spirits of the deceased. Myers was reported to have sent semi-encrypted messages after his own death.

The Society's repertoire included poltergeists, table tipping, spirit photographs, levitation, trumpets and accordions floating in midair and playing audible music, automatic writing (which later gave rise to Ouija boards), mediumship, crystal gazing, spirit knocking, ectoplasm, and telepathy (a term coined by Myers). These experiments had continuity with those of prior centuries, augmented with a new pragmatic empiricism.

Other nineteenth-century explorers of the paranormal ran the gamut from open-minded scientists to amateur sleuths like Mark Twain and Abraham Lincoln.

A bias of postmodern provincialism is to assume that all these researchers were gullible and myopic or lacked scientific methodology. But most of them conducted meticulous measurements while trying to disentangle multiple layers of coincidence and unexplained transfers of objects and information. Their trials were *at least* as thorough as those administered almost a century later at Duke University. Not only were parapsychology's early experiments conducted with *a priori* skepticism, they also were evaluated along impartial parameters that were abandoned in the later twentieth century under the fundamentalist protocols of scientism. Myers and crew had open minds about how the universe *might work* as opposed to current arbiters who ignore the paranormal and dismiss unexplained phenomena without puzzling over them.

By furnishing a quasi-scientific mechanism to explain most anomalies, Sigmund Freud played a role in the West's dismissal of psychic events. He modeled a fathomless unconscious mind with an indeterminate flow into the ego. If conventional thoughts and memories could be warped and esoterically malformed by normal biological drives, supernatural explanations were unnecessary for phantasms and cryptic events. Dreams and trances were declared psychotic fugues—brief, incidental breaks with reality. Poltergeists and past lives fell somewhere between sleepwalking and hysteria (with a dose of wish fulfillment).

An unconscious mind as complex and refractory as the one Freud adduced could concoct ghosts, reincarnation, or just about anything. The chain of custody to the Big Bang was preserved; within the universe's established boundaries, a kaleidoscope of fantasies, sublimations, and hypnagogic hallucinations perturbed cognitively endowed proteins. *Actual* other dimensions of reality became unnecessary. Freud and his contemporaries never considered that past-life memories could be *both* psychological and psychic, yet the universe is entangled in *exactly that way.**

At roughly the same time, quantum physics established an uncertainty basis—a minded refraction in matter—for *all* phenomena. Even though researchers were scanning only at a subatomic level, they installed a material cornerstone of anomalous action, eliminating the need for other anomalies by showing that *reality itself* was unstable and conditional. Physics came to serve not only "quantum mystical" camps like Penrose-Hameroff aficionados but also pious materialists as it "reduced" any potential aberrations (like consciousness) to paradoxical states of plasma issuing from the Big Bang. If a particle's position is measurable only in relation to its momentum (and *vice versa*), then matter behaved metaphysically *without metaphysics.*

Formulaic Christianity left its own parochial mark. Papal protocol decreed a single lifetime followed by a definitive Judgment. That was its defining commodity, and the faithful kept the faith.

The Real Search for Bridey Murphy

In this environment, Bernstein's regression of Virginia Tighe took the public by storm. After the publication of *The Search for Bridey Murphy,*

---

*I don't mean the literal quantum entanglement of subatomic particles. I am using "entanglement" as a placeholder for other unknown or undiscovered states of paradoxical affiliation.

newspapers and radio stations launched their own quests for the long-deceased colleen, Tighe's former self. For weeks, the *New York Daily Mirror* ran a front-page cliffhanger, detailing the adventures of its reporter in Ireland. Every day, it seemed, he was on the verge of finding Bridey and confirming reincarnation, but each promising lead petered out.

A consensus of investigators joined him in concluding that Ms. Tighe's "Bridey Murphy" never existed. No such woman inhabited Ireland during the years of her proposed lifetime as read by Tighe from her own tombstone: born 1798, passed 1864. The roster of churches, addresses, and artifacts cited by Tighe was deemed apocryphal.

In truth, the early nineteenth century, though relatively recent, is still too long ago to verify ordinary people and events. Locating the "real" Bridey Murphy is much more difficult than trying to pin down the identity of Jack the Ripper a few decades later, a gambit regularly attempted by historian-sleuths. It is more like trying to figure out if Shakespeare wrote his own plays. No records remain of most Cork habitants and occurrences from her era. About the only smoking gun was that, as a young girl, Bridey had shopped for provisions at a grocer named Farr and there *was* a shopkeeper of that surname in her purported neighborhood at the time. One random hit was par for the course.

Far more damning was the discovery that aspects of Bridey Murphy's memories were traceable to Tighe's childhood in Chicago, Illinois, including the name itself, for she lived across the street from a recent immigrant named Bridie Murphy Cockrell. Just about everyone jumped to the conclusion that Tighe's "reincarnation" was a conventional memory displaced in cryptomnesiac fashion.

Neither the *Mirror* nor other media recognized synchronicities—repeating anomalous coincidences—that might cause the former Bridey Murphy to reincarnate across the street from her prior namesake.

Ms. Tighe could also have recalled an authentic past life in Cork and subliminally conflated the name of her neighbor with that of her prior self, shielding her identity. A form of psychic sublimation or karmic privacy may have intervened, authorizing decryption only by displacing its phenomenology. Forbidden knowledge has its limits.

Instead, Bridey Murphy entered pop culture somewhere between a freak and a hoax, a discredited diva and star of a bad movie *(I've Lived Before)*, two popular songs ("For the Love of Bridey Murphy" and "Do You Believe in Reincarnation?"), and a 1956 satire, *The Quest for Bridey Hammerschlaugen,* in which comedian Stan Freberg hypnotized Goldie Smith (played by an actress named Joan Foray) and summoned her memories of different eras, each of which Foray hammed up. Then she turned the tables and, in a spoof of Bernstein, hypnotically regressed Freberg, who quickly recalled being Davy Crockett. Foray told him that he wouldn't be able to profit on the current fad of Tennessee frontier products, so Freberg declared that he would come back in his next life as Walt Disney.

The Search for Bridey Murphy also appeared iconically in novels by Thomas Pynchon and Ken Kesey, indicating less a rehabilitation than its influence over a new genre—magical realism.

Past Lives in Therapy

Since the days of Morey Bernstein and without fanfare, hypnotic regression has been regularly used by physicians, hypnotists, and therapists to disinter anomalous memories, including possible past lives, usually with a therapeutic goal. In an episode paralleling Bernstein's regression of Virginia Tighe, Brian Weiss, chief of psychiatry at Mount Sinai Hospital in Miami Beach, instructed a patient identified as "Catherine" to "go back to the time from which your symptoms arise." Weiss had failed to relieve phobias of choking, drowning, and being stranded in the dark— even after the patient recovered an age-three memory (under hypnosis) of sexual violation by her drunken father. Though not requested to recall a past life like Ms. Tighe, the patient responded similarly: "I see white steps leading up to a building, a big white building with pillars . . . I am wearing a long dress, a sack made of rough material. My name is Aronda. I am eighteen. . . ."[12] She identified the year as 1863 BCE. Aronda ultimately drowned in a flood.

In follow-up sessions, Catherine became a Dutchman named Johann whose throat was slit in 1473, a house servant named Abbey in nineteenth-century Virginia, a Welsh seaman named Christian, a German aviator, Eric, and a Ukrainian boy in 1758.[13] After weathering the assorted life crises and death traumas of each of these under hypnotic regression, she experienced a mitigation of her symptoms. Though clinical success could not be attributed to reliving a past-life trauma, her improvement was in contrast to *lack* of improvement following recall of abuse by her father.

While no one in 1863 BCE would identify their era by a prochronistic date, and despite the fact that Catherine's life as a Ukrainian boy overlapped her incarnation as a Spanish prostitute, the recall of these "lives" seems to have worked in the way that recovery of *an actual traumatic moment* does in psychoanalytic transference. When awakened from her regressions, Catherine not only did not remember any of her so-called past lives but also, when informed of their details, was mortified and quickly repudiated them. As a practicing Catholic, she did not accept reincarnation; nonetheless, she continued with the therapy because of its positive results.

Weiss finessed validating these "past lives" or their incongruities, conceding, "[T]he totality of the experience was such that these inconsistencies only add to its complexity. There is so much we don't know."[14]

Therapists consider either that symptomatic relief is proof of the legitimacy of the memories or, antithetically, that it doesn't matter if the "memories" are false because they tap into something primal in the patient's subconscious. Here the inquiry encounters a different dichotomy—real versus imaginal past lives. It will take preparation and lead-in to get there, but I will do a preliminary pass now.

Ailments that are unaffected by any other mode of treatment often clear up spontaneously after a past-life regression. But the cure doesn't require a past-life *belief system*. Stuck internalized energy— *cathected trauma* in Freudian terminology—transcends any specific content. If the energetic basis for a cure is triggered by therapist-patient transference, the content is ancillary. Since it doesn't matter if the "memories" are made cognitively conscious too—and they usually aren't—it also doesn't matter if they are "real" (see chapter 8, "Trauma and Redemption").

This model also accords with established spiritual views of the aura* as the repository of traumas as well as the only place where they can be released. In the aura, the many experiences and incarnations of a spirit or soul meld into a greater membrance, so unconscious associations can be triggered by *actual* past-life events, fictive past lives, or unresolved elements of the psychic field in general. In the aura, a fantasy is no less veridical than reality: each governs the same formation energy.

If reincarnation is added to the playing field, then all other meanings have to change to accommodate its context. Over thousands of years and recurrent death amnesia, forensics becomes both unverifiable and irrelevant. You can say that a trauma was caused 100 percent by a specific event in a given lifetime but also 100 percent by another event, or by many events from different lifetimes. They are simultaneously valid. An infinite number of antecedents are each sufficient to generate or reinforce a state: the universe *itself* is overdetermined, as we shall see, for multiple causes tend to cluster about one another and each "exclusively" causes the same effect, sometimes in multiple lifetimes.

In addition, the mind or psyche doesn't usually take in disorienting information directly or literally. It changes its context and location uncannily; the output—what becomes newly conscious—is contextually disconnected from the input. As meanings and contexts ricochet in the psyche, material passes from a liminal state and becomes known, though the link between it and the initial charge is counterintuitive. An innate intelligence seems to provide the necessary "meaning," which is always unexpected because it is a piece of what is being systemically camouflaged. It is the card, or divination, that the ego will never turn on its own.

In that regard, it is worth considering an episode I witnessed at the Berkeley Psychic Institute in 2009. Director Javier Thistlethwaite

*Like many states or meta-objects not recognized by science, the aura has multiple definitions, each legitimate in its way. Here I am emphasizing an invisible emanation, a psychic twin of the body, that is generated, along with its physical form, by higher-dimensional "seeds" during embryological development. The aura vibrates with the memories and emotional residues of all the lifetimes of the individual. It is also a boundary. Everything inside the aura, whatever its source, is the responsibility of the individual. Everything outside is not.

assembled an audience from the evening's classes in the commons, where he performed a series of past-life readings of students he had selected. Volunteers expressed a medley of "Yo dude, that was incredible; that was *so* my past life" to "How did you do it?" After the buzz died down, Javier teased the audience while pointing to the last volunteer, "Was that her real past life?"

No one took the bait.

"C'mon. Is any of this stuff really real?"

After about 30 seconds of silence, he responded, "I haven't the slightest idea. Her past life is past, and my reading is past. And the question is past too. We'll never prove anything one way or another. The only thing that matters is that energy was moving energy. Me as spirit was talking to her as spirit."

That is the long and the short of it. You can't prove (or disprove) a past life by a DNA swab. All you can do is follow a mystery thread, wherever it goes. Either it will become more meaningful or it will dissolve into irrelevance. As you keep at interrogation, unconsciously too, you dead-reckon your way to its rightful place in the universe and, remarkably, the universe itself. Reality is "view." That's how astronomers found us in a galaxy and our galaxy among other galaxies. A turtle emerging from its egg and heading straight for water creates a lake.

A Journalist's Journey

Washington Post journalist Tom Shroder, a longtime investigator of past-life claims, enumerates common objections to past-life explanations:

> If there was a soul, why could nobody detect it? How did it move from one body to another? Did it enter at the moment of conception? Of birth? Why did such a tiny percentage of people remember previous lives? Why were those memories so fragmentary? If souls were recycled, how could you explain the population explosion?[15]

After observing one of Weiss's regressions, Shroder reported nothing more extraordinary than "a contemporary American woman free-associating on a medieval theme"[16] —what a person with a high school education and a reading of romance novels could formulate by a mix of suggestibility, pseudomemories, and deference. Later, when he interviewed her, she told him, "It never made sense to me that we could be here for such a short time, and then . . . nothing."[17] To him, such wishful thinking was a red flag.

When undergoing hypnotic regression himself, Shroder experienced the same susceptibility he observed in others. He was eager to cooperate and "supply the hypnotist with what she wanted."[18] He concluded that past lives were fantasies similar to those of UFO abductees and children claiming molestation in preschools—false memories implanted by a hypnotist.

During a past-life reading, a menagerie of unconvincing characters paraded before him: an Australian rancher, a black Jamaican sorceress, and an arthritic Japanese sage. None of these had any resonance—in his words, "no fading scent of jasmine or sting of gin."[19]

I had a similar experience during my first visit to the Berkeley Psychic Institute. I went there at the urging of a friend, telling myself I could nab a class schedule and vamoose. As I approached the desk, a ghostlike man descending an Alfred Hitchcock staircase declared, "We've just had a cancellation for a psychic reading. Do you want it?"

I opened my mouth to decline but found myself saying, "Yes."

He led me down an unlit hall. We entered a large auditorium, and he pointed to a metal folding chair, a postage stamp on the space. I faced two young men in trance on folding chairs. Another man and woman stood alongside them, eyes closed. They reminded me of a Sophocles chorus—or the cast of a Woody Allen sitcom in which a naïf finds himself confronted by a klatch of batty channelers. No hypnosis was involved, but they proceeded to tell me about my past lives as a Japanese monk, cowboy, and society woman married to a scholar. None of it resonated.

Yet a woman in New Jersey, one of several participants on Skype, made surprisingly accurate observations about three of my family members, then tied them together in a reincarnational anecdote. She apparently read my aura through the video; that is, she read the universe at my vibration, which is why I chose to study there afterward.

Shroder went the other way. He confessed, after much soul searching, that he had "stared inward but never seen a ripple nor heard a whisper of any life but my own [and] seen people near to me disappear into death with an awesome and unappealable finality. . . . In my marrow, I could feel no trace, however faint, of a previous life. The universe before me was a void, a nothingness that flared into somethingness only with my earliest memories of *this* life."[20]

But he was searching like the nihilistically preconditioned Westerner he was, looking for a recognizable narrative, a Proustian opera starring himself. He was also trying to push himself through the existential opacity of his own denial rather than neutrally opening himself to an esoteric flow. Like SETI (Search for Extraterrestrial Intelligence) researchers with radio telescopes attuned to the heavens, he assumed that the "extraterrestrial" message would be in *his* terms. He did not consider that jasmine and gin essences, between lifetimes, might transmogrify, becoming talismans unrecognizable by a contemporary psyche.

One is not usually going to undo reincarnational encryption by tugging its knot in the direction in which it was tied—either by traveling hypnotically backward or having a clairvoyant flash of a pre-incarnation history. That's the sort of intrusion our biological system was designed to resist, and I don't mean that some high muckamuck designed it, just that it is *intelligently designed.* We are not supposed to know the cumulative history of our soul; it would interfere with the piquancy of the current lifetime and diffuse its singular focus. The universe's codes may bend, as Freud discerned—symbols and inversions tend to replace true mnemonics when a tabooed territory is threatened—but they don't break. Sublimation and reaction formation are designed to *protect* trances, not shatter them.

The Research of Ian Stevenson

Ultimately, Shroder shifted his focus to a different sort of testimony: the investigations of Ian Stevenson, a psychiatrist and research scientist at the University of Virginia who, to the chagrin of his family and colleagues, switched from microbiological psychiatry to parapsychology after a trip to India to check the account of a child who "remembered" a past life.

Before even departing, he learned of five similar cases in India, and he was informed of twenty-five more while there. Later, he spent a week in Ceylon (Sri Lanka), following up on seven reported cases. The commonness of such claims, plus—when a match was found—the verisimilitudes of children's memories to the lives of their purported past persons (PPs), indicated to Stevenson that he might have found an important, neglected rubric of psychology, a lacuna in science itself.

Thereafter, in a department chair endowed by Chester F. Carlson, the inventor of xerography, Stevenson specialized in past-life memories and related phenomena (near-death experiences, poltergeists, etc.). He abjured hypnotic regression, a potentially adulterating factor, and went straight to the source, hastening to wherever he got word of a child evincing an equivocal memory. He then attempted to match the accounts of the boy or girl to the life of his or her PP. This meant covering tens of thousands of miles in mainly the Middle East and South Asia. His goal was to corroborate (or refute) evidence before it was contaminated. In some instances, details had been written down or shared with multiple witnesses before the PP's family had been contacted.

Again, Stevenson was seeking spontaneous memories, not induced regressions. His cases "predominantly featured young children, ages two to five, who spoke of previous-life memories for a brief time, usually until they were about eight."[21] In the words of past-life therapist Carol Bowman, such young children "haven't had the cultural conditioning, the layering over of experience in this life, so the memories can percolate up more easily."[22] "Past-life" recollections tend to fade with immersion in the current lifetime. In Western culture, where such flashbacks are ignored or disparaged, they evaporate faster.

Stevenson filed 2,500 reports of varying completeness. There were no prior existences as Cleopatra or Napoleon or Alexander the Great or Pope Urban the Second, no memories of being in a pharaoh's harem or palace guard. Résumés featured ordinary people in mundane circumstances, a more likely PP census than the royal casting calls of many New Age regressions. A disproportionate number *did* involve violent deaths and deaths of children, suggesting that reincarnational carryover is traumatic—an unsettled or premature death picture needing resolution. This would explain why most "rebirths" take place within hailing distance of the previous life: "souls" are drawn back to matters left unresolved.

The following cases span a worldview foreign to a Western perspective:

☺ At an early age, a boy in Lebanon, Nazih Al-Danaf, told his parents that he had once carried pistols and grenades, was married to a pretty woman, and had many children. He said that his house was surrounded by trees and was near a cave. Repeatedly asking to be taken "home," he swore that he knew how to find the house. His parents delayed a search until he was six; then they followed his directions.

As they approached the alleged site, Nazih became more confident, picking which of six roads to take from the center of town. When interrogated by the widow of the man who had lived in the house, Nazih answered each of her questions accurately. The woman was convinced that he was the rebirth of her husband, Faud, father of her five children.

On a subsequent visit, Nazih recognized a man and cried out, "Here comes my brother Adeeb." The wary Adeeb demanded proof, so the child announced, "I gave you a Checki 16." Faud had indeed given his brother a pistol from Czechoslovakia, a model rare in Lebanon. Later attempts to trick Nazih by misleading queries—for instance, by asking him to "confirm" incorrect details about Faud—all failed.[23]

☺ About a year before he died in Angoon, Alaska, in the spring of 1946, Tlingit Alaska Native Victor Vincent had said to his sister's daughter of whom he was fond, "'I'm coming back as your next son. I hope I don't stutter then as much as I do now. Your son will have these scars.' He then pulled up his shirt and showed her a scar on his back . . . a residue of an operation he had had . . . some years earlier. . . . Mr. Vincent at the same time also pointed to a scar on his nose on the right side of its base as another mark by which his niece would recognize his rebirth."

Eighteen months later, his niece "gave birth to a boy named after his father, Corliss Chotkin, Jr. At birth, this boy had two marks on his body of exactly the same shape and location as the scars pointed to by Victor Vincent in his prediction of his rebirth."

When Corliss Jr., was old enough to talk, he rejected his name and said, "Don't you know me? I'm Kahkody." The boy had spoken the tribal name of Victor Vincent "with an excellent accent."

In ensuing months, he recognized and named several of Victor Vincent's relatives without prompting, including his son William and his wife, Rose.

Excited to see Vincent's stepdaughter one afternoon at the Sitka dock, the boy jumped up and down, calling out, "There's my Susie."[24]

☻ Chanai Choonmalaiwong, a boy born in Thailand in 1967, began talking at age three about being a teacher named Bua Kai who had been shot and killed while en route to school. "He gave the names of his parents, his wife, and two of his children from that life, and persistently begged his grandmother, with whom he lived, to take him to his previous parents' home," which he identified in a village fifteen miles away.[25]

After they arrived by bus, Chanai walked straight to the house of an elderly couple whose son Bua Kai Lawnak had been a school teacher and had been murdered five years before Chanai was born. Upon being invited in, he recognized one of Bua Kai's daughters and asked after the other by name. Though the family accepted him as the reincarnation of their son, his "daughters" refused to call him "father" as he desired, so he stopped talking to them.

Additionally, Chanai had two birthmarks, a large irregular one above his left eye and a smaller circular one on the back of his head, both hairless and puckered, which matched Bua Kai's exit and entry wounds.[26]

☻ A Turkish child, Necip Ünlütaşkiran, had numerous striking birthmarks on his head, face, and trunk. At age six, he began speaking about having been stabbed repeatedly in the city of Mersin, fifty miles away. He also remembered being married with children and cutting his wife on her leg with a knife during an argument.[27] One of his PP's widow's legs bore a scar that she said had come from a stab wound by her late husband. He was not christened Necip but insisted on being called by the name of his PP.

After the PP's family was identified, Necip correctly identified objects that he had owned. Also, Necip's grandmother in his present life turned out to be a local woman his PP had called "grandmother" too. Necip remarked that now she was a *real* grandmother instead of only being *like* one to him[28]—rebirth with synchronicity.

By the time Stevenson was able to examine Necip 2 at age thirteen and compare his birthmarks to those on the autopsy report of Necip 1, he found eight matching indications.[29]

☯ In July 1951, a boy in Kanauj, India, Ravi Shankar, was born six months after the death of another child, Munna, the six-year-old son of a barber named Jageshwar Prasad, in a different district of Kanauj. Munna "was enticed from his place and brutally murdered by two neighbors . . . and the motive for the crime seems to have been the wish to dispose of Sri Jageshwar Prasad's heir so that one of the murderers (a relative) might inherit his property. . . . The mutilated and severed head of the boy and some of his clothes were subsequently found and clearly identified by his father."[30]

Between the ages of two and three, Ravi gave explicit "details of his murder, naming the murderers, the place of the crime, and other circumstances of the life and death of Munna. The boy . . . kept asking his parents for various toys which he claimed he had in the house of his previous life." He accurately recounted numerous events from the life of Munna, plus he "had on his neck a linear mark resembling closely the scar of a long knife wound across his neck." He wasn't born with it; it appeared when he was three months old.[31]

☯ A New Delhi girl named Preeti told her sister, "This is your house, not my house. These are your parents, not mine. You have only one brother, I have four." Preeti identified her "real" family as living in a village twelve miles away. Her name there had been Sheila, and she had been hit by a car while running across the street. These and other details of her recitations fit the narrative of a recently deceased teenage girl in a nearby village. On a trip there, Preeti immediately recognized her PP's parents and began what became an ongoing relationship with them.[32]

When asked how she knew that Preeti was her daughter's rebirth, Sheila's mother referred to the girl's resemblance to Sheila at that age, a feature noticed by not only the family but also the milkman. A distinctive birthmark on the outside of Preeti's right thigh matched where Sheila had sustained an injury. Sheila's mother remarked, "When one of my sons pointed to Sheila's younger brother and asked Preeti, 'Is he older or younger than you?' she said, 'He was younger than me, and now he is older. . . .' One day, when I was taking Preeti in the street, she was afraid. She said, 'Don't, I'll get run over again.'"[33]

☯ Daniel Jirdi, a child in Lebanon, remembered having been Rashid Khaddage, a mechanic who had died when his cousin Ibrahim committed an act of road rage, speeding after an offending vehicle and flipping the car in which they were traveling, tossing and killing him.

At age two and a half, Daniel gave details of the accident and of Rashid's life. His parents first understood something about their son was strange when he corrected their pronunciation of Rashid's hometown, Kfarmatta, and explained *he was from there*. Daniel recalled the name of the driver, that he had been thrown from the car, and where the accident occurred; he also knew "that Rashid's mother had been knitting him a sweater."[34]

Later, as his parents drove past Military Beach, he put his hands over his eyes and began screaming and crying, "This is where I died."[35]

Daniel was born with a lump on his head in the approximate place of Rashid's head wound, though Stevenson conceded that delivery during birth could have caused such a swelling, adding he "wouldn't want to take that lump to court as evidence of reincarnation."[36]

Soon word got out, and the Khaddages showed up at the Jirdi's home, hoping to reconnect with their "son." As they approached unannounced, Daniel saw them through the door and called, "Bring bananas for Najla and make some coffee, my family is here."[37] Bananas had been Rashid's favorite food.

While investigating the Khaddage family, Stevenson found that Ulfat, the daughter of Muna, Rashid's younger sister, remembered a recent past life too. She had a vivid memory of being killed by Christians during the civil war, and her story closely matched that of one of the young girls massacred in Salina. She was twenty-three years old at the time. In Ulfat's account:

"It was at night, I was walking. I was afraid to go through an alley, but had no other way. There were about four men carrying guns." As soon as they saw her, they shot her in the leg. When they saw that she was clutching jewels to her blouse, they took them and tortured her.[38] She did not remember the feeling of being tortured or dying, only that it happened.

☙ In another case in Lebanon, Suzanne Ghanem, a girl of sixteen months old, suddenly grabbed the phone and began trying to call her "oldest daughter Leila." Her first words, in fact, were "Hello, Leila?"[39] Suzanne was born in the late 1960s, ten days after the death of a thirty-five-year-old woman in the area named Hanan Mansour. Hanan had warned her husband, Farouk, that when she was reborn, she would have "a lot to say about her previous life."[40]

Young Suzanne insisted that she was Hanan and promised that when her head was bigger, she would explain. The older she got, the more she looked like Hanan. Eventually, she remembered her old phone number (with two digits reversed) as well as provisions for jewelry she made in her will. She correctly identified twenty-five people from her past life.

She later took to phoning her PP's widower, Farouk, almost daily, interfering with his marriage to "the new wife."[41]

☙ Süleyman Caper, a child in Turkey, declared, as soon as he was able to talk, that he had been a miller and that an angry customer had hit him over the head with a shovel. The back of his skull was partially depressed and had a dark birthmark on it. Suleyman remembered the first name of the miller and the village. Again, there was a perfect match: death wound and birthmark.[42]

Western past-life memories follow similar motifs:

☙ When Bobby Hodges, a boy in North Carolina, began speaking, he asked his mother why she wouldn't let him live with his real family. By that, he meant his Aunt Susan. His parents paid no attention, considering it his way of expressing how much he enjoyed being with his cousins. One night at age four and a half, after his bath, he asked his mother if she remembered when he and his two-and-a-half-year-old brother Donald were in her tummy at the same time. She agreed that they had both been in her tummy but insisted that it wasn't at the same time. After rethinking the matter, Bobby said it was when they were in Aunt Susan's tummy and *didn't* get born. Then, to his mother's astonishment, he began yelling at his younger brother, blaming him for Susan's miscarriage: "I told you I wanted to get born real bad, and you didn't want to. How did you take me out of there, Donald? Why didn't you want to get born?" His mother had to stop him from attacking Donald.

Donald took out his pacifier and yelled, "No! I wanted Daddy!"

Bobby shouted, "I didn't want Daddy, I wanted Uncle Ron."[43]

Seven years before Bobby was born, Susan was pregnant with twins; they stopped moving at thirty-three weeks because one of them had rolled over on the umbilical cord.[44]

☻ William was born five years after his grandfather, a New York City policeman working a second job as a security guard, was fatally shot. William had birth defects corresponding to the wounds of his grandfather, including pulmonary valve artesia replicating damage from a bullet that had passed through his PP's back, lungs, and main pulmonary vehicle. The coincidence was more or less ignored until William, age three, spoke out after his mother threatened to spank him: "Mom, when you were a little girl and I was your daddy, you were bad a lot of times, and I never hit you."[45] He later remembered correctly that the name of his PP's cat was Boston but that he called him "Boss."

☻ Samuel Taylor, born in Vermont a year and a half after his paternal grandfather died, startled his father, who was changing his diaper at the time, by telling him, "When I was your age, I used to change your diapers."[46] Another time, he pointed to his grandfather in a family photo and declared, "That's me!"[47]

His mother asked if "he had any brothers or sisters when he lived before. He answered, 'Yeah, I had a sister. She turned into a fish.' When asked who turned her into a fish, he said, 'Some bad guys. She died. You know what, when we die, God lets us come back again. I used to be big, and now I'm a kid again.'

"The sister of Sam's grandfather, in fact, had been killed some sixty years before. Her husband killed her while she was sleeping, rolled her body up in a blanket, and dumped it in the bay."[48]

In a similar incident, Abby Swanson, a four-year-old girl in Ohio, told her mother after her bath one night, "Mommy, I used to give you baths when you were a baby. . . . I was your grandma."[49]

�} Gillian and Jennifer Pollack, twins born in Hexham, Northumberland (England), in 1958, remembered toys and events from the past lives of their older sisters Joanna and Jacqueline, who were struck by a car and killed while walking to church a year and a half before the girls were born. In fact, the two routinely talked about their sisters' lives as though they *were* them. On several occasions, their parents overheard them dispassionately reminiscing about the accident.

Gillian thought that she was Joanna; Jennifer claimed to be Jacqueline. When dolls and other playthings were brought out from the older girls' collections, each identified the objects belonging to her complement.

On one occasion, Gillian pointed to Jennifer's birthmark on her forehead and said, "That is the mark Jennifer got when she fell on a bucket." But it was Jacqueline, not Jennifer, who "indeed had fallen on a bucket, receiving an injury that required stitches and produced a permanent scar."[50]

Around age seven, the children forgot their PPs and stopped referring to them.[51]

�} When Patrick Christenson of Michigan was four and a half years old, he began telling his parents intimate details from the life of his older brother Kevin, who had died of cancerous metastases at age two, twelve years before Patrick was born. He said that he wanted to go back and live in their former house, the one that was orange and brown. He also asked his mother about his surgery, pointing to a spot above his right ear, where his brother had had a nodule removed for a biopsy.[52]

☻ Ryan Hammons, a boy born in Warner, Oklahoma, in 2004, told his mother at age four, "I think I used to be someone else." He remembered having been an actor in Hollywood, dancing on Broadway, traveling on boats to other countries, and being married.[53] Ryan's mother, Cyndi, a deputy county clerk in Muskogee, started keeping a journal of her son's accounts of a person he called "the old me." She did not initially tell her husband, Kevin, a lieutenant with the Muskogee Police Department. When finally presented with Ryan's tale, he said, "Damnit, Cyndi! Reincarnation? Where the hell do you come up with this stuff? We have a regular little boy who doesn't want to sleep in his bed and you just give in to him and let him sleep in here. He's a kid and kids have nightmares and I don't want to hear more of this New Age bull."[54]

Here is the gist of what Ryan recalled: He was a Hollywood movie star who occasionally tap danced on stage. (He demonstrated when cartoon music reminded him of one of his old routines.) After his acting career, he became an agent, and his agency represented famous clients. He lived on a street with the word "mount" or "rock" in it. He was very rich and had a large house with a swimming pool. He was married four times and had numerous girlfriends and affairs. The house was filled with children, but the boys weren't his birth children, though he gave them his name. He knew Rita Hayworth made "ice drinks." He had a green car that he wouldn't let anyone else drive and a large collection of sunglasses. These were among fifty-five later-verified memories.[55]

Ryan explained that his other self was always there, but "when you are a baby . . . you can't tell anyone because you can't talk."[56]

The identification of Ryan's "old me" came after his mother brought home a library book on the golden age of Hollywood. He recognized himself from 1932 as a nameless extra in Mae West's first film, *Night after Night*. "You found me, Momma! You found me! That's me and that's George and we did a picture together." Pointing to a man who stood alongside George Raft as a gangster, he added, "That guy's me. I found me."[57]

It took a year, with the help of Stevenson associate Jim Tucker, to match the picture with Marty Martyn (born Martin Kolinsky), an obscure Hollywood actor. Martyn had been both a performer and agent, was married four times, and lived on Rocksbury Drive. His death certificate had the wrong age; Ryan's memory of passing at sixty-one proved accurate.[58]

Once word got out, Ryan became a minor sensation; he and his mother were interviewed in *USA Today* as well as the international press. In a chapter she wrote for journalist Leslie Kean's book *Surviving Death,* Cyndi remarked that "Kevin and I were often struck by how much Ryan talked like an adult, although we were used to it by now. He seemed to have wisdom that was sometimes uncanny for his age."[59] She provided examples. "Some days when I picked him up from school he talked about being an agent, and when I asked him what he did at school, he would say, 'You know, agent stuff.' He also pretended that he was making movies. When he was four, I remember taking him to a birthday party where he assembled all the children there to direct them for his movie. He yelled at the adults that he needed help because it was hard to act in and direct a major production."[60]

When certain incidents involving a "Senator Five" (who turned out to be a real-life Senator Ives) terrified him, Cyndi explained that he wasn't Marty Martyn anymore and she just wanted him to be Ryan and happy. He said, "Mom, you still don't get it, do you? I am not the same as the man in the picture on the outside, but on the inside I am still that man. You just can't see on the inside what I see."[61]

Over time even Kevin came to believe Ryan. "In his more than fifteen years as a police officer, he had interviewed many people suspected of crimes, from stealing all the way to murder. He had learned to recognize when someone was lying."[62]

Marty Martyn had one birth daughter, who was eight when he died. When Ryan met her again as a grandmother in her fifties, she remarked, "The experience of meeting Ryan was strange. The first thing he said to me was that I was so old!"[63]

A comment by Ryan goes to the heart of the matter: "Why would God let you get to be sixty-one and then make you come back as a baby."[64]

Past-Life Dèjá Vu

What stands out in these accounts is each person's strong identification with his or her (or their)* PP, an intersubjective sense of *having been and still being* another person with a unique selfhood and vantage. "They *are* the previous personalities, and they resist the imposition of a new identity . . . they say, '*I have* a wife,' or *I am* a doctor,' or "*I have* three buffalos and two cows.'"[65] One boy told his parents, "See that rice field. It once belonged to me." Another insisted on shopping for size-eight shoes even though they were too large for him. "He wouldn't drop it," his mother told Stevenson. "We actually had to buy him a pair and take it home and make him wear it to prove to him that it was way too big."[66] The former self superseded proprioception of his own body.

Children are similarly attached to their PP's cultures and lifestyle. In some instances, a child may be upset by the diminishment of his or her social status. Jasbir Singh, a boy "reborn" into a lower caste in India, insisted on having his food prepared for him by a Brahmin neighbor for a year and a half before reluctantly submitting to his family's cuisine. Suzanne complained that her "real" house was larger and more beautiful.[67] Ryan Hammons "sometimes seemed confused about what was then and what was now, and what were reasonable expectations now as opposed to then. He thought he should pay his mom for cleaning his room because before he had a maid who came in every day to clean his house. He expected to see his buddies when he went to Hollywood, and said he might stay with them for a while and come home after his parents."[68]

His mother noted, "There were nights when he was very funny and I enjoyed hearing his stories. Then on other nights he just seemed to be mad at the world. Why couldn't I just fly him to Hollywood and let him eat at his favorite place? Sometimes our house would be too small in his opinion and he would rant about how he couldn't believe he was being expected to live in these conditions. His old room had been large and grand and he had his own swimming pool. Why couldn't we have servants? Do you know how much easier life is with hired help?"[69]

---

*I use the pronoun "their" to honor the new transgender convention.

Other piques by children include: "You aren't my mother. My mother was prettier and richer"; "You are not my family—my family is dead"; "You are not my parents. My parents live somewhere else."[70] They point out missing and altered buildings or landscapes with dismay; some comment on how much worse things have gotten, for instance, how unhappy they are that cars have replaced horses.

If their PPs died as adults, they may resist the transition back to childhood. One boy flirted inappropriately with his schoolteachers, using adult gestures and sexual language.

Reincarnational tracking can defy ordinary cognition. Ryan Hammons had fifty-five matching memory fragments of Marty Martyn—a few scraps blown against a wind barrier. Compare this to xenoglossy, a phenomenon wherein a child possesses a vocabulary and grammar he or she could not have learned in his or her current lifetime. A boy in a Druze family "spoke a strange language, which turned out to be Japanese." The family "only discovered what language [their son] was babbling when they were out with him and he saw some Japanese standing in the street and heard them speaking. He began shouting that he could understand, and he ran to them before his parents could restrain him. By the time they caught up, he was in deep conversation in Japanese."[71] You can imagine trying to explain to the strangers how their boy acquired their language!

Violence and Karma

Several boys and girls born in Burma after World War II remembered having been Japanese soldiers; they rejected local food as too spicy and asked for raw fish and sweets. They wanted to wear Japanese clothes and enjoyed playing battle games.[72] Stevenson speculated that soldiers who had mistreated civilians during World War II might have been "summoned" back to the scene of their crimes, taking on Burmese identities to pay karmic debts. (See chapter 5 for a discussion on karma.)

One Burmese girl who recalled a previous existence as a Japanese soldier craved toy guns and would play only with boys. She insisted on being addressed by the male honorific and eventually moved to the city and sought girlfriends.[73] However, most such children apparently adopt the gender of their current chromosomal identity.

Ramez Shams, a child in Lebanon, "reenacted the suicide of [his] previous personality by repeatedly putting a stick under his chin while pretending that it was a rifle"[74]—either a droll sense of humor or a compulsive counterphobia. Maung Aye Kyaw, a Myanmar man who grew up to marry the widow of his PP, threw stones at one of the men who he claimed killed him in his former life.[75] Other children have attacked the alleged killer of their previous self, kicking or punching them at first encounter.

Interpreting the Evidence

For almost all the past-life cases discussed above, reincarnation is the most logical and rational explanation, even by Occam's razor.*

What are other possible interpretations?

Some who accept telepathy but reject reincarnation propose super-psi whereby one person gains knowledge of another's life from a transpersonal information field or morphic resonance (to adapt biologist Rupert Sheldrake's term†). No one studies this sort of biophysics—the psychic version of a data "cloud"—so we have zero criteria for how a detached memory could be reassigned like a digital file.

Depersonalized clairvoyance does not explain how the narrative of another's life engenders such tenacious identification, though empathy does occur to a lesser and more ephemeral degree in emotional projection, for instance, during a movie when a spectator merges with characters played by actors. The subconscious mind blends disparate threads together—in fact, nightly in dream-formation—and some people have more active imaginations than others. Even so, transference of events from a novel or a play to a psyche is not as persistent as past-life remembrances;

Occam's razor is a problem-solving principle attributed to William of Occam (ca. 1287–1347), which states that "entities should not be multiplied unnecessarily," that the choice between competing hypotheses should favor the solution with the fewest assumptions.

†Morphic resonance is Sheldrake's theory that self-organizing systems store and share information and memory in a hyperdimensional field outside either brains or genes. They also acquire intelligence from prior *similar* systems and designs, inheriting it via telepathic-like signals. This frames a relationship that has both morphic and resonant qualities.

the former are transitory, and the man or woman experiencing them is aware of their fictive nature.

Other rebuttals of Stevenson's evidence are reductionist or ideological and discount the specificity of the testimony and its documentation. For example, it has been pointed out that in the case of Daniel Jirdi, who remembered having been Rashid Khaddage, both Daniel and Rashid were Druze, a sect that believes in reincarnation and soul transfer. Hence, they were prone to pick up a past-life narrative, identify with it, and embellish it. Here, a presumption of susceptibility to reincarnation fantasies is used to *preclude* an interpretation of reincarnation.

One of the more common explanations is that a parent might misunderstand or misconstrue the claims of children with overactive imaginations, weaving a child's fantasies into a narrative and then reinforcing it. One cynic claimed that parents "in their eagerness to confirm the existence of the past life, find another family with a deceased individual whose life shared some general features with those reported by the child."[76] The two families, as they meet and share details, delude each other or collude. By the time Stevenson (or some other researcher) arrives, the child has been coached or brainwashed. Then the parents get drawn into the game and consciously or unintentionally supply cues. The child comes to believe that the stories are her memories of her own past life.

One is tempted to ask, *"In every such case?"* In the University of Virginia's archives alone, there are thousands.

In an experiment to test (and ostensibly debunk) Stevenson's theories, Richard Wiseman, a psychologist in England, asked children to make up stories about their past lives, then searched through magazines and newspapers to try to match their tales with actual obituaries or new accounts in the genre of Stevenson's cases. Usually, he could find something suggestive.[77]

Wiseman's facile resolution—demonstrating that fantasies converge with real events in a universe in which there is enough information at multiple levels to make *any* association credible—may not be *the right interpretation even of his own data*. Wiseman and his subjects could have been drawn into a field of transpersonal clairvoyance or triggered a pattern of synchronous motifs (like Bridey Murphy being reborn across the street from her namesake). Wiseman also committed the mistake of which skeptics accuse believers: tailoring his analysis of data to his beliefs. A different interpretation of this experiment is that synchronicity, as a separate rubric from reincarnation, affects the basic status of information, both conscious and unconscious.

Looking Closely at Synchronicity

Synchronicity pairs events acausally with meanings or energy values we recognize. According to psychologist Carl Jung, these links are enacted on an unconscious level where life is always in psychosomatic unity with the cosmos.[78] Nineteenth-century philosopher Arthur Schopenhauer defined synchronicity as "an ultimate union of necessity and chance which links together all things, even those that are causally unconnected, and does it in such a way that they come together at just the right moment."[79]

The arc is uncanny. When people research synchronicity, they note sudden increases of coincidences in their own lives. Is that an illusion from increased attention to resemblances, or does the unconscious mind actually instigate links? More surprisingly, mystery writers find themselves involved, usually peripherally, in the sorts of crimes they are plotting literarily. Stage magicians faking clairvoyance end up with information they could only have gotten clairvoyantly.

I am going to discuss this sort of anomaly under Cosmic Chicanery in chapter 7, but I will point out here that the universe's complexity may reside in its paradoxes and reversals of the ordinary sequence of cause and effect, occasions that are overlooked because they are usually slight and incidental. Yet scientific stalwarts like electromagnetism and quantum uncertainty were once seined out of "minor" aberrations.

The parallels between Presidents Abraham Lincoln and John F. Kennedy, a century apart, though within statistical parameters of chance, are spooky. The politicians were elected to Congress in 1847 and 1947, respectively, and to the presidency in 1860 and 1960. Both were involved in famous debates (Lincoln with Douglas, Kennedy with Nixon). More strikingly, Lincoln had a secretary named Kennedy, who warned him not to go to the theater that night, while Kennedy had a secretary named Lincoln, who advised him against a trip to Dallas. Lincoln sat in Box 7, Kennedy rode in Car 7.

Still, no big deal: Lincoln and Kennedy are common enough names in the grand scheme. An early reader of this manuscript, physicist Piers Hutchinson, commented, "To my family, the Lincoln-Kennedy parallel was so obviously pure coincidence as to be funny." So let's concede that one.

What about Joseph Figlock, who in 1930, while passing a second time beneath a window, caught and saved the life of the same rambunctious infant?

What about the 1920 train on which the only three passengers discovered that they were Bingham, Powell, and Bingham-Powell?

What about a man, his son, and his grandson who were all struck and killed by lightning in the same backyard in Tarranto, Italy, decades apart, the first in 1919?

What about twin boys separated at birth, both named James by their adopting families, both trained in police enforcement, both marrying women named Linda, both getting divorced and remarrying a woman named Betty. Both named their sons John Allan, though one used a single *l*. Both had dogs named Troy. The coincidences came to light when they were reunited in 1979 at age forty.[80]

Again, with so many events and so much information flowing through physical and semantic universes, some of it is bound to entangle. But unless science can tell us how nature establishes frames of reference, it cannot *ex officio* reduce all synchronicities to coincidences.

Even as three-dimensional objects like machines cast two-dimensional shadows with motions too complex to be explained solely in terms of a two-dimensional landscape—a phenomenon known as the "kinetic depth effect"—an entangled four- or five-dimensional form might cast three-dimensional shadows as synchronicities. In either case, reality is more complex than its appearance.

Overriding Scientific Bias

Skeptical explanations for so-called past-life memories finally tend to be more cumbersome than reincarnation. What doubters are left with are claims that a child must have overheard gossip or that a parent is engaged in fraud.[81] Yet it is a stretch to imagine that a child of two or three could learn and accurately perform whole biographies. How did Suzanne Ghanem get twenty-five names right? Even if she had eavesdropped, how did she remember and assign them without a mistake? Did she have eidetic recall? What was her motive? The notion that children "somehow learned minute details about deceased strangers in other places without their parents' knowledge and then decided that they had been those strangers in a past life seems close to absurd."[82]

Hoaxing makes little sense either. We can't claim ulterior motives predicated on fortune or fame, as there is no financial reward for past-life identities and claims may lead to disputes. Yet we can't dismiss hoaxing solely on that basis because people make mercenarily motivated blunders and delude themselves into expecting windfalls or neurotically seek attention.

Because past-life recall is unusual even among the Druze, Stevenson proposed that its occurrences might be system errors, lapses of universal amnesia.[83] Either reincarnation is the rule and memory the exception or *reincarnation itself* is a system malfunction (as absurd a cosmological slip-up as that would be). The number of Druze cases *does* suggest that belief plays a role, if not in reincarnation, in its recall. In the West, by contrast, indoctrination takes place at such a young age that children become their own self-censors.

A tangential matter is whether reincarnation cycles are limited to one planet, Earth in our case, or whether terrestrial souls can reincarnate on other worlds, either in the Milky Way galaxy or other galaxies?

Some skeptics try for a *coup de grace* by claiming that there are too many people in Earth's expanding population for past lives to account for all of their existences. But there are plenty of solar systems in the universe, plus there could be other kinds of worlds, equivalent to planets but with different allocations of space, time, and matter or nonphysical modes of "embodiment." Souls coming from here could reincarnate in one of these. We don't begin to know the range of possibilities or have a basis for restricting them.

Dr. David Bishai of Johns Hopkins School of Public Health did the speculative math for just one planet. Estimating that humans had been on Earth about 50,000 years, he calculated that there have been some 105 billion *Homo sapiens* so far, as against a maximum planetary population of 10 billion in the late twenty-first century.[84] That would cover the necessary soul stock for now but doesn't address the ontological problem: if the inventory runs out, how can new people get born?

It is almost certainly not a quantitative matter, or, if it is, it likely operates at the demographics of the universe with its countless galaxies and dimensions as well as in the context of multiple personalities. Souls could land on other worlds or form simultaneous separate personae like Weiss's patient with her coinciding lives in Spain and the Ukraine. Various Tibetan lamas purport to reincarnate intentionally in more than one individual (see also the discussion of "death" in chapter 10).

One might more reasonably wonder why Stevenson's research never made it into even peripheral scientific discussion or received peer review and why so few people know about it. It's not as though he has been refuted or that more Occam-favorable explanations have been offered.

The reason is a prevailing view that reincarnation is absurd. It violates the laws of physics and biology, so it is not worth even discussing. This bias overrides any evidence, however compelling. Most scientists start from the premise that reincarnation *couldn't* happen, therefore it *doesn't*. In each case, there *has to be* another explanation. New School philosopher Paul Edwards's critique of Stevenson's work presumes that this assessment is plain to all:

> Which is more likely—that there are astral bodies, that they invade the womb of prospective mothers, and that the children can remember events from a previous life although the brains of the previous persons have long been dead? Or that Stevenson's children, their parents, or some other witnesses and informants are, intentionally or unintentionally, not telling the truth: that they are lying, or that their very fallible memories and powers of observation have led them to make false statements and bogus identifications?"[85]

If you believe in a materialist universe only—a humongous star-filled cosmos that happened to pop out of a nodule smaller than a beebee in the middle of nowhere—then Edwards's sarcastic caricature strikes the perfect chord: the only conceivable mechanisms for past lives are patently absurd. They don't happen, so there have to be other explanations.

If you consider, however, that what we know about the universe is far less than what we don't, Edwards's bias is a symptom of his own hubris and a dose of scientistic fundamentalism.

3

Transdimensional Physics and Biology

Neurologist Oliver Sacks's commonsense explanation for paranormal phenomena sets up shop where you'd expect: in the mirage-making chambers of the brain. "[T]he fundamental reason that hallucinations—whatever their cause or modality—seem so real is that they deploy the same systems in the brain that actual perceptions do. . . . Hallucinations, whether revelatory or banal, are not of supernatural origin. . . . [They] cannot provide evidence for the existence of any metaphysical beings or places. They provide evidence only of the brain's power to create them."[1]

Sacks is providing a neurological complement to Freud's psycho-symbolic displacement. From his vantage, out-of-body experiences are system distortions that read as real because they transude through the same neural circuitry and are interpreted by the same cerebral lobes as sensory phenomena: they register as "events" because the mind is tricked by its own electro-chemistry into believing them. The brain organizes neural artifacts into familiar pictures and then validates them like a stamping machine that has stopped looking at the documents it is authorizing.

But who is some guy sorting data on an outer waterworld in the Milky Way to lay down a protocol for the entire universe? I get Sacks's intent: the brain is a "bureaucratic" control center; it *does* homogenize information. But that doesn't *a priori* invalidate all paranormal experiences or expressions of nonlocal mind. It is also not proof that the brain *creates* consciousness or that its threshold in *Homo sapiens* sets the compass of experience-processing entities everywhere. And just because the brain can be tricked into registering *some* hallucinations as real does not mean that *all* psychic occurrences are *de facto hallucinations.*

Contemporary neuroscience closes its files prematurely, disposing of thousands of years of inquiry in shamanic, Hindu, Buddhist, and other psychospiritual lineages. That the brain is not the mind is axiomatic outside Western civilization. While consciousness is a local epiphenomenon of the nervous system, it may also be a nonlocal, transpersonal aspect of nature. Training this aspect of the mind, shamans practice transferring their identities to a plant, animal, or other entity. Tibetan lamas refine a specialized application, *phowa,* whereby an adept leaves his body while specifying where his identity will next attach, not only in life but also after death.

To those who value out-of-body arts, these spirit journeys are a fundamental feature of reality. You can't do *phowa* (trained reincarnation) without reincarnation itself.

To the scientific establishment, they are abject hoaxes, for they violate a sole and objectified chain of custody from the Big Bang.

Freeing the Mind from the Brain

In 2017, a team of neuroscientists based mostly at the École Polytechnique Fédérale de Lausanne in Switzerland adapted a form of algebraic topology to show how, in addition to its known cellular and cerebral activities, the brain conducts itself by what they called "kinetic depth parameters," which engage up to eleven different dimensions. Bound in spatial cavities, these "cliques" create complex structures that disintegrate as they assimilate information.

In language from the study, "neocortical microcircuits process information through a stereotypical progression of clique and cavity formation and disintegration, consistent with a recent hypothesis of common strategies for information processing across the neocortex. . . . A stimulus may be processed by binding neurons into cliques of increasingly higher dimension, as a specific class of cell assemblies, possibly to represent features of the stimulus, and [then] by binding these cliques into cavities of increasing complexity, possibly to represent the associations between the features."[2]

Cliques do not, in and of themselves, change the ontological status of the brain, but they provide possible staging ports for multidimensional and nonlocal functions. They could be the tip of a different iceberg too, for the brain's lobes may not even produce "mind" but serve as a transceiver (transmitter-receiver) linking synaptic activity in the nervous system with consciousness at large. The cerebral cortex may have evolved either to correlate biological systems with transpersonal fields or to individuate intrinsic intelligence in matter.

In this model, the brain has no capacity (or obligation) to create subjectivity or awareness, only to integrate it in a biological context. The receiving structure—in invertebrates a nerve net, in free-living cells a charged outer membrane—attunes a DNA-stipulated signal from a span of conscious information. According to Jeffrey Kripal, in his book *Secret Body,* consciousness is an invisible energy "with its own super-physics, one that is not bound by what our primate brains have evolved to cognize as space and time."[3] The brain actually restricts, filters, and channels consciousness. If an organism received its full measure, it would be overwhelmed.

It may not be the brain's electrical activity but its partial shutting down that affords the mind its greatest range, such as in near-death and other extrasensory experiences. Disciples of LSD and ayahuasca have described finding themselves floating outside the galaxy or in landscapes of unknown dimensions—places that, despite Sacks's reality-stamping device, they dead-reckoned as real. Patients in comas or brain surgery report having traveled in alien realms, met otherworldly beings, and ridden on giant insects (Harvard-trained neurosurgeon Eben Alexander in an exemplifying instance). It is as if without the bridle of a cerebral cortex, "mind" is free to explore an independent transcendent reality. The brain is apparently not a consciousness "machine" or exclusive generator of subjective experience.

Psychic researcher Frederic Myers speculated that the brain might have evolved as an adaptation of matter to being acted on by spirit: its biomolecular components are manifestations of subtle energies in the aura. Hindu cosmology locates a brainlike complex above the crown chakra.* This "structure" is said to process information extrasensorily. If an esoteric organ of consciousness is "thinking"—circulating thoughts at a higher vibration—the brain might function as its counterpart at a lower frequency, with "mindedness" entering living systems through nerves and ganglia. In other words, cliques in the brain transduce† a timeless self that we experience as ego.

Information passing from the aura into the brain transcends Sacks's obedient stamping machine.

Many nineteenth-century and twentieth-century crossover thinkers reasoned along similar lines. Nikola Tesla, Sir William Crookes, Sir Oliver Lodge, and Lord Raleigh, innovators of technologies from which radios and televisions were developed, each believed that consciousness was more accurately described as an exogenous "psychoplasma" than as electrochemical pulses of the brain.[4] If you smash a radio, the music stops, but that doesn't eliminate sound waves in the air.

Spirits seem to adapt electronic devices like televisions, radios, telephones, global positioning devices, and digital systems for communicating. Numerous elements converge here: the concept of consciousness as a form of energy, the notion of death as a mode of passage into a subtler energetic state, the human invention of electrical devices for communication and dissemination of information in various spectra of energy, and the attraction of all phases of energy to each other, whether the source is organic (a brain), psychic (an aura), or electronic (a television). One disparity is that while electromagnetic energies (radio waves, light, radiation, etc.) weaken with distance, psychic energy overrides spatial limitations, not needing propinquity and sometimes traveling between dimensions or emanating from disembodied entities or deceased persons. Mediums perform as well on the phone as in person, and remote

---

*Certain Hindu traditions identify seven major psychic-energy and embryogenic centers in the human body, culminating in one at the crown of the head. These circulate subtle energies from the sun, the earth, and the cosmic field for the development/nourishment of the body-mind and aura. Equivalent energy centers play a role in virtually every indigenous magical system and spiritual etiology.

†Transduction, used in in a metaphysical context, describes not only conversion of energy from one system to another but also a simultaneous transformation of form and nature.

viewers and psychic healers do not lose fidelity with distance.

If a radio suddenly switches itself on or an object moves for no apparent reason, the possibility of spirit action cannot be ruled out (unless, of course, you don't believe in spirits).

Mathematical savants reveal another grade of the brain-mind paradox. One heralded computing genius, Daniel Tammet of Barking, England, accurately multiplies four nine-digit numbers by each other, derives fractional square roots, and calculates pi to twenty-thousand-plus digits, all in his "mind." Is this an effect of his brain using "cliques" to operate as a computer or of his aura serving as a metacomputer? It could be both.

Whatever the nature of their interplay, consciousness and the brain—mind and matter—are correlated in ways that neuroscientists don't understand. No one could carry pi to that many digits using only *known* functions of the brain.

Tammet is one example of a mystifying phenomenon, savant syndrome. Calendrical savants can name the day of the week, even centuries ago, within a second of being given a date. Other savants have inexplicable mapmaking or musical aptitude. In addition, a high percentage of these geniuses have brain injuries, *reduced* intellectual and social capacities, or are on the autism spectrum.

Clearly, the brain is not merely a personified cellular machine; it is an imbedding of complex objects and operations that mimic machinery only from an artificially objectified view. Its anatomical elements and their functions embody many layers of conscious and unconscious adaptations, and their origins spread across time and space and perhaps other dimensions in ways that conscious functions of the cerebral cortex can't begin to comprehend.

Even as a conjectural receiver, the brain is more than a passive tuner of transdimensional signals. It is an organic capacitor/inductor/oscillator/microprocesser/amplifier and so on, made of layers of neurons folded into lobes with ridges and grooves to serve those provinces. It is also an emergent, self-organizing vegetative structure growing out of its own roots and branches—and not just a circumscribed foliage but also a fractally propagating colony that becomes sentient as its sectors clone other sectors and the sectors contact one another and generate the prerequisites of symbolic representation: qualia (subjective experience) and semiosis (sign-object interpretation).

The relationship between biology and metabiology might explain many of life's more baffling mysteries, including the origin and evolution of consciousness and direct transfers of information between organisms. Nonlocal mind may yet turn out to be a more transparent view of our situation and that of the universe than mind as an artifact of the brain—cosmopolitan instead of archaic.

Scientists, of course, deem such views romantically religious or pre-scientific. Most assume that consciousness originates solely from bio-chemical properties of the brain.

The Biology of Reincarnation

An aspect of Ian Stevenson's work—his matching of moles, scars, and birth defects in a child claiming a past-life memory to the wounds of his or her PP—provides potential game-changing evidence. If lesions in one lifetime can leave cellular imprints in a subsequent incarnation, that tells us something about the universe that physicists and biologists don't know, while raising fundamental questions about the nature of reality itself. There is *no ordinary explanation*—conventional thermodynamics isn't in the game.

Psychologist Jon Klimo, who studies anomalous and paranormal experiences, has no doubt about the implications of Stevenson's discovery, "Patterns such as birthmarks or deformities in the current lifetime that were correlated to experiences remembered from a previous lifetime . . . tied the past and present individual together. . . ."[5] Occasionally, such instances might be passed off as coincidences, but these matches are far too common to be anything other than what they seem: *forbidden biology.* Plus, investigators and laypeople tally only a fraction of these "mutations," as recognition requires a suspicion of reincarnation as well as access to medical records or autopsies of PPs and intimacy to some extent with their present embodiments.

In one notable example, a girl remembering the life of a man who had undergone skull surgery was born with "what Stevenson called the most extraordinary birthmark he had ever seen: a three-centimeter wide area of pale, scar-like tissue that extended around her entire head.[6]

This kind of stuff—spontaneous relocation of information, fluctuation between mind and matter—can't occur without a mechanism abetting ordinary genetic inheritance with Lamarckian* and transpersonal elements. Kripal credited Stevenson with introducing a new field: "the biology of reincarnation . . . [homologous] physical 'marks' from a previous life's violent ending by things like knife, ax, mallet, hanging rope, or bullet wound." He added, "The Ian Stevenson library . . . displays examples of such tools and weapons that Stevenson collected on his travels, which are carefully placed in glass cases near photos of the extraordinary birthmarks and birth defects in question."[7]

Stevenson speculated about embryogenic aspects in the case of Semih Tutusmus, a Turkish child who had past-life memories of being "killed by a shotgun blast to the right side of his head . . . born with an undeveloped right side of his face and . . . a linear stump [instead of] a right ear."[8] Pointing out that "the birth defect is [often] more extensive than the damaged tissues to which it corresponds," he surmised that the cause might be "a disturbance of a morphogenetic field." He described several cases for which this concept may be applicable, including that of Lekh Pal Jatav in India, "who had a birth defect of one hand that corresponded to amputations of [his PP's] fingers by a fodder-cutting machine."[9]

Morphogenesis is micromechanical differentiation of cells into tissues, ostensibly DNA-orchestrated and reshaped only by statistical variation (gene drift) and *random* mutations. A psychically induced doppelgänger would be necessary to convert traumatic lesions from a body that no longer exists into birthmarks or blemishes or glitches in the tissue of a successor embryo. Some combination of telekinesis and space-time relativistic telepathy would be required to transfer the identity of the source PP to a future child bearing correlative marks.

---

*The French naturalist Jean-Baptiste Lamarck proposed, counter to Darwinian orthodoxy as it was to develop, that characteristics acquired by an organism during its lifetime could cross the boundary between somatic and genetic cells and be inherited by its offspring and passed on to future generations. In more extreme instances, awareness or memories of experiences could be transferred from neurons to chromosomes or their psychic proxies.

An exotic trace gets introduced somehow, like a pebble tossed into a pond—an inexact replica of a pattern or design. It travels from a corpse or, more properly, a body that was once alive into a DNA strand (or a biological field) of a different organism. Disturbance of the morphogenetic field is hardly the showstopper here; Stevenson glosses over items that are: the telekinetic and Lamarckian aspects of transmission, the telepathic continuity of personal memory, and the nonlocal "time travel" of organized information. There is no diplomatic way to talk about quasi-genetic links between reincarnates and their PPs or extrabodily transfer of wounds as "mutations."

His colleague Jim Tucker compared these marks to the sudden appearance of heat blisters on a subject under hypnosis—at a spot where he was told that he was being burned but was not. When a hypnotist pressed an *unheated* object on the skin while pretending it was scalding, the "burn" wound consistently occurred in the shape of the prop.[10] If thoughts can produce a blister on skin, a mechanism for mind-to-cell transfer exists. (In modeling how such visualizations might activate nonlocal healing, osteopath John Upledger proposed a subconscious bio-encryption he dubbed "cell talk."[11]) That addresses mind-to-cell transfer, but it leaves out the telekinetic and reincarnational aspects as well as the transfer from somatic to sex cells.

There is *one* clue to the driver behind this phenomenon. Wounds that were experienced painfully or in states of terror tend to recur most often. By contrast, wounds that occurred when the victim was unconscious, for instance, senseless on the ground during combat or under sedation in surgery, rarely if ever leave indicia.[12] This suggests that an experience powerful enough to instill a death picture is telekinetic enough to imprint congenitally and telepathic enough to instill a carrier image that survives mortality to reconstitute in a new body with its own brain/mind.

Sheldrake's "morphic resonance" provides a mode of transmission: similarity or congruence travels though energetic and psychic fields, by-passing the genome. Perhaps the same touchstone that enables a child to recognize his or her (or their) PP resonates as well in the embryogenic field. Synchronicity is in play too, though morphic resonance and synchronicity are *phases* of a multidimensional depth effect. Note too that

scars can have delayed onset; the knife slash that killed Munna, Ravi
Shankar's PP, appeared when Ravi was three months old. That makes
relocation atemporal or fain to an indexable allele on a chromosome.

Reincarnational wound transfer—if that is what is happening—
suggests that information doesn't so much evaporate as sublimate. Hindu
philosophers and their latter-day theosophical colleagues propose that
experiences, emotions, and thoughtforms get deposited on a gigantic
"hard drive": the Akashic records or Book of Life. These annals cata-
logue every datum, either just human or from every entity everywhere,
regardless of species or planet. Though the physical universe might have
space for a metamagnetic platter, its repository is said to be in a vaster
dimension. From storage there, information can be transmitted elsewhere, biologically as well as psychically.

Birthmark telekinesis is validated by cultures that take past lives for
granted, and it is not confined to "cell talk." In parts of Asia, Stevenson
and his associates found people using soot or paste to mark the body of a
recently deceased relative while saying a prayer for them to carry this sign
into the next life. In thirty-eight instances where the process was tracked,
the mark recurred in some fashion on a newborn relative. A striking case
involved a daughter-in-law pressing a finger dipped in white paste on the
body of her mother-in-law, whose grandson then was born with a pale area
on the back of his neck corresponding to a major portion of the streak.[13]

In Tibetan Buddhist circles, a dying person or a corpse is marked
with ritual soot and paste or a smear of butter in expectation that it will
seep into a life imprint and show up as a birthmark on a newborn. The
body of a lama is tagged, not only to aid his rebirth but also to allow his
identity to be confirmed. Of course, application of oils to an inert body
contravenes a theory of traumatic telekinesis, but neither Stevenson nor
the lamas have unique claim on the mechanism, let alone its range.

If you think that metempsychotic* birthmarks that also cross the
DNA barrier lose credibility by violating two major scientific laws at
once, consider lab experiments in which mice inherit aversions to stimuli

*Metempsychosis is the transmigration of a soul, animal as well as human, into another
body after death.

generated by shocks *five generations after the mouse in which the original trauma was induced!*[14] Consider too the way the universe turns inanimate matter into life. The entirety of information blueprinting an organism is condensed, synopsized, and transformed into codes, which regenerate it inside the cells of another organism, forming chrysalises and turning them inside out and back again like origami balls, adding and differentiating fresh tissues and organs each time. Science considers embryogenesis ordinary thermodynamic activity organized by genes, but meticulous renditions for millions of species on a daily planetwide scale suggest that other forces may be at work too. I have no special insight on the matter, but in *Embryogenesis* I caught the sense of a pagan inscription, "The embryo is the universe writing itself on its own body."

Planes of Energy: Squaring Physical and Metaphysical Interpretations

For the remainder of this chapter, I will attempt to square physical and metaphysical interpretations of birth-scar phenomena and other past-life evidence. This discussion might get too mystical for some readers (and too steeped in cellular biology for others). At any point, feel free to skip to the next chapter.

I am first going to draw on a system known as the Seven Planes of Consciousness. I learned my version from John Friedlander, who inherited it from contemporary adaptations of theosophy while viewing them through a Sethian lens. But I believe that the recognition of seven creationary chords is universal. When I taught the Seven Planes system in eastern Maine in 2011, a visiting Penobscot healer told our group that his teachers imparted a similar grid with differently ordered divisions and native names.

The system basically describes seven tiers of energy in our overall human operating range, though only portions of three of them are ordinarily perceptible. These make up our everyday reality. Each plane is further calibrated into seven subplanes or finer differentiations. The subplanes have subplanes that have even more finite subplanes, and so on. Again, these gradations are frequencies rather than geographies. The planes don't climb as much as deepen and change pitch, though they are not objective energies in the sense of physics. They are *literally* planes (or maps) of consciousnesses because they imbue nature in such a way that their states of subjective cognizance are inseparable from their objective manifestations. The hierarchy operates at the intersection of energy, mind, and form such that each plane is tantamount to a whole reality *equal to this one.*

I am not asserting the validity of these planes in the way that one might attest to a sand dune or riverbed. They are attempts by psychic explorers to identify ranges of energy and dimensional shades they encounter, taking into account that our everyday consciousness is limited to the parameters of our nervous system while the universe is not.

The seven local planes have acquired traditional names. In the theosophical version, moving from "subtler" to "denser," they are called: Adi, Monadic, Atmic, Buddhic, Mental-Causal, Astral, and Physical-Etheric.* The Monadic is also called the Submanifestal, or Binah, when invoked on the Tree of Life in the Hebrew Kabbalah. It is Anupadaka (translated as "Parentless") at its Hindu source. The Astral plane is also the Kabbalistic Hod and Hindu Kama (or "Desire").

"Subtler to denser" does not capture the planes' full nature either, for they are *not* independent configuration spaces generating sovereign phenomena (though they function heuristically that way); every landscape in our universe—the physical space we live in—incorporates all seven planes even to manifest as a landscape. The higher a plane (or subplane within a plane), the more links and relationships it has—the more complex its consciousness and rich its dimensionality.

Early twentieth-century Russian mystic G. I. Gurdjieff proposed a similar cosmology in which a Ray of Creation, originating at what he called "the Absolute," penetrated zones of dormant intelligence, sparking manifestations at periodic octaves—each wave of seven mantralike notes

---

*My own conception of these planes, like everyone's, evolves. For a fuller but earlier description, see Richard Grossinger, *Dark Pool of Light: Reality and Consciousness,* Vol. 2, *Consciousness in the Psychospiritual and Psychic Ranges* (Berkeley, Calif.: North Atlantic Books, 2012), pp. 130–234. This covers each plane and many of the subplanes in depth. For a guided visualization of the planes by a skilled and experienced teacher, see John Friedlander's audio CD, *Navigating the Seven Planes of Consciousness* (Berkeley, Calif.: North Atlantic Books, 2011).

building to a cosmogonic shock. The octaves ignited a subzone's hidden properties of matter and mind. Most of the shocks and their manifestations were at higher frequencies than our universe; then the Ray imploded here as the Big Bang, injecting multidimensional information into a dark zone and actuating its kingdom of knowledge.[15]

If the Seven Planes (and the Ray of Creation and its octaves) are renditions of something genuine in the universe, they have to mesh with other natural phenomena, joining mass, gravity, electromagnetism, dark energy, dark matter, and so on somewhere in a unified field. Dimensional "rabbit holes" would bring each plane, subplane, or octave into relationship with not only the others but also known energies of physics. Yet I suspect that even if science significantly broadened its parameters, it would never come upon these sorts of vibrational tiers. Because they are generated outside our operating range, they only enter it *as other things*. Insofar as those "other things" are even recognized, they are assigned material causes, forfeiting any transdimensional provenance. Bertrand Russell may have intuited such when he said, "Physics is mathematical not because we know so much about the physical world, but because we know so little: it is only its mathematical properties that we can discover."[16]

Demonstrating how a system works on our own Physical plane—for example, how the sun is lit by the nuclear transmutation of hydrogen and helium—doesn't say *what it is*. Though electron microscopes and hadron colliders were conceived by sophisticated tactioceptors, we still perceive a star the way a flatworm does: as a "thing." We inherit the primal orientation of its statocysts.

The dynamics of the Seven Planes are finally as inaccessible to us as the Milky Way is to a flatworm. Even were such a creature to develop a telescope—and it could do so only in a thought experiment—it wouldn't "see." Likewise, we can't see behind the curtain, whether you call the hidden universe Seven Planes, octaves, superstrings, or something else.

The Human Operating Range and Its Physical Subplanes

The human operating range is limited to the lower tiers of the densest three planes in our system: the Physical aspect of the Physical-Etheric plane, the lowest five gradients of the Astral plane (which we experience as our emotional life), and the Mental tiers of the Mental-Causal plane.

The Physical plane is our baseline ambient reality. In this universe, everything we know vibrates at a material frequency. But matter is a subatomic oscillation, so even its "material" aspect is provisional (as particles and waves). In that sense, "physical" is a bit of a misnomer. All beings and objects vibrate—materialize—at the frequency of their plane. *They* are "real" (or experience themselves and their environs as "physical") because *it* is "real."

Since matter is also energy, a Physical realm is no less "energetic" than more radiant planes. For instance, the *meta*-"physical" Astral plane, though impalpable to humans, is as thick as matter to putative beings like the sylphs and fire salamanders who populate its landscapes and vibrate at its frequency. If we were primarily attuned to a more sublime frequency such as the Buddhic, we would perceive *its* vibration and objects as "material." Likewise, Atmic and Monadic planes, though seemingly too "exquisite" for real action or outcomes by our "thickness"-privileging standards, are just as rich and meaningful, possessing their own versions of jungles, oceans, and experiences, though these are not fabricated of atoms and molecules.

The Etheric Subplanes

What follows is a summary of the other subplanes and planes. Remember, though their activity is beyond human perception, they contribute essential flavors to our reality and the natural phenomena of our world as well as paranormal events at its dimensional hems.

The upper four subplanes of the Physical-Etheric plane transmit at a frequency slightly subtler than matter. Their surface fringe can be felt as "ethereal" stickiness. Try experiencing this range of Etheric energy by cupping the palms of both your hands and holding them facing each other, then moving them closer and farther and closer again; a soft invisible *chi* ball expands and contracts as it is squeezed between them. When it is rotated or propelled by martial artists, it can uproot opponents without physically touching them.

Chi is so close to tangibility that its flow through the body's meridians—the twelve major (and twenty or thirty minor) embryogenic formation channels depicted in traditional Chinese medicine—can be activated by metal acupuncture needles inserted at the fourth Etheric subplane.

The next highest Physical-Etheric level, its fifth subplane, is characterized as the source of *prana*, an even subtler energy that travels through the body's network of *nadis* (the channels of Ayurveda, an indigenous healing system of India). Finer than meridians, nadis are also far more numerous; in fact, they are numberless. The nadis conduct health and consciousness along with air (breath), blood, and other fluids as they draw on the vitality of the cosmos, pulling it through our Atmic vibration from its farthest galaxies and deepest-lying strings. Locally, *nadis* metabolize Etheric energy from air, sun, earth, and the remains of once-living plants and animals.

Even more celestial energies operate at higher Etheric discriminations. The "permanent seeds" of our bodies are said to congeal in the six and seventh subplanes before materializing here. These "atomisms" are interdimensional portals: terminals through which higher-plane rubrics interact with material forms. The "seeds" continue to maintain the subtle body (the aura) and the corporeal body throughout a lifetime.

Though the Akashic records are traditionally stored on sovereign Etheric planes, nineteenth-century theosophist Helena Blavatsky construed them as indestructible tablets of Astral light. Both could be true, for while all planes interpenetrate, Etheric and Astral energies, different as they are, overlap and mimic each other's energy.

The Astral Plane

The Astral body is the most polarized energy field in our universe, for every speck of the Astral generates a polarity. The Astral is why humans have strong emotions and desires, as the plane's envelope imposes sharp distinctions that lead to clashes, triumphs, and debacles—general havoc. There is no safe space in the Astral; yet it provides the turbulent landscape necessary for this incarnation.

While the lower Astral generates feelings, the upper Astral vibrates at the frequency of undines, leprechauns, faeries, and the like. Villagers in Ireland and Iceland recognize some mounds and stone circles as faery forts in the Astral, but that aspect is invisible to most humans because it is emanating at too high a frequency for our senses.

The Mental-Causal Plane

The Mental-Causal plane grows out from the higher Monadic realm and provides our intelligence and capacity for analytic thought. The four lower (Mental) subplanes transmit thoughtforms,* energy states that become both thoughts and forms. As thoughts, they make up constructs of science and philosophy—our understanding of nature from Newtonian dynamics to quantum physics and the holonomic theory of the brain.† As forms, they *become* atoms and molecules that construct that reality. Thoughtforms speak to a fundamental relationship between consciousness and matter (see chapters 7 and 8).

At its third, second, and first subplanes, the Mental-Causal plane becomes Causal, transmitting rubrics from higher planes and providing the logical and functional basis of this reality. The Causal realm is also where our soul encounters vibrations too dense for it to enter, so it disseminates aspects of itself into them: us.

Soul has a slightly different meaning here than it usually conveys. The Western personal soul is an individualized incorporeal essence—of just humans in the West's Judaeo-Christian religions and of any creature, even a mosquito or a bacterium, in Hinduism and most indigenous cosmologies. In the Seven Planes system, the soul *is* the self in the Causal plane, from where it gives birth to each of our physical incarnations. It continues as the imperceptible background of our lives, always present, always witnessing and guiding.

In the Causal landscape, each soul is the hyperspatial equivalent of a sun-star, with its own planets, moons, comets, meteors, and so on.

As we move "up" through the planes, the personal soul becomes a group soul and continues to expand, ultimately merging into the Atman in the Monadic plane.

Thoughtform is a twentieth-century theosophical adaptation of the Tibetan term *tulpa,* which has also been translated as "emanation body" or "intelligent entity created by focused thought."

†David Bohm proposed that requisites of consciousness arise from cerebral conduction of waves in hologram-like organizations in accordance with quantum theory and concomitant to Fourier analysis of the decomposition of other complex waves into sine waves. The "waves" are themselves an example of Mental energy nearing the threshold of the Causal.

The Buddhic Plane

The next plane above the Causal is the Buddhic, where we experience the collective (unity) basis of our existence. This is where this universe's consensus reality is put together (see chapter 13). By its cohesive nature, the Buddhic plane generates the coalescent energy of synchronicities as well as more refined versions of emotions that are individuated in the Astral. At the seventh subplane of the Buddhic, we share a soul with numerous other humans with whom we exchange experiences and even divvy up karma for future incarnations (though we each maintain an individual Causal soul).

At higher tiers of the Buddhic, our group soul goes wider and becomes more inclusive until, at its first subplane, we share a soul with every human—perhaps every sentient being—on our planet. No one knows quite how wide or discrete the Buddhic domain is; remember, it is beyond the human operating system with its modes of knowledge, so we automatically pare Buddhic spaciousness and connectivity down to Mental-plane equivalents.

The Atmic, Monadic, and Adi Planes

At the Atmic frequency, our souls intersect interplanetary and intergalactic systems. The fifth subplane of the Atmic is where laws of physics (like gravity, conservation of energy, and thermal equilibrium) are established, as they are incorporated into the Physical-Etheric by reciprocal interaction. The Atmic plane is what allows the Etheric to engender coherent, semistable forms. It is also the frequency to which yogis, forensic psychics, and saints attune to produce miracles, levitate, or gain impossible knowledge (e.g., solve "cold case" crimes) on lower planes. It is through the Atmic that yogis and lamas exit life in a "rainbow body"; that is, they raise their body's frequency to the Etheric and take all its information (except for hair and fingernails) through the Atmic with them. Otherwise, key experiences get lost or stuck at a Physical-Etheric level.

At the Monadic frequency, we interpenetrate other dimensional systems. If the Mental-Causal plane is where our soul passes into incarnations through Astral and Etheric energies, the Monadic is where our individualized spark of Divine Being, the Atman, kindles its incarnational cycles. The Atman stores an individual's beingness while coordinating its various aspects and experiences with those of other entities throughout All That Is (see chapter 11, "Multipersonhood").

The seventh ascending plane, the Adi, corresponds to the emptiness before an entirely different system of manifestation, so it holds the full unenacted potential of our domain. It isn't the terminus of Creation, just of our part of the haystack. Beyond the Adi, "higher" frequencies generate other realities and universes, arranged in their own haystacks, all the way to the source energy of Creation.

The Planes Beyond

Beyond the Adi is an uncertainty state before a new type of energy and consciousness sets in, perhaps like the termination shock and heliopause between solar systems. The space-time continuum that characterizes astrophysics as well as all seven planes of our consciousness is but one tier or emanation of All That Is. Myriad other universes and dimensional realms—Gurdjieff's ray-ignited zones—have their own sets of planes. Hierarchies of seven bind them to one another and to inaugurating octaves, all the way to the Absolute.

The next set of planes beyond the Adi does not necessarily run higher intelligence or propose super-realities; it conducts information irrelevant to our kind of universe or being human. Because it keys into All That Is in a different fashion, we are not equipped to recognize it or dimensionality itself at its level. John Friedlander told me that mystics who have accessed a plane above the Adi in order to untie certain knots report only a blend of gibberish or "interdimensional gossip."

No one knows how many planes there are or what kinds of realities they emanate, or if there are realities even beyond all tiers of seven and their octaves. Maybe there are forty-nine planes of Meta-Galactic Consciousness (seven tiers of seven) before they evanesce into the Ray of Creation, or perhaps planes are infinite and eternally changing in relationship to systems of consciousness and manifestation. A hyperplane making up this entire range of consciousness (and possible consciousness) could be something like a single octave in the Ecstatic Abyss of All That Is, no different from a frog beside a pond chirping and proclaiming its inexplicable appearance in the unknown bright.

Relating the Planes to Science

How might the Seven Planes lead to paradigms for transdimensional physics and biology? According to conventional science, life forms arise by molecular interactions under physical laws—gravity, heat, shear force—but, according the Seven Planes cosmology, their prototypes already exist as subtle bodies in the Etheric plane, emotional bodies in the Astral, thoughtforms in the Mental, karmic energies in the Causal, synchronicities in the Buddhic, laws and structures of nature in the Atmic, and interdimensional linkages in the Monadic. If Mental-Causal energy generates thoughtforms to ignite the physics and phenomenology of our domain, its germinal states still have to pass through the Astral and the Etheric to ground molecularly.

As mentioned above, embryos seem to defy solely genetic main-tenance, proceeding at times as if pulled by invisible self-organizing strings. Those strings might be energies coiling outward from deeper planes, knitting tissues together. This field would engage life at *at least* two levels: directly as information broadcast throughout nature and indirectly insofar as the Physical plane *is* a denser emanation of Atmic and Etheric energies.

Crick-Watson-brand DNA operates as a self-contained carrier of heredity here, but an Etheric twin-helical progenitor—perhaps a dwarf facsimile of the *ida* and *pingala** nadis—might provide its template. The Etheric plane would receive the patterning of trauma-charged lesions (perhaps from the Akashic records), then archive, encode, and implant them in new fetal tissue, transferring information from the aura of a PP into cicatrices in a successor. Assaults in one generation would recur as birthmarks or scars—morphogenetic distortions—in the next.

The thermodynamic landscape remains under full Darwinian traction.

---

*Ida and *pingala* are the two major nadis. The white, feminine, cool *ida* begins on the left side of the body; the red, masculine, hot *pingala* originates on the right; then they torque, DNA-like, around the central channel, the *sushumna,* itself a convergence of three subtle vessels.

There is no wiggle room between the two realms—one material, the other metamaterial. Seemingly incommensurate systems meet at frequencies of the same energy. Etheric "DNA" germinates Physical DNA.

The Akashic records are not books or files, even virtual ones; they are more like the universe writing itself on its own *subtle* body. When I proposed that sacred geometry could transduce Akashic information into genetic agency, I knew that is a lick and a promise on the Physical plane. The link must be more fundamental. Etheric DNA has to be the original hereditary molecule, perhaps throughout the universe, because without Etheric subplanes, there can be no Physical subplanes, no incarnation or embryogenesis on a planet anywhere. Every exobiological life form, though originating in tidepools and springs independent of Earth and pre-Cambrian evolution here, must reproduce by molecular configurations loosely resembling DNA in structure and function. If codon-bearing helices are archetypal, they transmit Akashic runes or esoteric spirals *pro forma*. Then Mental-Causal, Astral, and Etheric energies fuse with genetic indexing in cell nuclei.

Likewise, brains (or centralized ganglia) everywhere would be confluences of deeper energies flowing through neural sheaths and cliques, funneling sentience onto the Physical plane. The brain's vegetative and fractal structure might reflect buckling and integrating of Causal fields as they converge on neural-tube swellings and generate cerebral lobes. Atmic engagement with Etheric forces overgrows and prunes the vesicles and sulci, shaping them to a hermetic design. The brain, thus deemed, is both dimensional and transdimensional.

The Nature of Things

Aristotle provided four discrete modes of causation—material, efficient, formal, and final, each at the scale of the universe itself. That was the provenance of Western thought until the earnest watchmakers—the lineage of physicists—arrived. The Greeks couldn't take apart the watch—the atom or molecule—because they didn't have a lens sufficient to the pry; instead, they intuited how its parts worked collectively. Yet even Stephen Hawking, with all his can openers, couldn't account for the full range of Aristotelian causation. Unable to assign an initial state to the universe, he proposed that its present configuration selects its past from a superposition of possible histories. His trademark black holes, bosons, and time travel, though mathematically impeccable, turn into paradoxes against a greater night. That his tropes seem hip-hop or sci-fi compared with Aristotle's more cardinal notes doesn't mean that Hawking transcended Greek philosophy or beat the master at the West's oldest game; he merely switched the home court because modernity gave him three hundred years of equations and topological displays. He kicked the can—the *real* one—down the road.

Aristotle was, in principle, just as concerned as Hawking or Einstein with black holes and time dilation—or how anything happens that causes anything else to happen. He was talking about nature, and nature hasn't changed. Nature is a rainforest and a coral reef and thousand-miles-per-hour gas storms on Jovian planets. It is *the nature of things (rerum natura).*

What materialistic science confronts now at the frontier of particle physics is not a riddle of dynamics but a paradox imbedded in a lineage of causation that goes from the supervenient qualities of pre-Socratic philosophers to angels on a medieval pinhead to John Dee's sigils.* Because properties don't float freely, matter must get drawn into events, initially and again each time—whether we are talking about magic (sigils) or physics (gravity). Aristotle understood that this is a big, big problem: cause and effect, mind and matter, form and substance, the first plunk and all subsequent plunks and bumps, *whether or not there* is *a first cause.* You can't advance without resolving it—and we haven't. All we have done is mince the playing field to a Primal Implosion—then to ball bearings (or molecules) and their quantum derivatives.

Yet if you come at quantum physics not by way of entropy from Plato to Newton, but by an alternate route from Aristotle and Aquinas, Lao-Tzu, and Parmenides, you stealth through the back door, but enter you do. The door is nonseparability of cause and effect, multiplicity of causes combining in differential equations and noncausal correlations. No first

*John Dee was an Elizabethan magician. Sigils are activating symbols: runes, emblems, seals, glyphs, visualizations, or imaginal "objects" deeded in dreams and visions.

cause is needed because there is no beginning or linear progression.

An equivalent causality underlies indigenous cosmologies. The creation of the Apache sky begins with space indistinguishable from time: "[T]here appears a spot, a thin circular disk, no larger than the hand, yellow on one side, white on the other, in mid air."[17] This is so drop-dead seminal that its profundity is overlooked. Nothing is needed for cosmogenesis beyond an activated sigil with subconscious properties. The Australian Dreaming, Dogon Ogo (disorder), and Maori embracing sky-father and sky-mother propagate similar runes. When the universe moves from a Monadic to a Causal to an Etheric or Physical vibration— or when the Ray of Creation activates a dormant zone—the local frequency changes instantaneously and acausally. Cause and effect are subsumed in the thoughtforms and particles that materialize with them. If you don't have a cyclotron to demonstrate this (more or less), you summon mythic objects.

The Apache could no more propose the astrophysics of the Big Bang than could Aristotle or the Penobscot originator of a Seven-Planes-like cosmology, but they understood that something more runic and nimble than arrowheads and grinding stones was in play.

The Organizational Force of Absence

Thermodynamic systems, including biologically organized ones, operate according to rigorous natural laws. I have clearly violated that canon by proposing transdimensional ranges of causation, but before closing this discussion, I want to show how scientific nuancing can also provide glimpses of hidden properties in nature. Neuroanthropologist Terrence Deacon offers a set of reciprocal actions for dissecting biological inheritance, which gives us a fresh look at the possible interplay between physical and metaphysical systems. That is not his goal; in fact, he is somewhere between bemused and appalled by my use of his work, but I find its value in its universality: it introduces features of the universe that transcend the systems to which they are applied.*

---

*Terrence Deacon was gracious enough to edit this section of the book, correct significant errors and misunderstandings, and supply phrasing where necessary.

Deacon develops parameters to deconstruct nature's jumps across tiers of organization; he does more than just say "they are emergent." Life (and, later, the mind), he asserts, doesn't emerge solely from matter by cyclical loops among atoms, molecules, and ions, and then by nucleic-acid copying and genetic mutations under incremental feedback "but from the constraints (aka absences) that organize matter."[18] What does that mean?

First of all, the potential repertoire of a genome far exceeds any of its particular species or individual expressions, for the role of the chromosomes is not only to provide developmental information but also to confine its application to functional situations. This suggests that creatures do not arise, evolve, or get extinguished in lotteries as straightforward as "musical chairs." Evolution also depends on subcellular "ecosystems."

A genome is intrinsically deep and resilient, and that includes its large and mysterious complement of what scientists used to call "junk DNA." Depending on the factors analyzed, anywhere from 80 to 98 percent of the human genome and a significant portion of other genomes fit into the former "junk" (noncoding) category. Why is there so much of it, and why does it survive, reproduce, and consume biological energy?

Noncoding DNA sequences are not without purpose or function; they don't correspond to a protein, but they do play a role in the organization and interaction of encoding sequences and in the origin of the DNA replication function.

There are both highly conserved noncoding DNA sequences and highly variable ones. Those that are highly conserved—varying only minimally in evolution—are likely constrained by the functional importance of their particular sequence. One of the most common functions of conserved noncoding sequences is as binding sites for regulatory molecules: a specific sequence determines a specific twist of the DNA double helix that corresponds to the structure of a regulatory protein that fits into this shape and serves one of a number of possible functions, such as promoting or inhibiting expression of some downstream coding region. Other noncoding segments might produce RNA molecules that themselves can serve various inhibitory, facilitating, catalytic, or regulatory functions in the cell. Even highly variable regions of the genome may play a simple quantitative role. For example, animals with atypically large genomes and massive redundancy seem to be highly dwarfed, with unusually large cells and very slow development, while animals with atypically small genomes and very little redundancy tend to be flying species, in both birds and insects.

In part because of nonlinear "coding," recalibrating of proteins and other codons, or regulatory functions of both coding and noncoding DNA, creatures are more stable and developmentally inventive than their extant genotype.* Different codon patterns can lead to similar or even identical phenotypes, while the same codons may incubate new organisms under changed cellular and environmental conditions.

A "Micro" View of Natural Selection

Most people's view of natural selection is a "macro" one: when environmental conditions cross tipping points, some species die off and different ones arise or flourish, as when an asteroid struck the earth off the coast of Yucatan 66 million years ago, precipitating a changed climate and contributing to the extinction of dinosaurs and the rise of small mammals. In a more recent instance, soot from the early factories of England darkened leaves in surrounding regions, expediting a decline of lighter-colored moths camouflaging themselves from predators by alighting on trees (as they had done for generations). Populations with darker tints replaced them. Likewise, the introduction of a new predator to a region affects differential survival: usually a decrease in species on which it preys along with an occupation of their niches by other species.

But events in the external world are only part of the selective equation. Selection also occurs on a genetic, nucleic level where the potential for traits to be favored or eliminated is organized, for it is in the cell's nucleus that novel codon possibilities and organisms arise. Environmental factors still affect the creatures carrying the genes, but the genes and their alleles (alternative forms on the same chromosome) also juggle formats and their expressions. The traits that get preserved

---

*The genotype is the entire DNA makeup of an organism, as opposed to just its physiological phase. Its phenotype is its current observable appearance or expressed traits.

or expressed depend, in part, on the thermodynamics of the cells' molecular environment (activities like nucleation, unstable saturation, macromolecular phase shifts) as well as expressions of other genes and noncoding sequences in the same organism; so organisms are bred not only by predators, prey, and climate, but also by intra- and inter-cellular factors.

Deacon uses the term "lazy" genes to highlight the fact that genetics takes advantage of any nongenetic constraints that are reliably available in context. For example, the self-organizing dynamics that produce the quite precise geometric relationship of Fibonacci spirals in plants is not "coded" in genes but emerges from the interactions between cells in a plant's apical meristem as cells differentially respond to the concentrations of signaling molecules released and diffused away from other cells in all directions. With all the cells interacting with one another in their way, collective concentration gradients tell each cell whether or not to transform into a rapidly dividing cell line destined to become a seed producer. The genetic contribution is the determination of what change in concentration induces the cell to change behavior via a shift in the pattern of its gene expression.

Extragenomic influences play an important role in selective gene expression that determines cell and tissue differences and the large-scale structural features of organisms. Persistent nongenetic influences will "tend to mask selection maintaining corresponding genetically inherited information . . . the genome will tend to offload morphogenetic control in the course of evolution, in a way that takes advantage of the emergent regularities that characterize many epigenetic* processes."[19]

Offloading is, in a sense, a form of emergence. While organisms are in constant dialogue with the external world, receiving, ordering, and integrating feedback, their subcellular domain runs its own environment. Unexpressed traits and contexts—dormant features of the genome—and unrealized nucleic potentials arise from a shift, usually a reduction, of degrees of freedom in a broader life system. Organisms or anatomical

---

*Epigenesis refers to the nongenetic and heritable cellular traits that arise from external and environmental factors (the phenotype) and influence organism development by the way these reliably interact with gene expression.

features that might have become extinct can be restored, as though from backup genetic databases but as new genotypes with fresh evolutionary potential. Deacon and his coauthor Tyrone Cashman explain how these counterintuitive liaisons work:

> [C]onstraints in the world are intrinsically relational phenomena. They are reflected in relationships between degrees of freedom that are excluded and those that are not excluded. And these are always degrees of freedom of some physical process of change. So, when we argue that the constraints that characterize autogenesis* actively preserve themselves we are not mentioning the fact that this active preservation necessarily involves physical processes that by virtue of these constraints do the work of preventing these same constraints from degrading. And because these constraints are preserved, whenever thermodynamic conditions enable the resumption of chemical work, this energetic change is again channeled into autogenic catalysis and linked self-assembly processes. The chemical reactions that are thereby prevented are those that tend to degrade the capacity to prevent these deleterious reactions.[20]

The authors are trying to decipher complex nonlinear feedback loops. The genetic script and its performance have different agendas or meanings, but these converge in real organisms. It is *because* genes interact in nonlinear and semirandom ways (from the standpoint of natural selection) that their control can be transferred to epigenetic influences. Deacon calls it "a non-Darwinian mechanism which acts as a complement to natural selection in the generation of functional synergies, because its form-generating properties derive from self-organizing tendencies of molecular and cellular interactions rather than from relationships to environmental conditions."[21]

---

*Autogenesis is Deacon's minimal model of the process that distinguishes the origin of life from nonliving things; as such, it describes the thermodynamic synergy of the first living creature and is an aspect of the dynamics distinguishing life in all its forms.

The Teleodynamic Universe

The accessible DNA grid is like a thin layer of taffeta atop a dense glob of information spun by billions of years of evolution wherein each line of primal organisms got wrapped intermittently (and unevenly) in branching sequences of successors many times over, a fractal ball of yarn with helical threads. The pearls (information) on those threads were expeditiously abbreviated, synopsized, and recoded. Pathways of storage, interaction, and expression retangled at such deep levels that they developed their own attractors, dynamic phase states, and recursive motifs during later embryogenic playback, and some of these got locked in by organismic successes. This is where mutations under incremental feedback encounter constraints imposed by prior systems. Effects may get organized randomly, but that organization becomes an anchor and compass for the next generation. The developing embryo doesn't have to know where its ballast comes from; it was already there, so it points the way.

A constraint functions teleodynamically as its own outgrowth. Like transit in a Klein bottle—a one-sided surface across which a traveler is flipped upside-down in returning to her point of origin—inside and outside fuse as a continuous interdependent flow. A form never has to disclose itself or its etiology, for its identity emerges from within *without a without*. An entity persists by continually undermining its own integrity, which allows it to maintain far-from-equilibrium states. It does not just insist, "neg-entropically," on its own existence; its potential nonexistence *becomes* existence by maintaining disequilibrium, advancing by fluctuations of constraints, delaying its own obliteration. All the action is inside the shell—the cell membrane—because there is no "shell," only a temporal matrix. *Re*cursion becomes *ex*cursion.

Ultimately, you *can* squeeze an organism through the eye of a needle, teleodynamically.

The autogene—the hypothetical first cell—encompassed a shift of positive and negative feedback loops. As active values of efficient cause brought about random changes, passive ones integrated them, leading to membrane-enclosed organelles. That's how Deacon's version of nature managed to go from inanimate chemistry to unicellular membranes to a broad multicellular taxonomy. It kept placing and removing constraints, as former sea mites turned into crabs, birds, otters, whales.

A nonlinear process frees neo-Darwinism from having to be a billboard for its own effects in the way that a copier *can't* be the genesis of what it is copying.*

For Deacon and Cashman, this mechanism is as irreducible as it is unpredictable.

> Although it seems convenient to think of the DNA in a cell as being the source of these constraints, as though these are the blueprints created by some extrinsic influence like natural selection, this is too simple. DNA itself is replicated by this cellular machinery, as are all of its other components, and so it is also just part of this synthetic reciprocity. Moreover, it is because organisms are incessantly working to preserve their critical functional constraints (in themselves and in their offspring) that there is anything susceptible to natural selection. These constraints are not a consequence of natural selection, but its precondition.[22]

In a sense, negative feedback becomes positive feedback because the system is so eclectic and reciprocal it can't distinguish between them. Deacon and Cashman are talking about thermodynamic activity and its biophysical levels. They are *not* talking about theosophical planes. But the universe makes no systemic distinctions. A similar mode of constraints could operate between planes of reality as energy "hypnotizes" itself into fewer dimensions, more constraints, and more specific sets of experiences. Form-generating atoms and molecules become self-organizing compounds and organisms as their Astral and Etheric states bind—that is, restrain—Atmic source energies. The Physical plane becomes physical by providing a denser, more discrete field of expression, encouraging finer vibrations to disclose hidden traits as they engage reciprocally with the plane itself. Proteins and enzymes could be Mental-Causal energies catalyzing at lower frequencies by constraint of some of *their* Monadic

---

*This is challenging information. For my own slower-paced entry to Deacon's work, I refer the reader to my book *Dark Pool of Light: Reality and Consciousness,* Vol. 1, *The Neuroscience, Evolution, and Ontology of Consciousness,* pp. 198–208.

properties. The brain might be formed by teleodynamic constraint of the aura in the Etheric, as the aura summarizes constraints of higher planes. The twists of the DNA double helix might constrain more fluid *chi* and *prana,* drawing strands of information onto this plane.

Each dimensionality continually undermines its own minimum number of coordinates, generating microcosms by maintaining disequilibrium while delaying its own reversion to a macrocosm; that fits Ilya Prigogine's nonequilbrium thermodynamics too. However many dimensions—or cosmic frames—there are, feedback, constraints, and scale are universal.

In Deacon's version, "Emergent properties are not something added, but rather a reflection of something restricted and hidden via ascent in scale due to constraints propagated from lower-level dynamical processes."[23] This befits Hindu planes as well as cell nuclei or particles of string theory.

Sheldrake's morphic resonance, despite its range, is still, literally in fact, morphodynamic. It is imposed abstractly and impersonally—disembodied—from without. What it lacks is a *teleodynamic* basis of organization. Once constraints are introduced, the absence of degrees leads to embodiment and personification (or individuation) from *within* the system, and that has to be part of any discrete, living, evolving mechanism in an actual planetary environment.

By itself, morphic resonance could not cause wound transfer, biogenesis, evolution, or consciousness ("ordinary" or telepathic), for it has no way into molecular dynamics. It is part of a neo-Platonic, archetypal universe that I accept implicitly, even as I accept birth charts without believing in astrobiology (beyond sun and moon). Synchronicity is a powerful organizer. Yet *self*-organizing systems generate their own processes.

Deacon explains how a teleodynamic process

shifts the focus from a disposition to grow and reproduce to a disposition to produce a specific unrealized potential—an end, which is a type of condition rather than any specific bounded structure. The autonomous generation of precisely those constraints necessary to specify a complete dynamical system with a disposition to do this incessantly is . . . the defining attribute of biological selfhood.

Only with respect to such a self-reconstituting, self-individuating disposition can an actualized state of things be about another un-actualized state; i.e. be information about something. In this way, the origin of teleodynamics is the emergence of both self and semiosis at the same time.[24]

Teleodynamics organizes (disorganizes) an informational helix and then a speaking hominid. Yes, morphic resonance is an elegant application of congruence (or sacred geometry) as a depth effect, but all those genetic molecules, organelles, and cells are simultaneously interacting, coordinating, and layering in membranes and designs inside *their own* three-billion-year dense ball of chaos and information. Selfhood is both potential and innate. Constraints drive information outward from micro- and macro-molecular levels into novel forms, even as archetypes impose signatures. The paradigms clash and combine as the universe proceeds, paying no more than lip service to either.

To be teleodynamic is to be teleological *without teleology*.

Modernity's Need for a Reality Compass

Whether constraints are imposed transdimensionally (me) or thermo-dynamically (Deacon), flexibility increases with dynamical depth: the universe—at least the universe of meaning—expands.

Terrence Deacon and I navigated this topic without me conceding my metaphysics or him requiring me to. After I drew his attention to neuroscientist Gary Marcus's *New York Times* article, "Face It, Your Brain Is a Computer," (see chapter 1) he wrote me: "Mind-as-computing is a classic version of the unconscious metaphysical propaganda that is implicit in much of modern science today. The result is that my work is sometimes treated as scientifically uninformed mysticism by one group and as reductionistic materialism by others."

Modern science overlooks its own self-imposed irony. That neither mystics nor materialists can figure out whether a given paradigm is meta-physical or material exemplifies our want of an ontological purview, especially when things get very tiny, in the cell nucleus or the electron. If mind-as-computing is the real McCoy, then constraints become metaphysical addenda (and *vice versa*). And that's without crossing into real metaphysical territory. Deacon added (in a subsequent email):

> I believe that despite its counterintuitive negative framing, this figure/background reversal of the way we conceive of living and mental causality promises to reinstate subjective experience as a legitimate participant in the web of physical causes and effects, and to ultimately reintroduce intentional phenomena back into the natural sciences. It also suggests that the subtitle of my book [*How Mind Emerged from Matter*] is slightly misleading. Mind didn't exactly emerge from matter, but from *constraints on matter*.

That's because Deacon's figure/ground reversal allows autochthonous "spirits" to take the place of exogenous ones (even messengers with morphic resonance). My own view is that there needn't be a distinction between constraints out of the Big Bang into primeval Gaian oceans and constraints from the Adi down the haystack into *the same primal waters*. Laws of nature that cross scales must also cross dimensions.

Deacon concluded by gently chasing me out of my supernatural bias:

> I would add that a tendency to "substantialize" the phenomena that are effects of constraints (absences) is also a danger for those who assume that consciousness, meaning, purpose, value, etc., reside in a parallel nonphysical realm. It leads to a tendency to prematurely abandon the scientific enterprise in favor of uncritical mysticism.

Guilty as charged! I summarized my rebuttal in an email to him:

> 1) The parallel nonphysical realm, if it exists, is consolidated in such a way that there is *no difference* between its physical and metaphysical expression, nor should there be. At the level of constraints, they converge. We are viewing the contour of a far vaster, *more* occult system.
> 2) Materialism, even your nuanced brand, is unaware of its own roots and unconscious dependence on rootless constructs and mathematical

models, so it is more truly *metaphysical* materialism. There is no way around the mind/matter paradox; you can only invert it.

3) The statistical derivation of a Big Bang is not the same as a Big Bang (likewise the autogene)—nobody was there to officiate. You can't back-apply logic to prior conditions without a sense of what the original terms were.

4) Idealists and spirtualists, on the other hand, fail to appreciate, regardless of deference to materialization of "spirit," that the universe is operating on a physical plane here.

5) Neither side seems to recognize that the phenomenological depth of the system is *already* a measure of how accountable a model has to be. I mean, you can't have a paradigm of consciousness that is less subtle than the consciousness performing it. You can't have a universe less implicate than us.

4

James Leininger or James Huston?

James Leininger was a cheerful toddler in Lafayette, Louisiana, unnoteworthy except to his adoring parents, Bruce and Andrea. On May 1, 2000, three weeks after his second birthday, he began having nightmares: "[T]he screams came out of nowhere . . . his sounds were blurred and blunted inside the high-octane howl of a very young child who looked and sounded as if he were fighting desperately for his life."[1] These bouts occurred up to four times a week.

Since Bruce was dealing with a stressful situation at work, he persuaded Andrea to troop down the hall to investigate and provide comfort. Night after night, she became sole witness to James screaming and kicking his feet in the air while emitting blood-curdling moans in a strange voice.

Her pediatrician consoled her that night terrors were normal and would diminish over time, that it was better not to wake a child abruptly from a bad dream. She accepted his advice, quieting her own premonitions. Neither a yokel nor a naïf, Andrea was a former ballet dancer and an educated, discerning mother.

James's fits gradually took on definition. As Andrea explained to a newspaper reporter, "In the throes of his nightmares you couldn't work out what he was saying. But two or three months in, I was walking down the hall and I heard him saying, 'Airplane crash, plane on fire, little man can't get out.' It chilled me to my bone hearing this."[2]

A few months later, when James had more language, he explained that his plane had taken off from a ship and was shot down by gunfire; the little man was unable to escape the burning cockpit. Though ominous, this was at least in the range of childhood fantasy.

Then, during daytime and while fully awake and being read a story by his mother, James rolled onto his back and began kicking in the air like in his dreams. He announced, without the dream fright, "Little man's going like this." She asked who the little man was.

"Me."[3]

Andrea fetched Bruce, and James repeated his assertion.

Bruce asked who shot down his plane. James flashed a disgusted look as if the matter should be obvious: "The Japanese!" he called out cheerily. Later, he told his aunt that anyone could identify the enemy plane from "the big red sun."[4]

The Leiningers recalled an incident from when James was a toddler in diapers. As he looked at a toy propeller-driven plane at Hobby Lobby, Andrea called his attention to a bomb attached to the bottom. After examining it closely, he countered with similar exasperation, "That's not a bomb, Mommy. That's a dwop tank."[5] A drop tank is an extra gas tank added to extend a plane's range.

Other foreshadowings gradually came to mind. Before the onset of the nightmares, Bruce had taken his son to an air museum. They had finished looking at older planes and were headed to modern ones when James ran back and climbed into the cockpit of a World War II fighter. He would not get out even when bribed with ice cream, usually a foolproof lure. On a subsequent visit, he was so excited that he could barely contain himself as he raced to the World War II planes. Bruce described his behavior in the cockpit as having an intense adultlike focus, not at all like his playfulness on trampolines and jungle gyms.

At home, James also liked to buckle a pretend seatbelt like a pilot and put on pretend headgear, so Bruce built him a toy cockpit from an old car seat and concocted a helmet from a construction hard hat. The boy made his own parachute from old canvas bags and a backpack. Using these props, he conducted aerial battles for hours, chattering things like, "Roger . . . Zero at six o'clock . . . Hit him!"[6]

On a family flight east, the boy impressed a commercial pilot with his grasp of the instruments and later, at another museum, demonstrated a professional aviator's knowledge of aircraft structure and function.

Those events were now seen in a different light.

Down the Rabbit Hole

After the nightmares began, Andrea was dropping off Bruce, already a nervous flier, at an airport for a business trip. From his car seat, James called out, "Daddy's airplane crash. Big fire!"

Bruce exploded. "Do not ever say that again. Do you hear me . . . ? Airplanes don't crash! Daddy's airplane will not crash."[7]

Soon after the "indiscretion," Andrea was spying on her son playing in the sunroom when she saw him pull himself to attention, strike the pose of a soldier, bring his hand smartly to his head, and declare in a deep sotto voice, "I salute you and I'll never forget. Now here goes my neck."[8]

The adultlike character was eerily real and somehow *not* James. Yet her belief-system—the Leiningers are devout Christians—did not support reincarnation. Also, Americans these days don't consider it as a possibility. "Having a past life is not the initial conclusion you come to," Andrea conceded. "You try to figure out any other way he could have. . . . Did he see something? Has there been anything on television? Anything that we've discussed? There has to be some other explanation."[9]

While Andrea was at least provisionally open-minded about past lives, Bruce's response was "Baloney!"[10] He too felt that if they pursued their search for the source of their son's behavior, the airplane fantasy would be cleared up by a rational explanation.

From that point on, the parents' actions betrayed their emotional and ideological schizophrenia. On the one hand, they interrogated their son and exhaustively researched his responses as though *he might have had a past life as a World War II pilot;* at the same time, Bruce was determined to discredit the story and prove that James was making up stuff out of his imagination. Either way, an analytical process had begun.

When Andrea asked the boy if he remembered the name of the little man, he answered, "James." She assumed that he didn't understand her question. Taking a different tack, Bruce asked what kind of airplane he flew. James countered promptly, "A Corsair."

The response surprised Bruce, who knew that Corsairs had been launched from World War II aircraft carriers. But how did *James* know? Not only did he know, in a later conversation he added an insider tidbit: "That's a Corsair. They used to get flat tires all the time! And they wanted to turn left when they took off."[11] Both details turned out to be correct! Still, he might have picked them up off the television.

Bruce asked his son the name of the carrier, certain he would invent something nonsensical. "Natoma!" James shot back.

Bruce breathed relief. "Natoma" sounded like a child's make-believe word. Yet an online search revealed a United States aircraft carrier *Natoma Bay* stationed in the Pacific during World War II.

After the cat was out of the bag, Bruce admitted that the repeated coincidences perplexed and disturbed him. A problem solver at work, he could not clear up simple enigmas created by a four-year-old in his household. His son was attacking his belief system, almost goading him into a sacrilegious view.

While tucking James into bed one night, he tried a lighter touch, "No dreams about the little man tonight, okay, buddy?"

The boy said, "The little man's name is James, Daddy."

"Baby, *your* name is James."

"The little man is named James, too."

James often signed his drawings "James 3." When asked one time for an explanation, he declared, "Because I'm the third James. I am James Three."[12]

Though James 3 could not provide James 2's surname, he was able to identify one of his fellow pilots: Jack Larsen.[13]

They were now at a crossroads. If Jack Larsen turned out to be a real person, it was down the rabbit hole.

That Christmas, as father and son were leafing through a book called *The Battle for Iwo Jima,* James pointed to a photo and said, "That's when my plane got shot down."[14]

Upon checking, Bruce discovered that, yes, the carrier *Natoma Bay* had been deployed at Iwo Jima. That was pretty much the last straw.

In September 2002, despite misgivings, Bruce attended the *Natoma Bay* veterans' reunion in San Diego, identifying himself as an amateur historian doing research for a book about the ship's exploits. He couldn't think of a way to tell the truth and not be discounted as a kook. By then, he wasn't certain what he believed himself:

> If James' nightmares were truly a manifestation of a past life—a proof of reincarnation—then, as I saw it, it would threaten the biblical promise of salvation. If the immortal soul can randomly transfer from person to person, generation to generation, then what does that imply for the Christian orthodoxy of redemption? What happens on Judgment Day if the immortal soul is handed off like that? It goes against the evangelical teaching of rebirth through a spiritually transformed personal life.
>
> The impact of James' story on my spiritual well-being . . . well, it felt like spiritual warfare. My purpose for disproving what was happening to my son was to establish that this was all a coincidence, as astronomically remote as that possibility seems. . . . [A]ll the while I was getting closer and closer to something . . . dangerous. It was like putting my hands in a fire.[15]

During his weekend in San Diego, Bruce got corroboration on several points. There *had* been a Jack Larsen on the *Natoma Bay;* he was living in Arkansas but never came to reunions. There were no Corsairs on the ship, only FM-2's and TBM Avengers. There *was* a "James" among the *Natoma Bay* dead, James M. Huston Jr., a nuance that might explain "James 3." Bruce also discovered that Huston had died at the location that his son had pointed out in the book, about a hundred and fifty miles from Iwo Jima.

It was time to entertain the unthinkable. No longer disguising his motive, Bruce called Larsen and then drove to Springdale, Arkansas, to interview him. After greeting his visitor, Larsen described the day on which he and James Huston flew together. It was March 3, 1945, when they took off from the *Natoma Bay* to strike at Chichi-Jima, dubbed by one pilot "the hellhole of the Bonin Islands." Their mission was to stop a "Japanese build-up of troop replacements and supplies."[16] Though not scheduled to fly that day, James Huston volunteered. It was his squadron's final mission before being shipped home. They winged through heavy flak, which Jack presumed brought his shipmate's plane down.

Later, Bruce learned that James M. Huston Jr. was the only pilot lost during the attack on Chichi-Jima. Age twenty-one, he perished on his fiftieth World War II mission, far more than enough to build up aircraft lingo and fighter-pilot ritual.

As Bruce left the Larsen house, Jack handed him a present, his old flight helmet with goggles and oxygen mask still attached. "I was wearing this on the day I flew off *Natoma Bay,*" he said. "On the day James Huston was shot down."[17]

At home, young James "put it on firmly, professionally, slapping out the air bubbles, shaping the fit, as if he were going to work."[18]

Prebirth Memories

Not long after his visit to the Larsens, Bruce lofted James in the air and declared how happy he was to have him for his son. James responded, "That's why I picked you; I knew you would be a good daddy."

Instead of letting the compliment pass, Bruce requested an explanation. James complied. "When I found you and Mommy, I knew that you would be good to me." The boy provided details: "I found you at the big pink hotel. I found you on the beach. You were eating dinner at night."[19]

Bruce and Andrea stayed at the Royal Hawaiian Hotel approximately five weeks before Andrea became pregnant with James. Not only did the boy apparently "see" it in his mind's eye, he also responded as if, "Doesn't everyone choose their parents before they're born?" Maybe everyone *does.*

Maybe everyone also travels back and forth to the land of the dead. James had named his GI Joe dolls Billy, Leon, and Walter, and when Bruce somewhat gratuitously wondered "why no Buzz or Todd or Rocky," the boy said, "Because that's who met me when I got to heaven."

Bruce later learned that his son had correctly identified, by name (and later by hair color), three men who died before him on missions between October 25 and November 17, 1945: Billie Peeler, Leon Connor, and Walter Devlin. Billie Peeler had dark hair like James's Billie doll; Leon Connor had blonde hair, as did the Leon doll; and Walter Devlin had the reddish hair of James's Walter doll. These "accumulating flukes and strikes of accurate details connecting to the GI Joe action figures were dumbfounding."[20]

About 20 percent of people who have memories of events from before birth also recall some combination of their PP's funeral, his or her time in another realm, the interval between death and rebirth, choosing new parents, and conception, gestation, and being reborn, though a child may rationalize bewildering metamorphoses by juvenile iconography. One boy reported that "God gave him a card to come back from heaven . . . it looked like a business card with green arrows on it."[21] A Sri Lankan girl recalled being an old woman in a village three miles from her home and "being lifted up, even though her body was buried, and flying like a bird." She met "a king or governor whose reddish clothes and beautiful pointed shoes were never taken off, never dirty, and never washed. Her own clothes were also always clean, but they were golden. The king's home was made of glass, and had beautiful red beds. As she played there, all she had to do was think of food and it appeared. She didn't have to eat it, for its mere appearance satisfied her hunger."[22]

Marta Lorenz, a Brazilian girl who remembered having been an adult friend of her mother's in an earlier lifetime, commented after the disheartening death of her own sister, "Emilia is not in the cemetery. She is in a safer and better place than this one where we are; her soul can never get wet." As her father retorted that the dead never return, she interrupted his diatribe, "Don't say that. I died also and look, I am living again."[23]

A patient of Brian Weiss recalled how when "floating in a shining void, she would become the host for disembodied spirits who revealed the mysteries of eternity."[24] Bridey Murphy danced.

At age sixteen, my own daughter, Miranda, informed my wife and me one evening at dinner that she had picked us to be her parents and take care of her. We had done a good job, she said, but she was able to handle things now on her own. Soon after, she underwent a change of appearance and personality. Her blonde hair turned black at the roots, and she matured into a cutting-edge artist.

The Reincarnation of James Huston

Bruce Leininger eventually learned—no thunderbolt by now—that while most planes at Iwo Jima took off from the *Natoma Bay*, James Huston's last flight had been off a different ship, the *Sargent Bay*. This information surfaced as Bruce continued to interview survivors in James Huston's squadron and weave together accounts of James 2's death. A participant pilot's journal entry from the scene that day read: "One of the fighters from our escort squadron was close to us and took a direct hit on the nose. All I could see were pieces falling into the bay."[25]

Another flier recognized James Huston in a photograph Bruce brought along. Recalling the 1945 day, he began to sob:

> We were no more than thirty yards apart when the pilot deliberately turned his head and looked at me. I caught his eyes and we connected with each other. No sooner had we connected than his plane was hit in the engine by what seemed to be a fairly large shell. There was an instantaneous flash of flames that engulfed the plane. It did not disintegrate but almost immediately disappeared below me. . . . Mr. Leininger, I have lived with that pilot's face as his eyes fixed on me every day since it happened. I never knew who he was. I was the last guy who saw him alive. I was the last person he saw before he was killed. His face has haunted me my whole life. . . . Now I know who he was.[26]

He also supplied a possible back story for an odd detail in James Leininger's play. The shell took off James Huston's plane propeller, and "James' toy aircraft were always left [by him] without propellors."[27]

In a parallel quest, the Leiningers hunted down and made touch with James Huston's last surviving family member, his sister Annie. By phone, Bruce told her to sit down and pour herself a drink, then recited an incredible tale. She was not as surprised as he had expected. Annie told him that several friends and family, including herself, had received ghost-like visits from James Jr. on the day of his death. His spirit had come to bid each of them goodbye. She knew that he did not depart easily.

The four-year-old and his PP's eighty-four-year-old sister later talked on the phone. James shared intimate family details with her as if she were still his kid sister, recalling things that no one could have known except her brother or parents.[28] Annie later remarked that James 3 didn't so much look like James 2 as *radiate him.*

The "reincarnation of James Huston" had gone public by then. The Leininger family was interviewed on ABC *Primetime,* so Bruce confessed to the alumni of the *Natoma Bay.* To a one, they were sympathetic and welcomed young James at their next reunion. As the boy walked around, he recognized many, greeting them by name. He aced a few friendly spot quizzes, for instance, showing accurately where a five-inch gun was located.[29] He told his father later that it was sad to find them all so old. James Huston, inside him, was still a young man.

After the show, a Japanese production company flew the Leiningers to Tokyo, then brought them by ship to Chichi-Jima. As he took in the scenery, James tugged at his father's sleeve and pointed, "This is where the planes flew in when James Huston was killed."[30]

They floated flowers over the site and conducted a ceremony for James 2's soul. James 3 put his head in his mother's lap and sobbed for fifteen minutes. "He seemed to be weeping for himself and for James Huston—and for all the world of woe that he had ever seen or felt."[31]

Bruce experienced his own breakthrough. "I had a kind of revelation. James' experience was not contrary to my belief. God, I thought, gives us a spirit. It lives forever. James Huston's spirit had come back to us. Why? I'll never know. But it had. There are things that are unexplainable and unknowable. . . . The secular culture demanded facts and proof, and I had done the heavy lifting. I had made a leap of faith. I believed—truly believed—in the story. I did not need a reason."[32]

The Response of the "Atheists"

Professional skeptic Paul Kurtz, who made it his duty to debunk such claims whenever they arose, gave an ABC *Primetime* reporter his own "expert" opinion of the Leininger case:

"I think that the parents are self-deceiving, that they are fascinated by the mysterious, and that they built up a fairy tale. . . . He's overhearing conversations of his parents, he's looking at cues. He may talk to his little friends or hear from neighbors. And then this notion builds up that, yes he was this pilot, he will come to believe that himself."[33]

He nodded to accentuate his point, then smiled condescendingly at the camera.

"Little friends" indeed! Kurtz's comments do not address the Leiningers' scrupulous behavior or their diligence, only his assumptions that they must be deluded or perpetrators of a hoax. These are compelling explanations *only if paranormal options are* a priori *excluded.*

Bruce, initially a disbeliever himself, responded to Kurtz via the show, "We're talking to a two-year-old. What am I going to do, sit him in a corner and say, 'Now we're going to concoct this elaborate scheme and you're going to imagine that you went through those things?'"[34]

Kurtz's view, of course, was that this kind of phenomenon is impossible. He didn't pause to think the matter through. His duty was to protect the public from disinformation.

Along similar lines, Daniel C. Dennett (of "we're all zombies" fame) is reported to have said that "he would commit suicide if paranormal phenomena turn out to be real." What an odd impulse, even as a quip! Did he mean that he couldn't stand to live in a nonmaterialistic world? That he couldn't bear the humiliation of being wrong? That he was so certain of his view that he would *bet his life on it?* If the latter, it is a self-contradiction, almost an oxymoron, for if paranormal phenomena *do* turn out to be real, he might *not be able to "kill" himself.* Holistic physician Larry Dossey explained, "Special contempt is reserved for the possibility that humans might survive bodily death, for this would be the death-knell for the mind-equals-brain assumption on which physicalism rests."[35] (See more on "special contempt" in chapter 9, "Worshipping the Algorithm.")

Another materialist dismissed a case of nonlocal consciousness by commenting, "This is the sort of thing I would not believe, even if it really happened."[36] A self-sanctioned worldview and belief system mimics empiricism while supplanting it. An observed effect may have been real, but it doesn't count. The dissenter was saying, in essence, "If it happened on my watch, my tribal loyalty to science precludes my acknowledging it. And I certainly wouldn't broadcast my experience." That is how physicists and engineers at the University of Colorado responded to parapsychologist Jule Eisenbud's demonstration of Ted Serios, a Chicago elevator operator who allegedly projected hidden target pictures as well as images from his mind into camera lenses. After Serios sent numerous "hits" through an electromagnetic-wave-blocking Faraday shield onto randomly purchased strips of film, attending scientists talked faculty gossip and college basketball at lunch, as if nothing notable had happened.[37]

Skeptics know that one-up events and anecdotal evidence can be ignored and that despite the documented fieldwork of Stevenson and Tucker and the careful experimental set-up of Eisenbud, there is no valid protocol for past-life memories or nonlocal image projections.

Philosopher Charles Eisenstein described the logic underlying sectarian faith: "The debunker must buy into a world full of frauds, dupes, and the mentally unstable, where most people are less intelligent and less sane than he is, and in which apparently honest people indulge in the most outrageous mendacity for no good reason." Since the witnesses seem sincere, the debunker assumes "either (1) that this apparent sincerity is a cynical cover for the most base or fatuous motives, or (2) they are ignorant, incapable of distinguishing truth from lies and delusion."[38]

The issue here is not even that skeptics presume that phenomena like out-of-body experiences and past lives are preposterous, hence they must be fake; they also uphold a higher fiat: that there is no meaning, spirit, or innate intelligence in the universe. To seek it is blasphemy. To "find" it is casuistry or treason. They would remain unconvinced if a Cheshire cat deliquesced out of thin air and extended an ectoplasmic paw.

The modern universe bottoms out here. Its texture may get more intricate and dicey, but it never goes beneath this "absolute" bottom.

Why such fanatic antispiritualism as if honorably upholding truth against heresy? No coven of traitor scientists or paraphysicists is seeking a reversal of human progress. Yet skeptics react as if nonlocality of mind would automatically sabotage the technology on which the world's societies and economies stand. All the jets would come tumbling out of the sky; suspension bridges would collapse; the internet would crash.

Others fear that if they even tacitly pondered a hoax, their achievements would be nullified and their lives made worthless. This came up in an interview I conducted with Carl Sagan in 1972. I was young and artless enough then to raise the possibility of visiting Mars on the Astral plane.

"In my mind," Sagan rejoined, "there's a big difference between something I want to be true and therefore pretend inside my head is really true and something that's really true. . . . Suppose you lived your whole life in a very subdued and puritanical and uptight way because that was what you had to do to get to heaven, and then you die and that's it. Well, I think you would have been had."

"You wouldn't know it," I said.

"Nevertheless, it makes a difference to me. The fact that you would have foregone all sorts of satisfactions and pleasures for a supposed infinite reward and then that infinite reward was never delivered."[39]

So that's it? The main point of life is not to be scammed? The fear of being "had" is so strong that it supersedes both the search for truth and respect for the universe's complexity? Brilliant and sophisticated as the author-to-be of *Cosmos* was, he did not understand the true nature of "pretend." Even wishes have profound etiologies, and Astral planes have archaeoastronomies too.

This is the shadow side of modern civilization: ephemeral prosperity and technological zealotry masking dearth and shibboleth.

Taking Responsibility for a Conscious Universe

Scholar of religion Jeffrey Kripal pinpoints a counterphobia with its own sophistry:

We [meaning "they"] allergically avoid all . . . those religious experiences that strongly suggest that quantum effects *do* scale up into human experience—all that mystical interconnectedness, all those entangled people who somehow instantly know what is happening to a loved one (or a beloved pet) a thousand miles away (nonlocality) or, worse yet, what is about to happen (retrocausation). Instead, we go on and on about how we are all locked into our historical contexts, how religion is only about dubious power, or bad politics, or now cognitive modules and evolutionary adaptations, how these fantastic stories are all just "anecdotal" statistical flukes or perceptual delusions—*anything,* as long as it is depressing and boring.[40]

"Depressing and boring"—these are a concession to existential fatalism as well as unwillingness to bear the responsibilities for a universe that subsumes souls and afterlives. Perhaps they are a defense mechanism against fear—fear of one's own hidden powers and of nature's deeper meanings and mysteries. In a convenience-first culture, it is better to be a robot that will eventually get shut off for good. Death is a commodity too.

One of the least acknowledged facets of modernity is its unwillingness to be responsible *for the implications of existence itself.* People take faux responsibility for just about everything else, or everything they consider important: the pleasure principle, their material equity, their discontents, the *entire* extant universe. Just not themselves.

The perils of an unexamined "I" came up dramatically in an interview I conducted with Jule Eisenbud in Denver in 1972. As we touched on human aggression, his tone turned histrionic and indignant:

Thoughts alone can kill; bare, naked thoughts; isn't all this armor of war, this machinery, these bombs, aren't they all grotesque exaggerations? We don't even need them. . . . To put it schematically, and simplistically, and almost absurdly, because we don't wish to realize that we can just kill with our minds, we go through this whole enormous play of . . . killing with such overimplementation; it gets greater and greater and greater as if . . . it's a caricature of saying: how can I do it with my mind; I need tanks; I need B-52 bombers; I need napalm, and so on, and so on . . . I have examples of people who died this way. Not that I could see them do it but if I put together the jigsaw, it looks as though this one was responsible for that event.[41]

I mentioned a classic article, Harvard physiologist Walter B. Cannon's "Voodoo Death" from an issue of the 1942 *American Anthropologist,* but Eisenbud was frying bigger fish:

Yes, of course, of course. But the whole point is that there a man deliberately said, "I'm going to kill you." We mask it. It goes on unobtrusively. Which doesn't make a damn bit of difference. What's the difference whether I do it or streptococci do it. We have cover stories, you see. All science has produced cover stories for the deaths we create; it's streptococci; it's accidents, and so on. But, what I'm trying to say is, there must be, I feel, a relationship between this truth, which we will not see, and this absurd burlesque of aggression that goes on all around us, as if we're trying to deny that the other is possible.[42]

Eisenbud is proposing that voodoo (a combination of telepathy and telekinesis) is not only consciously trained throughout the indigenous Weltanschauung but is also an innate function of the human psyche. Aboriginal cultures heed what the civilized world has repressed and forgotten: hexes, charms, and unconscious projections *work*. We prefer the burlesque. Even nuclear weapons are less terrifying than mind control, for the latter not only changes the rules of engagement, negating all politic rationalizations for violence, but also exposes us to poltergeists, goblins, and monsters from the id. Our denial is ravenous and insatiable.

The internet provides cover for what Eisenbud suspected in 1972: a covert "dark zone" of bloodthirsty lusts and projections. Only shamans, in the fullest sense of their calling, can commute that energy at its source.

While secular fundamentalists acclaim sociology of knowledge, cultural relativism, universal positivism, and deconstruction of mere contextual information, they aren't even truly postcolonial because they do not accept indigenous realities on their *own* terms—shamanically inculcated totems from Asia, Africa, Dreamtime Australia, aboriginal North and South America, and so on. Yet each of these ethnographically diminished or cyber-colonially rejected landscapes represents *a full working reality.*

Kripal adds, "Do not the logics of basic doctrines like reincarnation and the ultimate nature of realized consciousness . . . imply, indeed demand, that *consciousness precedes culture?* Consciousness is transhistorical and cosmic in these systems, not just some local ethnic epiphenomenon constructed by brain matter, social practice, language and an ethnic group."[43]

Yet mindedness is treated as alternately an accessory and an intruder. In its fascination with information and prophylaxis, science disparages contexts, especially the most encompassing ones.

Multiple Yardsticks of Reality

The truth is, the universe is folded into itself tortuously enough to impose multiple yardsticks of reality simultaneously. Consciousness can bore a hole through materialism without abrogating *even the physical aspects of its operation.* Conversely, materialism can operate with cesium-clock precision despite flurries of ghosts and other anomalies.

To dismiss the entire body of Ian Stevenson's work as if it were *prima facie* self-delusion *and* an embarrassment to the University of Virginia (as some protesting alumni did)[44] is not a defense of science against religious obstruction. That effectively ended with Galileo's *"E pur si muove."*

One can dispense with God as a personified patriarch or avenger of aborted embryos, but that's not what's at stake. "God" designates a focused intelligence at the vortex of a cosmic mystery. Theologian Gordon Kaufman called it "the religious name for the profound *mystery of creativity,* the mystery of the emergence, in and through evolutionary and other originative processes, of novelty in the world."[45] God is the placeholder for formal cause, not a patriarch fashioning universes out of whipped cream or hydrogen atoms.

On the other hand, to declare past-life memories proof of reincarnation (like actors taking on roles in successive plays) is as reductionist as the skeptical position. In a universe of ephemeral states, there are *never* going to be final verdicts.

A woman I met in Bar Harbor, Maine, in 2009 was convinced that a ninety-five-year-old patient whom she befriended at an assisted-living facility returned two days after her death, as she had promised, in the alias of a dragonfly, her favorite animal and a motif of many of her brooches. The insect hung around on her friend's arm for an entire day, rode in her car with her, accompanied her into the kitchen on her elbow to the amusement of her teenage children, and sat at dinner on her shoulder. The woman took this as an unmistakable sign of the woman's continued existence.

Ten years later, Betsy MacGregor, a speaker at a conference on Cortes Island, British Columbia, told an almost identical story about her mother and a small bird that tapped at the window after she passed at age eighty-one. Prior to her death, Betsy's mother had confided that she was scared of dying, and Betsy had said, "I don't think you need to be afraid. You might even discover that your sense of who you are doesn't end when the body dies, but continues on in a different dimension from this one."[46]

Her mother was skeptical, keeping faith with her late husband, who avidly pooh-poohed consciousness surviving death. Betsy said, "Maybe you can send a sign of some kind to let me know if I was right, Mom. I've heard that sometimes birds can deliver such messages, and you've certainly been a friend of birds, what with all the bird-feeders you've maintained in your yard. I bet one of them would be happy to do that if you asked!"[47]

On cue, after her mother's death, a bird began appearing daily, frantically flapping and pecking away. Betsy worried for its safety so, on a friend's advice, she summoned an animal communicator, a profession she had not previously heard of. The woman explained:

The reason the bird is still coming to you is because *you haven't fully believed what is happening*—which is that it's coming on behalf of your mother, exactly as you asked, to say that you were right: dying isn't something to be afraid of, for life simply continues in another form. The bird can't accomplish its mission as long as your mind is filled with doubt about this![48]

Animal totems dispatched by the recent dead are recognized in just about all aboriginal societies. In this pancultural belief system, loved ones use feral or theriomorphic intermediaries to bridge the gap between worlds. Because incarnate and disincarnate renditions of the same meaning clash and nullify each other, a different mode of communication and messenger is needed. The literal truth would not compute in our terms, and no symbol is as vibrant and mysteriously cogent as a living bird or dragonfly. Yet dead-reckoning (a telling pun) and divination are status-less in the exclusionary empiricism of the West. Pragmatists not only want the road to Mandalay but also to call home when they get there.

Nonlocal mind does not mean only "mind unaccompanied by brain or singular personality," it also means "consciousness without ontological status or spatiotemporal venue." "Bird" or "dragonfly" validation is not anchored anywhere and, more to the point, doesn't anchor anything else. We have no way to determine if Virginia Tighe *was* Bridey Murphy, let alone the "Ms. Murphy" of the *Daily Mirror*'s investigations. She could have inhabited the Ireland of Bernstein's regressions or another "Ireland." She could have also lived on an alternate world akin to psychonaut Robert Monroe's "third space." Or she could have been a cryptomnesiac displacement. Without a psychic GPS or Google All That Is, woman-to-dragonfly mapping is beyond our range *in every sense.*

We can't know what the old woman herself experienced, whether she knew herself as a dragonfly—whether the dragonfly was a poltergeist cascading from the fissioning of her soul. Or did her soul enlist an entomological bug in the way Betsy's mother dispatched an ornithological bird? The events could have also been synchronicities, each set in motion by psychic ricochets from the women's deaths in the context of their prior discussions of survival; they were linked by meaning rather than by causal succession. Like the after-death ghost visits of James Huston (and countless others in reports from every culture on Earth), they affected only the immediate participants (living and dead).

The "dragonfly" could also have been (as most scientists would insist) coincidence, the human mind imposing meaning on a chance event. Yet even a conventional biological event may not be what it seems, as contexts are erased and rewritten from epoch to epoch. An Egyptian scarab does not belong to the same "order" as a New England ladybug or a Thai rhinoceros beetle. The scarab contained regenerative sun rays but no DNA. Likewise, an Aramaic-speaking Israelite practiced different incarnational hygiene from a Belfast Irishman, though the latter attends the church of the former.

Christ's Rainbow Body

Father Francis Tiso deconstructed one of the most transformative icons of Western civilization by juxtaposing Christ's resurrection with rainbow-body reincarnations of Tibetan lamas. Though working for the

Church of Rome, Father Tiso did not take an exception for Divine intervention in nature. He proposed that resurrection shifts culturally with the meaning of the physical world. The Crucifixion and Resurrection, if they took place today (and in many ways they *do*), could never be the same as they were at Calvary, even if we allow another immaculate conception and divine trinity.

> We no longer think of protoplasm in the same way that we did a thousand years ago; microbiology and biochemistry have completely altered our knowledge of bodily processes and even our idea of what a human body is; we now need to take into account microorganisms and even organelles, such as mitochondria, that have their own DNA and evolutionary history. From this perception, what rises [as Christ] on the third day is in fact a community of living beings, symbiotically supportive of the self-emergence of consciousness, in accord with a physical, scientifically accessible genetic program.[49]

The resurrection (or rainbow body) of Christ was far more profound and multidimensional than appreciated by his apostles and priests. They assume some sort of divine power play or facile costume change without recognizing the depth of cellular and soul transformation required. No one gets resurrected without encountering the incarnational root. The man Jesus was carrying both terrestrial DNA and a higher vibration of Christ consciousness. He meant to incarnate a celestial archetype in a human context. His vibration is still tolling through the planetary body, attempting to raise our own vibration to its octave: service, compassion, revelation—biological event as theophany.

What Survives?

Nicole Keller, a Facebook "friend," asks, "What or who the heck is 'I'? This bouquet of higgledy-piggledy conscious lifetime experiences and thoughts claiming to be myself in the first place?" Part of each of us is memory; another part is a continually reconstructed internal dialogue, some of it inadvertently fictionalized or revised. If core identity and personal history are that fungible in life, they are more so after death.

Reincarnation is *not* continuity of identity; it is our incompletely parsed reification of a phenomenon for which we have no name. What we have been talking about as if sequential—linear consecutive—lives is a *different* conflation of information, identity, and temporal existence.

What was established by Stevenson is that "memories, emotions, and even physical injuries can sometimes carry over from one life to the next."[50] That's it. The *life itself* doesn't carry over. It is *not* like going to sleep at night and waking in the morning with the same self. Shroder likened fragmentary flashbacks to "a bad carbon copy—here and there you could make out a word, or even a phrase, but it was impossible to get a sense of the whole document."[51]

Look at it a different way: if James Leininger isn't the proximal legatee of James Huston's soul, what *is* the relationship between the two? And where is James Huston Jr. now if he is not James Leininger? Does he continue to exist independently? Does the fact that young Leininger possesses strands of Huston's death picture and other memories preclude Huston's existence elsewhere (because he has been transformed)? Or can aspects of spirit be separated as they are transferred between auras? Can memories and identities exist in multiple hosts simultaneously?

If a Viking longship's timbers are replaced section by section at successive landfalls in Greenland and Labrador until there are no staves left of the original knar, is it still that ship? If the old timbers are stored in the hold and upon arrival in Vinland another ship is constructed from them, which ship is the original one? I say that it is the one with *none* of the original boards.

James Leininger has access to a chunk of James Huston's life within his own selfhood, but he is *not* James Huston, a zombie arisen from an airplane crash, seeking more Earth time. He has snippets of James 2's memories and death picture *but not his existential thread or selfhood*. He has no continuity with James Huston's beliefs, desires, or experience. *He is another person.* James Huston *cannot* impose his identity or values on James Leininger; they are independent egos psychically connected, not the progression of a single personality.

If that seems equivocal, back it up an iota or two: there is no intrinsic explanation for existence in any form, let alone states of incarnation. We don't know if individual creatures are complete and final as birthed or whether they are phases of greater creaturehoods. The mystery of the two Jameses is not solely psychological, phenomenological, demographic, mnemonic, or chronological; it is ontological but in a way few philosophers address. Because the formal discussion of "being" does not generally include cleaving identities, there are few, if any, forays into what, if anything, could be fissioning and how its parts get weighted, personified, or redistributed. Since reincarnation is either accepted (in many traditions) or not supposed to happen, past-life memories tend to be all or nothing: you *are* the PP or you're not. The reality is far more prochronistic* and convoluted.

The details that James 3 possesses of James 2's personhood are less than a billionth of a percent of James Huston's total existence—and this is true to the same relative extent for all who experience past-life fragments. Even Ryan Hammons, with a much larger archive of Marty Martyn's "memory," does not encompass the actor-agent's rollicking life.

Similarly, Daniel was not Rashid. He had none of his mechanical skills and did not remember most of his PP's experiences. He had scraps, remnants—that's it.

Most children forget their past lives, either by late childhood or their teens. James 3's interest in the fighter-pilot routine waned as he aged. Some memories lingered, but they came to seem less important; his nightmares ended. He accepted his current life as his self. Ryan Hammons told his mother that it was time to become a regular kid. Just like that: Marty Martyn gone!

Even among those who have persistent past-life memories, flashbacks come and go and are more and less intense at different ages, eventually lapsing into reincarnational amnesia. As with a dream, a person may remember events intensely at one moment and forget them a moment later. Favorite times for recalling prior "lifetimes" appear to be after baths, during car rides, at bedtime, and upon awaking from sleep. These

---

*Prochronism (see also chapter 2) is a chronological error or glitch, invalidly displacing an event backward in time or into a spurious past. Here I mean a chronological juxtaposition of an unknown kind.

memories are often soporific or hypnagogic; they interrupt ordinary consciousness with a different presentation that is briefly lucid. Perhaps they come more from the aura than the brain.

Not only do people recall details of past lives best when they are young and forget them later, they also forget even that *they once remembered them*. A child in Stevenson's files, when taken to the house of a formerly vivid past-life memory, remarked to his mother that his PP's mother looked familiar. "Why is that, Mom?"[52] Yet he once knew *exactly who she* "was."

Most children lose their earlier memories by age six or seven—not *past*-life but *this*-life, a process dubbed "early childhood amnesia." If current childhood memories fade or disappear, exponentially greater amnesia occurs with memories from other lives. James 3 could have carried incomplete fragments of *other* prior lifetimes. The premature loss of James 2's life was no more exigent than any of those. Each was lived in its time with its own unique ego and view.

Accounts of near-death experiences, past-life memories, and channeling from spirit entities don't fully tide the waters between the living and the dead because they can't; the two realms are separate and can only function as they do by being quarantined. Otherwise, the "living" wouldn't be fully alive, and the dead couldn't enter their own realm. (I will pick up this thread in Chapter 7.)

It looks like a cosmic masquerade or a square dance in which selves rather than partners get traded. But if spirits can flip bodies and manifestations like ghosts at a rodeo, why do we have an entire process of evolution from stellar dust through elemental synthesis, molecules to cells to life forms to consciousness? Remember, this is science's ace in the hole to play against all spiritual and metaphysical rivals: conscious being is an emergent property of inanimate matter. Mind took billions of years to evolve. It is a nontransferable property of *closed* systems. Yet it is worth noting that physical incarnation seems to require phylogeny (evolution) as well as ontogeny (embryological development) and, surprisingly, cosmogony (the unfolding of the universe). It is *both* teleodynamic and morphodynamic, as each frequency recapitulates and insinuates the others, from macrocosm (multidimensionality) to microcosm (the human sphere) to nucleocosm (the nanosphere). Science-savvy mystics like Rudolf Steiner and Pierre Teilhard de Chardin have addressed how spiritual evolution is mirrored in physical evolution in order for souls to cross into material worlds. Cycles of water vapor, photosynthesis, and glycolysis draw on vital properties and, as it were, esoteric "meanings" of hydrogen, oxygen, nitrogen, carbon, phosphorus, water, chlorophyll, and other atoms and molecules in expressing attributes of life.*

From a purely spiritual perspective, our identity needs aloneness to apprehend the stark reality of its own presence. Jane Roberts considers this our protection: "The selves we know now . . . exist in bodies that bloom only for a personal time . . . closed to all other beings who came before or who will come after. We have the world, for a while to ourselves. . . . [T]he gracious focus of our physical senses gives us that privacy and protects the personal space we've made in a world of moments."[53]

Forgetting one's own past lives, which *everyone* pretty much does, means (to me, anyway, because I am fundamentally an optimist) that there is a greater essence that all—however many—lives feed, and from which all of them (including this one) trickle like fading dreams. That essence is our anchor and final outpost, the great remembering to offset the great forgetting.

Consider how many languages and peoples have been lost on this planet alone. The last speakers of Native American tongues like Spokane and Mohegan have died or are dying, taking with them not only the grammars, sounds, and lexicons but also the myths, songs, history, tribal wisdom, and *symbol-symbol representations and sound-object relationships.* This will happen to English too someday—all the words you are reading now or have written and spoken yourself as well as the seemingly immortal notes of John Keats's nightingale, the King James Bible, and *A Midsummer Night's Dream* will become babble and then get washed away or incinerated for good. Yet their strings of deeper syntax and meanings,

---

*This is a complex topic that I can only introduce peripherally here, but if you are interested, I have speculated on it at length in *Embryogenesis: Species, Gender, and Identity* ("The Materials of Life" and "The First Beings," pp. 25–60, and "Spiritual Embryogenesis," pp. 695–724) and in *The Night Sky: Soul and Cosmos* (pp. 361–364 [Teilhard] and 561–562 [Steiner]).

unconscious as well as conscious, may be preserved as psychic glossolalia: silent drumbeats and panpipes at the cosmic core.

Each "known" or "news" is known for a time and then erased, shadowed by countless "unknowns," before, during, and after. They trail like infinitely diverging kite strings through the depth of the unconscious, the undesignated universe, and the sheer multiplicity of dimensions and meaningnesses. Nothing "known" is meant to subsist, here or anywhere, yet everything known is connected to everything else, known or unknown, forever.

If we could access all of time and self from every vantage, self would be surrendered to a timeless entity. It is not *just* an exaggeration to posit that, without privacy and separation, there might be no stars, galaxies, or worlds.

5

Karma, Nonduality, and Meaning

Reality and Illusion

A Buddhist precept states that one personality gives rise to another *without carryover of personal identity.* Ego identity wasn't real to begin with. At death, it ceases to exist because it *never* existed. The self either becomes enlightened, that is, recognizes the basis of its reality and enters a Buddhafield, or it dissolves back into its own essential nullity. Like a dying candle lighting a new wick with its last embers, the charge of one ego-state *transfuses* a new identity—but without continuity of personhood. The PP is gone forever while a new person is shaped around the former ego's karma. Instead of a continuation of personal identity, there is transfer of psychic energy.

The continuity of lives rests on the degree to which each existence potentiates a future emanation. A Buddhist homily strikes at the core: "If you want to know who you were in a past life, look at who you are now. If you want to know who you will become in a future life, observe your present actions."

In that fashion, the dead person lives again; James 2 passes an aspect of his own torch to James 3. Zen master Shunryu Suzuki addresses the underlying paradox:

After some years we will die. If we just think that it is the end of our life, this will be the wrong understanding. But, on the other hand, if we think that we do not die, this is also wrong. We die, and we do not die. This is the right understanding. Some people may say that our mind or soul exists forever, and it is only our physical body which dies. But this is not exactly right, because both mind and body have their end. But at the same time it is also true that they exist eternally.[1]

This limns the true depth, complication, and interconnectedness of All That Is.

In the sixth century BCE, Gautama Buddha made a determination not to track a deceased person beyond his or her initial change-states. It was a matter of neither belief nor ontological priority; it was a focus of practice. He was concerned with how to end suffering *here and now.* When the Buddhist-defined self shatters from the fallacy of its own existence, the mirage holding it together breaks into pieces, none of which continue to exist discretely.

In other words, much like modern science, Buddhism assigns consciousness to a delusion. But while science deems the mind a vagabond mirage, Buddhism sources the mirage in a self-arising luminosity. Its "ego illusion" is attributed to five conditional interdependent aggregates *(pancakkhandha)*: body or matter *(rupakkhandha),* sensation *(vedanakkhandha),* perception *(sannakkhandha),* mental formation *(samkharakkhandha),* and consciousness *(vinnanakkhandha).*

How do these latent "energies" discover or recognize and attract one another and then federate as life forms and personalized identities? How at death do they come asunder and redistribute their vital energy and essential beingness?

Karma, a traditional Sanskrit term rendered in English variously as "action," "work," or "deed"—or, more popularly, "payback"—is an *energy,* though it operates at a subtler frequency than electromagnetism or gravity and, as such, may participate in their formation. If gravity is mass plus motion plus relativity (the space-time continuum), then karma is a predisposition to particle acceleration and attraction—cosmic and planetary settings—as well as incarnation *in* them.

The breadth of karma is expressed by its multiple indices of action: simple cause and effect (gravity and mass, thirst and quenching of thirst), destiny (unmanifested deeds and events from previous lifetimes manifested in a present life), and potentiation of later effects (electromagnetic-like waves stored in the cosmos as Akashic memory).

The Buddhist universe arises as a lesion between cosmic abeyancy—the fundamental dormancy of nature—and egoic recognition. I am calling it a *lesion* because it is a gap that cannot be bridged, or it can only be bridged by a core metamorphosis *of everything*. That's the "moment" of recognition. Through the primal tear, a ground luminosity ignites sub-atomic vibrations, inaugurating secular time.

Karma predicates beingness and suffering. The cause or basis? That lies in some prior theogony or Apache dawn and reflects a latency beyond thought, a *true* bottoming out. As a temporal condition, nature is *only conditional,* dependent. Being is dependent too.

Dependent origination means that as human beings we exist only in, and because of, our relationship to everything else, depending on this relational nature for an almost axiomatic belief in our felt existence: our sense of self as well as our apparent discreteness in space, persistence through time, and status as centers of knowing in relation to an ever-shifting array of sensory objects.[2]

The goal of spiritual practice (for an individual ego once it exists) is to dissolve the lesion with its bias toward duality and attachment and to observe its illusional and situational entrapment. This leads to both enlightenment and the cessation of suffering.

In antithesis to scientific dogma, which wipes out whole universes with the panache of keystrokes, the Buddhist "real" universe never perishes, for nothing real could cease to exist. Essence cannot be repealed; it shifts from one state to another toward its basis. Even if the ego-self is an illusion, its predilection to existence is not—this is what creates our conviction of inviolable identity.

The distinction between existence as a mirage and existence as a self-arising radiance marks the divide between Eastern and Western ontologies.

For creatures in the game, meaning *all* creatures, "being"—temporal selfhood—is indispensable because they have nothing to put in its place, no way to exchange where or what they are. Since the choice to *be* wasn't a choice, it cannot be repealed. If you try to annul it by suicide, you alter its frequency but not its basis. Karma assures continuity. We go only (and inextricably) from reality to reality.

Consider then how marooned we are. *This* may not be real, but *reality* is real.

Buddhist philosopher Dustin DiPerna posited this with exquisite succinctness: "We are always in some sort of state. States are an ever-present part of our experience."[3] Each realm is a bardo, a bridge or transition to *another* realm or state. Suicide is a bridge too.

From within Western ontology, Shakespeare's Hamlet pondered his own problematic beingness ("to be, or not to be"), then hailed "the undiscover'd country from whose bourne no traveler returns" (*Hamlet,* Act 3, Scene 1, lines 56 and 79–80). Centuries later, Albert Camus would invert his existential elegy, "There is but one truly serious philosophical problem, and that is suicide."[4] Suicide, adds Arthur Schopenhauer, is "a question which man puts to Nature, trying to force her to answer. The question is this: What change will death produce in man's existence and in his insight into the nature of things? [Yet] it involves the destruction of the very consciousness that puts the questions and awaits its answer."[5]

This is because the issue isn't really consciousness; it's personal identity, subjective beinghood, the little man or little woman—or little Gila monster—with its sovereign and subjective self. Existence is "waz happ'nin', waz going down."

Most Buddhist teachers set nonduality—primordial intelligence without ego, without subject or object—as the ultimate goal of practice, the way out of this bind, for the universe as well as the self.

From a Sethian standpoint, to make a priority of nonduality and ego-dissolution overlooks how egoity came into being, how profound it actually is. Karma did not locate us in a fix to see if we could get ourselves out of it, nor did it consign us to conditional beingness from original sin or because our soul was too stupid to make a better choice. Ego nature is neither a defect nor an aberration. It is the effect of *an already enlightened intelligence* choosing to explore personal existence. The soul is intentionally incarnating in this world as us because it is the *nature* of consciousness to explore every dimension.

And the universe is not just a lesion; it is an exquisitely designed reality. Whether the architect is divine energy or our own higher intelligence, reality is giving rise to beingness (and *vice versa*). Essence (*essentia*) is identical to existence (*esse*).

Seth spoke elegantly on this matter:

> God may know itself through a million or a thousand million other worlds, as so may I—but because his world is, and because I am alive in it, it is more than appearance, more than a shackle to be thrown aside. It is a privilege to be here, to look out with this unique focus, with these individual eyes; not to be blinded by cosmic vision, but to see this corner of reality which I form through the miraculous connections of soul and flesh.[6]

The sundry merchandise pouring out of factories and sun-stars is reality's subtlest and most irreconcilable aspect. The banal and ordinary are as profound, for occurring at all, as the most sacral or weighty thing. Each vista is a glimpse into a mode of beingness: Hopi entering their kiva to conduct a corn ceremony or a band having arrived with their instruments, sitting on Eighth Avenue outside Penn Station. The tags on the guitar cases and luggage say everything about our situation in the cosmos, as December solstice turns Earth's indigo vault an early black.

What Is Reality?

Buddhists teach that the "reality" mirage can be snapped only by equally deep-seated nondual practices: meditation, mantra, guru devotion, and sacred visualization.

Western-oriented scientists see neither the mirage nor a reality it conceals. Making themselves and nature—the world of atoms and molecules—objective on each other's terms, they conclude that the hullabaloo is real but meaningless. It has no intrinsic meaning, it just happens—stars, meteors, oceans, jellyfish, jungles, us, and so on.

But modern science has it backward when it says that this is real but meaningless. In fact, *none* of it is real, but it is incredibly meaningful. Reality doesn't have to be "really" real; it has only to generate experiences. The desires, joys, and hardships of mortal existence are "real" enough.

It is finally more real to be meaningful than it is to be real—for to be "only" real in a realm of molecular objectivity is to be circumstantially configured and then expunged. To be meaningful is to explore the open-ended possibility of each conditional or ephemeral reality while it is arising.

The soul is curious about its own nature—the contradictions and paradoxes that lie within its unconsciousness, without which it does not have a full sense of itself. It has questions it cannot answer otherwise: What am I? What will happen if . . . ? How can I be in both loving unity and deadly disparity? How is the profundity of my experience joined to the profundity of existence itself?[7]

Existence plunges the soul into extrinsic reality, opening a pathway to its own actual depth. Illusory or not, the reality is profound and valid. The richness of creatures' lives is its warp and woof. Feelings of bliss and despair are as elemental as molecules of hydrogen or tungsten. Each combines and converts energy to resolve innate tensions. Difficult conversations are tantamount to bodies of water or geologies elsewhere.

It is materialism's bias to think that subjectivity is not as real or veridical as objectivity; in fact, it is *realer.* This universe goes as far as its greatest epiphany and most excruciating agony. It has the texture of its sprightliest mirth and dizziest nausea. Beingness is, in fact, the fiercest situation in Creation, fiercer than sun-stars and black holes, for it provides their ferocity.

When novelist William Faulkner wrote, "Between grief and nothing, I'll take grief,"[8] he meant it literally, and the truth *is even more literal than that.* We are, as Elena Ferrante proposed in *The Story of a New Name*—and she is hardly a metaphysical author—"[an] infinitesimal particle through which the fear of every thing becomes conscious of itself."[9] The love of every thing too.

Even narco lords trying to spread fear by the most horrific tortures they can imagine can't go deeper than the universe itself goes and can't cast a darker shadow. Their very consciousness turns back on them as they try to drive it into their victims, for they are as vulnerable to their own existence. They are answering "what if?"

What is profoundly terrifying is also terrifyingly profound.

The Soul Chooses a Dualistic Perspective

It would be the epitome of New Age naïvité and arrogance to compare a Sethian view with Buddhism. Yet what I am calling "Sethian" in this book is not a formal liturgy. It is a combination of interpretations of Seth as Jane Roberts and others have channeled him mixed with Hinduism-informed theosophy as well as Buddhism itself (via both its Hindu roots and modern Buddhist inflection on all ontological thought).

When John Friedlander* puts Buddhist nondualism in a Sethian perspective, he is speaking as a student of Dzogchen as well as a disciple of Seth:

> Ken Wilber[†] said something to the effect, If you have dual awareness, it's like trying to rearrange the deck chairs on the *Titanic.* You're in catastrophic mode, whether you know it or not. But it's more like rearranging the deck chairs *in the movie Titanic,* which in itself is a very rich, exciting, and valuable experience. Or the movie *Some Like It Hot.* In other words it can be a drama, comedy, or a romantic comedy, or bitter cynicism. All those storylines are possible as a human being and all of them are rich and they add to the universe. . . . That's what neutrality is for. Neutrality is not the same thing as

---

*John was present for some of Jane Roberts's later Seth channelings; he also continues to channel Sethian entities himself and has synthesized Seth with contemporary Buddhist, philosophical, and psychic thought. Before joining Jane Roberts's Elmira, New York, group, he studied at the Berkeley Psychic Institute. Later, John earned a law degree from Harvard and practiced as an attorney for seventeen years. His secular training is useful, for he represents Seth with precision and nuance. Because I studied with John myself, I often quote him by first name when characterizing material that is not otherwise publicly available.

†An American nondual philosopher and transpersonal psychologist, author of *A Brief History of Everything* and *The Marriage of Sense and Soul.*

nondual awareness. Neutrality is, you're inside the illusion of separateness, but you have a sense of humor about it. You are open to life as it is.[10]

Life is neither real nor unreal; it holds *both* possibilities and accepts the terms given.

In a later class, John clarified the existential nature of our storylines:

Our soul incarnated as us *because of* the limitations of being human. These limitations then provide a very specific context in which we develop stories, and our stories are what the universe gets out of us. . . . I have this image of humans going around the universe, stepping up to whatever kind of beer hall there is, say in the Monadic—or sort of like the bar in *Star Wars* with creatures from all those different worlds—and saying, *"Do I have a story for you!"* And that's a kind of story that no one other than human beings can tell. And people gather round, "Wow, what an amazing story you human beings have, full of horrors and wonders!"[11]

Elsewhere, John called life "a virtual reality machine," proposing that when we awake from the roller-coaster ride, we may think it was terrible and fantastic and a bit too rough and intense. We might say, "I'd like to try that again, but I think the next time I'd rather go on the merry-go-round."[12]

Some people think they are getting on the merry-go-round and it turns into the Mad Mouse. This is the "one encounter, one chance" a warrior chooses.

"There is nothing to evolve beyond," John submits. "The soul has chosen to enter into a dualistic perspective and to develop a new form of group consciousness* that retains the kind of individuality that we wouldn't have had without this process. . . ."[13]

Upon hearing these precepts, a longtime Buddhist practitioner

---

*He means unity consciousness through a collective Aquarian expansion; see chapter 11, "Multipersonhood."

groused, "The guy is not equipped to understand nonduality; he doesn't have the spiritual credentials. Who is some dude from Georgia named John Friedlander, who used to be an attorney, to say anything significant about the universe compared to great lamas and Himalayan saints?" He didn't use exactly those words. What he *did* say was, "The man is deluded!"

John told me that most sophisticated Eastern practitioners usually "assume that I just don't understand the basic concepts here, that my argument simply misunderstands that the laws of the universe generate the 'fact' that nondual awareness retains all the advantages of human dual consciousness minus only the suffering."[14]

Yet nondual awareness cannot retain all the advantages of dual consciousness. If it did, there would be no rationale for duality. An original harmony would project its own profundity through timeless time. There would be no basis for stars, worlds, or beings.

Later, John nuanced a dual path to nonduality while affirming his Buddhist loyalties:

> Some advanced Buddhist practitioners recognize that there's nothing in my argument that violates the Buddha or disagrees with subsequent Buddhist ontology or its understanding of interdependence and impermanence. I too am talking about an interdependent, impermanent process, not a *thing*. But I am saying that everyone eventually finds that nondual process. You incarnate to light up certain storylines that were unavailable in nondual awareness. It makes sense to dive in with a sure and certain promise that you will be able to wrap all the alienation of your dual consciousness into an already present nondual awareness in a way that will treasure it.[15]

For that you have to track identity beyond the death of the individual. Drawing again on Sethian ontology, John proposed that the personality and the soul are *both* real and survive. When a personality dissolves at death, it breaks into fragments, each redistributed according to its karma. At least one of the fragments continues to track the life from which it came—*to know it as itself.*

"Duality is not a problem," John explained. "In fact, it's more than not a problem. *It's the whole point.* It's who we are. The soul survives, *and* the personality survives. You are your soul, not added on to you but as a center of awareness. We don't own our soul, nor does our soul own us. The broader your perspective, the more you see that this is how the universe operates and why we're presently in this dual phase and also why we *don't see it.*"[16]

The fact that we can't presently see beyond a dualistic mode is *the way in which we are seeing it* as well as the reason we exist in it. It's how we got on the roller coaster while forgetting that it was just a ride. John also likened the experience to a "mud run":

There are people who will actually pay money to get up very early in the morning, like five a.m., in forty degrees, and run through an obstacle course filled with wet mud and slush. And they enjoy it, or most of them do. In some of the mud runs, wires will shock you if you don't get low enough. So you really have to get down in the mud. And people do this on purpose.

But you don't have to slosh through mud. You can go to a thing called a motel room and take a hot shower and watch television on which you might even see other suckers running through mud and going under wires and ropes and stuff like that. Or you can sit in an RV and listen to Bach. But then you wouldn't have the experience of a mud run. You'd be missing something. You'd have a different experience. . . .

In a sense, this life is a mud run, a mud run for the soul that it chose willingly. Your multidimensional self says, "I think I'm going to explore time and space. And I'm going to set these rules for myself. I can't fly and things have to happen, one after another. Won't that be interesting?"

Nonduality is sort of like doing everything in the mud run except running through the mud. In other words, you're missing something quite profound. When you're done with the mud run, it becomes part of the richness of your life. The mud run may be over, but it's part of a story you tell twenty years from now.

What I'm saying is, "Welcome to Planet Earth. It is a mud run. You signed up for it. You may not have understood that you were signing up for it, but that's part of what makes it real."

Here's a slightly different perspective. When I was in the eighth grade, we had our first summer football practice. It was 102 degrees. Now if that were my entire life—I was born at 2 o'clock that afternoon and I died at 5 o'clock that afternoon—then football practice would make no sense at all.[17]

Yet football is no more arbitrary than wind or igneous rocks. It arises as "real" within conditional reality. None of these are arbitrary rides, and the amusement park is not merely virtual or for diversion and entertainment alone. While being amused (or terrified), we are exploring the inside of creation and our own beingness *simultaneously*. Where they come together is an imprimatur that drives everything. The reason we feel texture, cadence, and profundity is that there *are* depth, elation, joy, and sorrow at the heart of Creation. But if we were to go at their gravitas by the lucid singularity of unity consciousness, it would fragment into lesser states and lose its sumptuousness.

John put this succinctly in an email to me:

The innumerable constituent parts that we ordinary human beings lump together, such as bodies and auric energies, themselves continue, within and outside time, to grow, to expand subjectively, in all directions, together and separately, "forever" (language fails, as time itself is only a *form* of consciousness). In a universe where no single consciousness arises by its self, it is nevertheless true that every subjectivity, from subatomic particles to universes and thus to the human personality, expands in all directions and thus retains an eternal, though ever changing and interdependent subjectivity that is divinely meaningful. (Again, language fails, because our concepts of eternality rely on time, which is itself, an energy construct, a particular form of consciousness that is just one of many others which are incomprehensible to embodied humans.) In this multidimensional world that ecstatically breaks outside human experience, our human experience of duality is something to be treasured, even though it involves suffering that can be avoided. It is humans' gift to other dimensions of ourselves, a gift that they and we human personalities can luxuriate in and continue transforming forever.[18]

From a nondual perspective, this Creation is a mess, a delusion, a catastrophe, and shouldn't be here to flout nirvana or to disturb cosmic unity and the soul's—or illusory self's—eternal bliss of emptiness. The sooner we get released from the roller coaster, the sooner the amusement park itself is quenched, the better.

From a dual perspective, what is happening is *exactly* what is meant to happen, the only thing that *could* be happening, right down to its short hairs—those wily preons and quarks with their lesion. Each of our individual "flares" of beingness and their cycles of rebirth are indispensable to an *already* indispensable situation.

This relationship between duality and nonduality is a central dichotomy to consider as we look not only into past lives and personal identity but also the riddle of why there is something rather than nothing—or why we are in the middle of it all. Past lives are not inaccessible; they are not even past. They are not even *lives,* or lives alone. Buddha's concept of nonduality *requires* that there are no objects without subjects—no universe without beings—dependent origination, for subjective and objective views are equally necessary to create phenomena.

But I am not trying to write either a Buddhist book or a non-Buddhist book. There are countless Buddhist interpretations of reality and existence in multiple languages going back centuries. Most of these are sophisticated, subtle, and comprehensive at keener angles than I am able to tack. Addressing even a few of their shades and distinctions would be like trying to capture a caucus of water bugs (or subatomic particles). Yet this text would be specious and extraneous without visiting its own tacit Buddhist assumptions.

There isn't even finally a difference between what most Buddhist teachers say about the nature of reality and Sethian memes: this universe is an illusion, a thoughtform, a temporary state of projected energy.

While Buddhist teachings, especially in the West (where they are sometimes applied as if a cosmic operating manual), tell people to practice with urgency and diligence and make personal sacrifices to clear the mind, end suffering, and find peace, Seth proclaims that all experiences are valid and of value, even the most vulgar, twisted, and cruel. They are all sacred and consequential and get redeemed. Each incarnation ultimately finds realization and enlightenment, in itself and in participation with others. That doesn't mean that there aren't better states or more graceful lives—more refined practices—just that there is no operating manual. We are what Dzogchen practitioners call "spontaneous presence." Our fullness of being is complete *in itself.*

In itself does not mean *for itself.* Only as "being" awakens empathy for fellow creatures does it experience its own wholeness. Kindness and generosity are converted into everyday experiences and fed into the soul. Compassion doesn't bottom out the universe in its vast and myriad conditionality, but it provides sanctuary and safety within bottomlessness.

6

The Universal Basis of Past-Life Memories

Dolores Cannon, a military housewife and freelance writer in Arkansas, began practicing hypnosis in her late forties as a way of retrieving past-life memories. Like Morey Bernstein (who elicited Bridey Murphy), she was an amateur, yet she regressed hundreds of volunteers successfully, at least by her own standards, curing phobias and traumas in the process. In *Five Lives Remembered* and *Between Life and Death: Conversations with a Spirit,* she documents several of her regressions. In another book, *A Soul Remembers Hiroshima,* she spotlights "Kathryn (Katie) Harris," who recovered her past life as a Japanese man in Hiroshima at the time when the *Enola Gay* dropped the first atomic weapon on the city.

Memory of this apparent past life arose in Harris spontaneously six months before she met Cannon. During a chance viewing of an interview with a Japanese woman who had survived the attack, Katie recalled *being there too.* No footage of the blast or its aftermath was shown, but, as the woman recalled a blinding light, people running and screaming, and things crashing down, "something just 'clicked' inside her head and suddenly she could *see* what was happening. Horrified, she turned the TV off, but she couldn't turn off the pictures and scenes that flooded into her mind."[1]

Like the previously discussed Ryan Hammons, Katie experienced her impromptu recollection as another being inside herself. "I knew I was an old man and was watching from his viewpoint. I was feeling his feelings and thinking his thoughts. As I watched the scenes in my mind of the horror after the explosion, I knew that he was thinking, 'This can't be happening.'"[2]

Floodgates had opened on another identity.

Twenty-two years old at the time, Katie was a junior-year high school dropout from Texas. Her father, like Cannon's husband, was in the military, so she moved around while growing up before deciding that she couldn't deal with continual adjustments to new teachers and friends. She quit early junior year and earned a high school–equivalency diploma; then she worked for the Air Force. She was not otherwise formally educated and had not traveled outside the United States.

Described by Cannon as short, blonde, buxom, blue-eyed, and charismatic, Katie expressed curiosity about past lives at a 1983 party without tipping her hand. Like James Leininger (and Ryan), she grew up in an orthodox Christian family—Pentecostal in her case—and reincarnation was a taboo topic. Cannon took steps to disguise her subject's identity: her name is not Kathryn (or Katie) Harris.

In Cannon's initial regressions, she noticed her subject's receptivity to past lives. The young woman slipped into trance with all five senses, as she adopted the "I" of former beings and crossed gender lines effortlessly. When experiencing her first "other lifetime," she described a white house "sitting up there all lonesome" in a landscape of hills and valleys, a place she later identified as Colorado Territory before statehood. The girl (named Sharon) could smell her mother's bread baking in the oven.[3]

Only after trust was established did Katie confide her Hiroshima flashback. Using Sharon's dating of her death as sometime in the late 1870s, Cannon subtracted the Colorado timeline from her subject's birthdate of 1960, clearing a gap of about eighty years. The women agreed: let's go for it!

Not wanting to plunge Katie into the traumatic events of World War II, let alone Hiroshima on the day of the attack, Cannon picked 1935 as a safe starting point, instructing her subject to go back to then. Katie landed, as hoped, in Japan, becoming Suragami Nogorigatu, "a man in his late fifties making pottery at a kiln in back of his house. He was at a small farm located about 20 miles south of Hiroshima in Nippon (the Japanese word for Japan)."[4] Through several hypnotic regressions, Katie drew a rich and flavorful portrait: oxen, bean sprouts, water chestnuts, charcoal heaters; Nogorigatu's primary school (with scrolls, brushes, and calligraphy of thousands of characters); procedures for growing rice, differences between water gates and water wheels in the irrigation of fields, uses of animal dung for fertilizer; architecture of a seven-room house with a sod roof and pagoda gables; the birth of two boys (aged twenty-nine and thirty-three by the time of the attack); how to cast traditional Japanese pottery, designs and kinds and sources of herbs used to dye pots; Japanese clothing of the era (caps, sandals, sandal straps, names for gis, kimonos, obis, and other costumes), plus other museum-level relics and accouterments.

Needless to say, neither Cannon nor Katie had backgrounds in any of these matters prior to the hypnotic regression. Whether Nogorigatu existed once or not, Katie performed his character like a master thespian. Cannon recalled getting chills at how *real* he was; his energy filled the room.

He reported being married at fourteen. He saw his wife only once before their engagement; his parents had picked her out. They were wed in the late 1800s. He described dressing for the big event in his ceremonial kimono. "I am scared! It is strange . . . to know that I bring someone else into our house . . . I don't know this person."[5] He depicted a Japanese wedding in striking detail: ceremonial knots in his bride's hair, his wife-to-be's white pan makeup and cherry-blossom silk pink kimono, musical instruments (harps, kotos, drums, and flutes), sake, rice cakes, honey cakes, and more. When asked whether the woman's pale makeup looked strange, he said, "I think it looks nice." When asked next whether his bride was happy, he said, "Who can tell with girls?"[6]

During another session, Cannon regressed Nogorigatu/Katie to a later stage of life, 1920. He described taking his pots to market twenty miles away in Hiroshima. He explained that by then he had sold his share of the family farm and bought his own plot south of the city. Upon request, he accurately enumerated different roads leading to the Hiroshima metropolitan area as well as the bridges across the separate branches of the river that runs through the city.

Subsequently, he gave a nuanced account of the prewar era of the late 1930s: the *feng shui* of his house and land, the isolation of rural Japan in the events leading up to World War II, the spiritual kinship of the emperor and the sun; the melding of Shintoism and Buddhism in religious training, the tea ceremony and other rituals. Another time, he described the effects of militarization in the countryside—how soldiers took over fields and other property, putting citizens under virtual gang rule: "Many strangers and soldiers come through and they take what they want. So we are hiding things. . . . They took our oxen and our goats and destroyed the fields. It was a shortcut. They marched right through them, and then they laughed. . . . Because they are in power and they are soldiers."[7]

Later, he commented wryly, "No one ever sees the orders but them, if there are any orders."[8]

None of this comes across as fantasy or fabrication, yet it is not the worldview or droll wit of a provincial girl from Texas. "Probably kill [our goats and oxen] and use them for food. . . . Whatever food stores they could lay their hands on easily, that they could take with them, they took. Things like salted fish and rice, things that would keep. . . . Now we have no way of plowing except by hand and I am too old. But they don't care about this. . . . Every time we start to grow things, something happens. Either the soldiers run through the fields or there is nothing to plant with."[9]

He discoursed on the fallacies of war and the illusion that you gain honor or dignity from military power. He analyzed Japanese feelings of inferiority, of being played down by the rest of the world, and how the warrior class thought that they could exhibit superior skills and bravery and demonstrate what it means to be courageous in battle to the Americans, who had become weak and effeminate.

About the military cult of the kamikaze, he remarked, "I think they are a little crazy, maybe more than a little crazy."[10] He added, "Who knows what they have filled their minds with. What hopes of paradise. How can anyone promise something that they themselves have never seen?"[11] He lamented: "We are at war. . . . I cry for Nippon. She is fallen, she is losing her majesty."[12]

Against Nogorigatu's advice, one of his boys moved to Hiroshima with his family to take a job in a factory, then thought better of it and tried to return to the homestead. Too late—the farm was already in ruins. Soon after that, soldiers in trucks strong-armed both of Nogorigatu's sons into service.

When Katie was counted forward to 1944, Cannon was stunned to hear, "I see the grave of my wife."[13] Expressing shock, she offered sympathy. Nogorigatu said simply, "She was walking along the road in the village. And the jeeps came by and ran her over. They didn't see her and didn't care to. None of them stopped. . . . She was trying to get things for us to eat. Anything."[14]

Katie's voice had shifted to match Nogorigatu's grief, becoming almost inaudible at times as if "s/he" were about to cry. When Cannon asked what happened next, Nogorigatu described leaving the farm and moving into town with his children and grandchildren. "We must all walk our own path. If this is mine, so be it."[15]

What Does This Mean?

Is Nogorigatu *in* Katie, *of* Katie? Was he ever a real person—Katie herself once—or merely her contrivance? Could all this drama have been feigned by Ms. Harris's subconscious?

Of course, she might have been a naturally gifted actress with an unrecognized talent. People diagnosed with multiple personalities evince convincing *alter egos* far more discrepant than Katie's "Nogorigatu." The narrative isn't evidence of reincarnation as much as it is of the inscrutability of the human psyche.

At the conclusion of Nogorigatu's session regarding the death of his wife, Cannon observed, "He was exhibiting such deep, deep sadness and sorrow, it was overwhelming. I felt so sorry for him, this man I had come to know so well, that I could not leave him there. . . . I could not, in good conscience, end the session on such an unhappy note. Maybe it was more for my benefit than Katie's, because on reawakening she would have no conscious memory of the events she described."[16]

Cannon counted Nogorigatu back to 1930. He went there at once and quickly adopted a festive spirit: "They're having the procession through the village. It is the celebration of the blooming of the cherry trees. They have the priests at front, throwing the rice and calling blessings, hoping that this will be a good year for prosperity. And we have the young men and women of the village all dressed up in their most beautiful kimonos. They are wandering through the streets singing. . . . [There are] paper streamers and they have kites flying from the houses."[17]

Just like that, from sorrow and mourning to celebration and delight!

Yet no matter how many times Nogorigatu got returned to happier times, he would travel back to Hiroshima. His path had no other course.

This is an essential enigma of the "past life" gambit, from Bridey Murphy falling down the stairs in Cork, Ireland, to young James Leininger waking from a nightmare of a plane on fire. The one-way flow of identity and meaning is shattered. Where does Nogorigatu's later identity go when his earlier one is evoked? For that matter, where *was* it prior to its recall? Are there many "Nogorigatus" in simultaneous existence? How do their concurrent realities intersect each other? Is there a level at which they meld into integral beingness?

Note the unavoidable juxtapositions in Cannon's framing. She can't "leave him there" but must "count him back." Cannon's time travel, though imaginal, violates Heraclitus's irreversible current into which no man, or warthog, can step twice.

From the recounting, it seems that every temporal self arises timelessly, no matter what will follow, traveling like ripples outside time. Nogorigatu's 1944 self does not gobble up or supersede its 1930 predecessor. They remain independently evolving and supporting each other. The greater entity can reexperience any of them as present. We do not know how finite the selves get—whether every minute or second has integrity. When Freud said, "There is no time in the unconscious," he meant the individual psyche, but he could have been intuiting a transpersonality imposing its timeless "clock" on the ego's temporal selves.

Perhaps a soul sends out myriad selves like a multidimensional octopus to experience aspects of its identity in different realities. Each of its arms—far more than eight—savors an exclusive realm. In Jane Roberts's metaphor, "Our greater consciousness or 'source self' dips in and out of time and has existences in other dimensions, showering aspects of itself out in all directions. These aspects are alive, active, but latent in each of us, where their abilities help form the stuff of our own personalities."[18] Each self has its own evolving integrity. They neither are isolated nor totally overlap, merge, or cancel each other out.

Cannon confronts her own muddles around Nogorigatu:

> Upon awakening from a session, Katie would feel fine. Because she was virtually asleep, she had no ill effects. *I* was the one who was troubled. I could not shut out his suffering. . . . This man had begun to actually haunt me. His pain was my pain. I would hear again his words as I tried to sleep at night. He filled my waking thoughts as well as my dreams. He became very real to me and it was as if his turmoil was happening now instead of 40 years ago.[19]

Who was Cannon to Nogorigatu? Whom did he "see" as she drew him from the slumber of Katie? Was he in dormancy at her call? Does he dwell eternally in his soul, reexperiencing timeless events from each of his selves?

Cannon felt he was calling out for recognition, affirmation. "This was no cardboard imaginary character. I came to know Nogorigatu very well. I liked him and he became my friend. I often wonder what he thought of me. Was I just a still, small voice in his head asking questions?[20] . . . He seemed to be pleading with me to tell his story, to give his death meaning. . . ."[21]

Indeed! An American woman addressing him decades after his death was a witness in the void, but he was also engaging his own internal voice through her. I can't picture him as a figment in Katie Harris's unconscious mind, and I can't picture her as a ghola* of him. Cannon's supposition—"a still, small voice in his head"—is a haunting trope, given that this "head" was also a figment in Katie's psychic field.

---

*The term *ghola* was coined by Frank Herbert in his *Dune* series. He used it to describe a person artificially cloned from a dead individual in Planet Dune's Axolotl tanks, sometimes from as little as a single cell of the original being. I am adapting it here to mean a psychic "clone."

Reliving Hiroshima

In subsequent sessions, Cannon edged Katie closer to the attack. Cannon had promised her that she would approach the bombing gradually and then visit it only once. As she counted deeper into 1944, she feared that Nogorigatu would appear as a broken man. She was right; he had no idea what to do next as he stoically described the situation: "I can see the troops. They are moving. They have decided that they want the head-quarters closer to town. . . . They are all in their trucks and have their guns and they're moving. . . . Sometimes I stay in the village, sometimes in Hiroshima."[22]

In town, he roomed with his daughters-in-law, who, by then, helped make jeep parts in a factory. "We spread the mats on the floors and we sleep on them, and there is enough room for that. . . . We have a brazier, which is a charcoal one, that is in the one room. . . . This is no life to bring up children in."[23] When Nogorigatu walked between his farm and town, the journey took three days: "One does what one must. A man can do anything if he sets his mind to it."[24]

Food was rationed. Those who toiled for the government received larger portions, allotments dispensed at the factories. It was mostly rice, occasionally bread or grains. Otherwise, they found wild beans and grew their own sprouts. Workers were paid in scrips, an emergency currency that could be used to purchase items only at government centers.

Cannon opened her next session with, "Let's go to the spring of 1945. It will be spring when the earth is waking up and things are beginning to grow again. What do you see?"[25] The shift in tone was dramatic: "I can see the planes flying overhead. It seems like they are stalking us. . . . There are . . . four or five of them. . . . They are not ours. . . . It's just as if they watch us. They do not drop bombs. . . . I wonder if they are looking for a good place to drop their bombs. I don't know."[26]

To that point Hiroshima had been spared aerial attack. Routine drills were conducted. Sirens sounded, requiring people to clear the streets. Nogorigatu said, "I do not desire to go to the shelter. I would rather see what is coming at me than run like a frightened squirrel into a tree and hole up. If I die I would like to see what kills me."[27]

Progressing toward the fateful day, Cannon counted forward to July 1945 and asked Katie/Nogorigatu to describe what s/he saw. He was watching his daughters arrive home from work. His three grandchildren were playing on the floor. When queried as to how things were going, he said, "Extremely bad. There are many problems. They've had bombings around the city and everyone is worried and tense. . . . Two of the outlying factories have been hit, no *serious* damage, some deaths. They manage to keep working." When asked what the bombs sound like, he says, "There is a shrill whistle before the explosion. They say you never hear the one that hits."

The soldiers fired at the planes. "They almost treat it as if a big game is going on. As if nothing serious."[28]

Nogorigatu's daughters had been told at work that "the Americans don't wish to bomb us, or something . . . I don't know. They say they are not strong enough to fight us . . . that the war is almost over because we are no longer fighting with them. Who knows?"[29]

As Cannon subsequently counted Katie forward to August 6, 1945, she noticed an abrupt change in her complexion and posture.

> She turned white as a sheet and her body stiffened. When she tried to talk, only gasping sounds came out. She had great difficulty forming the words. . . . She seemed to be in a state of shock and when she did manage to speak, her voice trembled. Sometimes her body would shake. I had never before heard such heart-rending emotion and pain in a voice. It came from somewhere deep inside her subconscious memories and had no connection with Katie at all. . . . Phrases came out disjointed with pauses between them as Nogorigatu confusedly groped to find the words for an experience that words were useless to describe.[30]

The subject took deep breaths as Cannon asked her what was happening; she could barely form the syllables at times. Cannon had to reassure her that this event was no longer present and she had the capacity to terminate the session and wake herself up whenever she wished. Finally, Nogorigatu spoke:

"There was . . . there was a great flash . . . a blinding white light. And . . . then a great . . . boom. And . . . and . . . a *giant* cloud. It went straight up, and . . . and . . . it went out. . . . And then the winds rolled . . . they were like fire. . . . The people, they fell down, and they . . . and they just lay there, and . . . and. . . . [Cannon adds, "the voice was full of utter disbelief."] *The screams! . . . People are dying everywhere. WHY?*"

"It was a cry from the depths of his soul, and it sent shivers down my spine."

"People are . . . those who can run are running. Some just stumbling around, holding their arms out . . . Everything is gone! It's been destroyed! Buildings are as if they've never been. [. . .] Some . . . when the cloud hit, they . . . disappeared. Some, the great wind, it knocked everything to the ground. [. . .] There's nothing left! *WHY?!*"

"I am alone. (Bewildered) I don't know where *anyone* is. Everything is gone. The city is as if . . . there is no *center* to the city! *IT'S GONE!* The buildings have . . . *disappeared!* There's nothing but rubble . . . and the *screams!*"[31]

Is this what it seems: a grim revisitation by *someone who was actually there*? Or is Katie cathartically imagining an atomic attack, fulfilling her hypnotically induced role? Could it be a clairvoyant reverberation of the bomb itself, bending space-time-consciousness with its malign *thwack*?

"My . . . hands! My hands . . . are black. [. . .] My . . . face feels as if there is nothing . . . no skin. (He moaned.)"[32]

Cannon had to push the image of scorched flesh out of her mind in order to continue. Meanwhile Katie/Nogorigatu was wandering among stunned Hiroshimans, stumbling and falling, getting up but not knowing where to go. He wanted to escape, but to where? There was no city center anymore.

He didn't understand how a weapon could cause so much wind or such an unnatural fire. He imagined some sort of explosion or spontaneous combustion. Cannon asked if the devastation was connected to the planes flying overhead.

"The planes this morning . . . Could they . . . ? They . . . must have . . . dropped . . . some horrible . . . *thing!* (Gasp) How could anyone *do* that? How? Don't they know what they have done? Do they care? *How* could we get to such a point where anyone would want to do this? Even *think* of doing something like this? How could anyone?"

The words were like a forlorn voice crying in the wilderness.

"They've killed the town! A *whole* town! It's gone! (Suddenly he moaned.) I feel like my insides are on fire. Everything is . . . it's . . . as if . . . someone struck a match and placed it inside of me, and it's become a bonfire. And it's ablaze!

"My daughters . . . my grandchildren! (He sobbed that word) [. . .] They are probably dead. [. . .] All dead!"[33]

This doesn't sound like a theatric performance to me, and it isn't a young Texas gal either.

Cannon knew she had to get Nogorigatu out of there. She quickly counted him back to 1930; he transitioned with startling alacrity and ease: "I am working on my pots. I have taken them out of the kiln and they are cooling. . . . They are very beautiful. Each unique in their own way. I take care in my work. My love shows in every piece that I make."[34]

Another being replaced the devastated man: Nogorigatu in happy times. Was the artisan working on his pots a man who had *never* experienced Hiroshima or one who had *already* experienced it and sublimated his "future memory"?

Is there any way out of "Hiroshima" for him, perhaps a parallel future? Can he can travel through probabilities to where he *didn't* experience the attack? I will discuss this issue in chapter 11, but I refer the reader to the 2011 movie *Source Code,* in which the "hero" escapes an eight-minute reality loop by becoming conscious *within* it. After he *re*-incarnates from a soldier killed while flying a helicopter around Khyber Pass, Afghanistan, into a civilian on a commuter train entering Chicago just before an explosive device is ignited (the eight-minute reel into which his mind has been transported by computer technicians trying to catch the terrorist), he goes rogue from *both* personae as well as the programmers, fleeing the source code with a woman passenger "killed" in the blast by establishing a different probability. Free will *becomes* freedom.

What about Katie and her predicaments? Even though she remembered none of what she recited in trance, like other past-life "patients" she exhibited discernible relief after the regressions.

Cannon recalled a memory trace she recovered from her subject before summoning Nogorigatu. While entering this world in a home delivery, the girl had been declared stillborn. The doctor had given up. Only an aunt working on the lifeless body drew a feeble cry. Guessing that the clue to Nogorigatu lay there, Cannon asked Katie to return to the moment when she first entered the body of Kathryn Harris. The hypnotist had guessed wrong—she expected a stillborn baby and an alert aunt—so she was in for a surprise.

> Instead of preparing to enter the body of a newborn baby, I found her standing at the foot of a bed getting ready to enter the body of an adult. She was preparing to exchange places with the spirit that had inhabited the body of Katie for 21 years. That entity had taken on too many problems to be worked out during this lifetime and when she found that she was not strong enough to handle them, she had asked to be relieved of the situation. Because the two entities had known each other previously and had very similar personalities, they agreed to swap places for the remainder of the physical body's life.[35]

The entity answering Cannon was Nogorigatu, not Kathryn of her own first twenty-one years. That young woman was gone, as the Japanese man stepped in, changing genders, languages, ages, nationalities, and historic frame. That is why s/he recognized Hiroshima when s/he viewed the television interview—and also why the past-life memory had not been previously triggered. *It wasn't there.* Katie had *become* Nogorigatu by the time she saw the television interview, or he had become her. *Cannon never met the real Katie.*

But how did the walk-in* also "remember" Katie's past life in Colorado or the rest of her American identity? How deep did the pair's linkage go? Were they habitants of the same group soul—"arms" of the same "octopus"?

When Katie was told that she was a walk-in who had acquiesced to an exchange of souls, "she was startled, to say the least. She said that she could not believe that. She felt no different and believed that she was still the same person."[36]

How could Nogorigatu merge so seamlessly with the persona of the previous occupant of Kathryn's body that s/he did not notice the difference? How did a Japanese man take on Katie's personality and language? Are sexual identity and personal history so fluid and commutable? Can one soul be traded for an entirely different one and lived as authentically, without the ground individual missing a beat?

The historical connection and affinity of these two souls must have transcended the discrepancies between their most recent lives.

In Cannon's view, Nogorigatu entered Katie's body with her permission. This sort of reincarnation-like event, conducted between auras, could explain why some people begin remembering a past life at an older age: it is not the past life of their womb self but that of a newly arriving guest. The walk-in's identity is transposed subliminally so that it is not a heinous intrusion; it seeps through layers of unconscious identity as it subtly revises them. By the time it is introduced to consciousness, it feels natural and endemic (like Ryan Hammons's "man" inside). If such possession takes place before birth, it is, by definition, reincarnation.

Apparently, personae can be simultaneously latent and manifest inside and outside of time. Katie did not discern Nogorigatu as a characterological intrusion, despite their clashing identities, because he *used to be her* (as she used to be him) or because their egos were "cloned" from shared experiences of their group soul on the Buddhic plane. One aspect of personal identity is that all souls sharing an incarnation, regardless of their source or status, seem to recognize the same self and are recognized

*Traditionally walk-ins are spirits, usually of deceased people, who enter a body to replace the spirit who was living there. They can also co-habit and share the body and ego.

by the same self as "I." They meld into a cohesive personality despite their individual comings and goings through a lifetime. What each soul brings is of a karmic rather than a memorabilia nature.

Perhaps "languages" get regenerated from syntactic strings underlying all human tongues, as they are posited to have come from an original root parlance or common deep logic and universal grammar.* (That is the science-fiction justification for beings on other worlds speaking "English." They are not *really* "speaking" English but a "cosmic Esperanto" transmitted telepathically between sentient minds. Animal communicators and "whisperers" use a similar clairsentient *lingua franca*.)

Again, chronological reincarnation as the sole option for existence beyond single lifetimes is a limited view of beingness. There are countless ways for knowledge and experience to crystallize that are reenacted in occult traditions from Haitian voodoo to Pawnee vision quests. Others are beyond our ken or even imagining, yet quotidian for an expanding universe with an esoteric rulebook. As you read further in this book, particularly the chapters on Multipersonhood and Seth, other explanations for Nogorigatu's and Katie's interchange will factor in, not as alternatives to a walk-in but as additional layers of possibility.

Cannon interrogated Nogorigatu on his status before Katie.

I learned . . . that "she" had entered the spirit resting-place on the other side for a while after the traumatic death at Hiroshima. This is a special place that is reserved for deaths such as these. She felt she had gotten rid of a lot of karma by the lingering death she had experienced. She then attended the school on the spirit plane where the masters and teachers helped with the evaluation of that life. That was where she was when she was called for this assignment and the exchange of the souls with the entity that had previously occupied Katie's body.[37]

---

*See glottochronologist Morris Swadesh and cognitive linguist Noam Chomsky, respectively, for these theories.

Olden Times

Past lives that surface in individuals like Katie Harris and James Leininger are intact versions of elusive flashbacks that everyone has. Some moments feel different, as if experienced through someone else's senses, or as if Earth were seen by an alien creature. Obscure figments flit by, images and feelings that evaporate as we try to identify or place them: faces and moods, wisps and fragments of landscapes that lack context. "They were valid," Jane Roberts explains. They *did* exist but

> in reference to something else, some other reality that we translate into sense terms or pseudo-sense terms in order to perceive it at all. . . . Each of us at some time or other is struck by a moment that is timeless, in which we "know what we know" in a way that has nothing to do with words, in which the focus personality almost stands at the summit of itself and views the inner skies of its own soul. . . .
>
> [The] human personality [is] getting a glimpse of its own entire nature . . . for there are bleed-throughs, when we almost see who we "were" in a past life or who we "will be" in a future one.[38]

Seth adds:

> A portion of you has lived many lives upon this planet, but the "you" that you know is freshly here, and will never again encounter space and time in precisely the same way. . . . The soul, or . . . greater personage, does not simply send out an old self in new clothes time and time again. . . . [A] rich psychic heritage connects it through memory and experience to those who will "come after." Or those who have "gone before."[39]

This is the incarnational set-up. Everyone awakens from an unknown source and dimension. I remember lying in my crib at age two or three, coming to terms with reality. I felt the lingering presence of something I couldn't identify. My parents claimed later that I pointed to each car on the street and identified it: "Studeybager, Olds, Bluick, Cadiyack." I lost the ability by age four.

At three, my grandson Hopper told my daughter Miranda that he remembered when she and his father Mike saw each other as children. That was possible since they briefly overlapped in the Oakland-Berkeley area. He also told her that he had been to a restaurant at which they were dining for the first time and had seen cowboys there, not a character type she recalled his knowing about. When she asked if it was perhaps when he was very, very young, he replied thoughtfully, "Before that. Long ago, in the olden times."

"Olden times" could be a child's veridical chronology for a past life.

Journalist Tom Shroder eventually concluded that past lives "are less important for what they say about what happens after we die, than for what they say about how the world works—that it's mysterious, that there are larger forces at work, that—in some way—we're all connected by forces beyond our understanding." He adds, "If [that's] not science, maybe it should be."[40]

We float inside an amplituhedron-like field reflecting in multiple dimensions and things beyond dimensions. The reason most of us don't remember our past lives is that we can't remember (or even place) much of anything. But amnesia is not a system flaw or cruel trick. We are well taken care of by the universe; its greater context is simply beyond egoic percipience. Our passage from state to state—what we remember of who we were, what we intuit about who we will become—is subsumed in a general flow of metamorphoses, which has its own stability and framing.

"Past life" is the wrong answer to the wrong question. Each lifetime stands—and can only stand—in relationship.

· · · · · · · ·

Transmutations

look for me
in the critical mass of a high easterly rain . . .

MICHELLE BELLEROSE, THE OPENING LINES
OF THE LAST ENTRY IN THE TORONTO ARTIST'S
BREAST-CANCER JOURNAL

7

Cosmic Chicanery

Cosmogenesis

There are two ways to think about cosmogenesis, the creation of the universe. One is to accede to the scientific worldview: reality began with the Big Bang and nothing existed prior to it. The physical universe appeared 13.8 billion years ago and incubated the conscious universe, which discovered it. The body-mind by which we stalk its landscape took almost all of those 13.8 billion years to develop here on Earth, though it might have arisen sooner in other star systems. Whether anything preceded the Big Bang is an issue that I will discuss in chapter 10, though, of course, reality before the Big Bang is inaccessible by telescope, microscope, spectrograph, cyclotron, or *any* tool of discovery and measurement. The application of scientific instrumentation begins with tracking the background noise of an inaugural implosion.

The second option is to consider that the universe began as consciousness. It will take me the remainder of this book to interrogate this. But in order to satisfactorily bottom out the universe in a way that diverges from both science and conventional metaphysics, I need to show how a physical (objective) reality and a psychic (subjective) reality are reciprocal and in balance. In that regard, little is advanced by saying either "the universe began as consciousness" or "the universe began as matter." The deeper dialectic is "the universe was always both."

If consciousness preceded a starry initialing of the void, the Big Bang is ontologically secondary. We don't have to guess what came before it or assume that *this* universe is the first and only one. Instead, we infer that our own consciousness *reflects* a prior state of All That Is. Excavation may be impossible materially, but philosophy and meditation go beyond materiality.

In chapter 3, I introduced the notion of "thoughtforms": items that are both thoughts and forms and fluctuate between them. In the Seven Planes system, these rubrics arise as primal energies and flow from the Atmic plane through Causal into Mental subplanes. They manifest here as Astral or Physical-Etheric hybrids.

Psychotherapist Carl Jung defined pretty much the same amalgams as "psychoids," archetypes at the invisible, transcendental end of the psychic spectrum (see chapter 1). They anchor states in which psyche and matter are each manifestations of "eidos" (primordial form). Psychoids have energetic, even physical existence but only take on the shapes of the psychic energies projected onto them. They must be experienced to be known. As noted earlier, undines and faeries are psychoids, but so are neutrinos, UFOs, and sasquatches.

In psychoid cosmology, modes of consciousness and experience can be turned into matter, and matter can be turned into objects, even cosmoses—that is how a macrocosm can begin as both mind and matter, a union of polarities like Taoist yin and yang. It also speaks to the source or precondition of the Big Bang.

In cosmogony, ancient thoughtforms lie behind the present hydrogen/helium universe, unimaginable events from much longer ago than a "mere" fourteen billion years, but atoms and molecules are what those realities look like by now. In Hesiod's *Theogony,* they are Titans and progeny gods like Zeus, Hermes, and Athena, but those are place-holder personifications, predilections and attributes of entities in another dimension (on Mount Olympus or in Asgard, outside of common time). Such gods can become forces like gravity and electricity (lightning), diseases like AIDS or schizophrenia, or deities and worlds again.

We have no way of deciphering what sort of primeval events led to the Big Bang, but they were karmic in nature and yielded the alchemy (or nuclear synthesis) for their next expression. Likewise, we do not know what psychoid energy caused the emergence of this world out of spiraling solar dust, but whatever it was, Earth is it now. I am speaking of such vast parameters that they transcend space-time as we conceive it.

What is *not* remembered—the lesion at its source—creates life forms, egos, worlds. Nothing carries over except archetypes. This is where alchemy is senior to chemistry. Remember, you can't destroy essences or archetypes, you can only transmute or transubstantiate them.

My use of the same term—*lesion*—to describe cosmogenesis, the Big Bang, and the ego's awakening to reflective mind draws my nethermost strands together. It posits that karma is powerful enough to render entire planets and galaxies to receive the tattered energy of realms that have completed their cycles long ago. That rescales the Big Bang against a background of prior consciousness and form. I will pick up this thread in the next chapter.

The same union of opposites played out as the reciprocity of mind and matter in the evolution of culture. Hominids learned to survive by raising a social milieu out of signs and signifiers. They applied these in at least three ways: as pure mind, as mind onto matter, and as evocatory magic or thoughtforms. In the rivalry of technocrats and shamans, the toolmakers seemingly won because they got quicker and more reliable results. Shamanic invocation has effectively no impact on mineral formations: tens of thousands of years got called the Stone Age for a reason. On the other hand, empirical applications modified matter quickly and durably in circumscribed formats, such as a hand axe or chopper. While shamans psychically "traveled" to distant worlds, they couldn't engage in standard behavior when they got there. Similarly, you can't transport folks and their belongings across oceans by astral projection.

Thoughtforms are, however, as real as snow on Pluto or trucks on a Mongolian highway. In Sethian as well as Seven Planes cosmology, concentrated mind vibrates on Etheric and Astral levels, transforming "energy into physical form" according to a person's ideas and beliefs.[1] It takes quite a bit longer than physical transformation, yet if you look at the planet today, you see the fruition of a collective Pleistocene thoughtform, the realization of Stone Age shamans' unconscious projections and prayers. They manifested the current landscape out of their desires for food, shelter, safety, power, and mobility. Translating inchoate shapes into imaginal counterparts, they projected items too vast to be manifested in their lifetimes or contained within the minds of any individual or group of individuals: wheels, engines, electricity, cities. They did not understand the nature of their objectifications, for they had no templates and did not directly charm matter. They were drawing on subconscious aspects of thought and its psychoid properties.

Once such aspects become physical rather than shamanic, they address matter directly. That is why we have such a vast technological exposition: humans have turned millennia-long psychic projections into artifacts that maintain an entire civilization. But they began as chants, sigils, and mantras and, since the universe is fundamentally psycho-physical, even their scientific modes retain psychic aspects.

Humans could not have fabricated machines out of matter unless matter had an aspect of mind in it. In Sethian ontology, "Objectified mental states [are] constantly interacting, formed automatically by conscious energy's intercession with the three-dimensional field."[2] Not only all of science but also the cosmos itself may represent conscious energy's intercession with a nuclear/gravitational field that turns intelligence into artifacts. Magic works (when it does) not because the mind moves matter telekinetically but because *matter is, at crux, a thoughtform too.*

Magic and prayers may be slow going and subliminal, but they are ultimately cosmos changing. Minerals and life forms coalesced on Earth from the same geochemical deposits at different epochs. A seemingly random distribution of molecules and their compounds, many of them located underground, became modifiable into everything *Homo sapiens* needed, from weapons and clothing to huts, vehicles, and eventually microscopes and computer networks. That speaks to either an uncanny ability to turn lemons into lemonade or an intrinsic relationship between mind and matter.

Just about anything can be made if it is imagined long enough. Some things take hundreds of thousands of years, and in the case of hominids, the physics and chemistry to support the creation of an object have to be developed first. What is being made magically is unknown until it manifests, which may be epochs later. Cars zooming through modernity were once shamanic sigils. They are also the outcome of empirical thought applied to stone. Over long periods of time these converge. Seth doesn't hedge:

> Man dreamed his world and then created it . . . from the first tool to . . . fire, or the coming of the Iron Age . . . and the units of consciousness first dreamed man and all of the other species that you know. . . . [They] are the building blocks for the physical material of your body, for the trees and rocks, the oceans, the continents, and the very manifestation of thought itself as you understand it.[3]

If you are a member of a Plains Indian warrior sodality or a Tibetan lama, you start your education from this premise. There isn't any other. You can't enter a universe you don't believe in. Stone Age shamans believed, and what we are living today is the materialization of their beliefs. I take poet Charles Stein axiomatically here: "To participate in the possibility of a magical cosmos is . . . [not] technological production without technology—the creation of change according to will—so much as the capacity to project upon reality a picture of being itself."[4]

A picture of being itself has been projected "upon reality" since the dawn of our species, perhaps since the Big Bang.

The question is, What unknown landscape are we evoking today?

Trickster Arts

An indigenous healer told an academic friend of mine that he used sleight of hand and other duplicity in his practice, yet he insisted that it was fair play—a ploy to shift stubborn beliefs, stuck thoughtforms that had metastasized as tissue pathology. "Western doctors open people up like car mechanics," he explained, "and they try to fix them by changing their parts. We heal them by changing their belief systems."[5]

Quesalid, an elderly Koskimo shaman interviewed by anthropologist Franz Boas, admitted that the bloody down he pulled out of a sick person's body was crumpled feathers darkened from biting his own tongue. In his youth, he had thought to expose this technique as a fraud, but he gradually arrived at a more profound understanding. It was *transforma-*

tional theater. Each of his patients assimilated the totem object into their psychic fields and converted it into parasympathetic or cellular energy. Even knowing that the bloody down is a sham, a medicine man calls on a fellow practitioner to treat him in this manner if he becomes sick.[6]

Jeffrey Kripal interpreted these and similar practices in terms of an overlooked psychokinetic principle:

> It is almost as though the real needs the fake to appear at all, *as if the fact relies on the fiction to manifest itself.* . . . It is not as if the appearance of the sacred can be reduced to a simple trick, as if the shaman is just a sham. It is as if the sacred is *itself* tricky. Even the well-documented medical placebo, after all, is a fake that has real effects. . . . Psychical researcher Russell Targ . . . first became aware of the reality of telepathy when, as a young stage magician in New York, he realized that he was receiving genuine telepathic information *from within the mentalist trick he was performing on stage.* The trick was a trick, but it was also, somehow, catalyzing the real deal.[7]

According to Kripal, fake fortune-tellers and séances lead to "accurate and veridical information, [for instance] about the time, nature, or details of the death, all unknown and unknowable to the supraliminal self until the subliminal or telepathic communication occurs."[8]

When we are in dialogue with a transpersonal intelligence, a trickster element comes into play, using psychic counterparts to Freudian defense mechanisms like sublimation (concealing by conversion) and reaction formation (exaggeration of the opposing tendency). The intelligence also interposes synchronicities and plays with space-time itself, teasing us in ways that Native American clowns like Coyote and Raven fooled humans and other animals in the myths of the dawn time. A similar gremlin may be in play with crop circles. The goal is not to mislead but to guide us to a paradoxical, inherently self-contradictory reality to which there is no direct route and that cannot be assimilated in one piece or at one time. This is not just an occasional back channel or synchronicity. It is the fundamental structure of nature.

Similarly, science-fiction tales, though *meant* to be imaginary, can represent "the greater reality from which we spring [and] . . . send messages from there to the selves we know."[9] Magical powers in superhero movies and comics cue fallow human capacities, sometimes ones experienced in less extravagant form by the authors. You become a superhero by first *pretending* to be a superhero (or shaman). Athletes play above their abilities at game-changing moments because a picture of their feat almost imperceptibly precedes the feat itself. Targ became such an accurate remote viewer (depending on whom you ask) that he was hired by SRI and the CIA to locate Soviet military installations. Others "see" through time, preperceiving earthquakes and plane crashes. These knacks suggest that when we engage the cosmic trickster, we take on some of her numinous powers.

Messages from the Afterlife

No aspect of the relationship between objective and subjective universes affects creatures more significantly or intimately than birth and death. Birth swathes conscious beings in a physical universe. Death ends the relationship, though it does not necessarily terminate identity. In addition to people's memories of past lives, accounts of near-death experiences, and other reincarnational artifacts and poltergeists, channeling from the afterlife provides glimpses of how consciousness might separate from a physical envelope and reconstitute itself in another dimensional field.

A popular 2013 book, *The Afterlife of Billy Fingers: How My Bad-Boy Brother Proved to Me There's Life after Death,* summarizes Annie Kagan's dialogues with her brother after his premature passing.[10] In life, Billy, who nicknamed himself Fingers at age sixteen after he lost the tip of one finger while working in a welding factory, topped out as a petty criminal and drug addict. He was hit by a taxi after leaving the emergency room of South Miami (Florida) Hospital, an ID cuff still on his wrist. He described the sensation of being sucked out of his body by a rush of energy. After that, in a state of bliss incompatible with the human body, he entered a welcoming zone, a festive land of silvery lights.[11]

Later, he recalled floating weightlessly through space with "gorgeous stars and moons and galaxies" glimmering all about him, while he noticed a faraway intoxicating sound, a celestial choir like wind or rain or ocean waves but more musical and with a rhythmic pulsation that kept fluctuating and becoming more melodic.[12] A stream a few yards wide shimmered with the colors of chakras. As the pulse escalated into sacred music, Billy realized he had heard it unconsciously throughout his recent lifetime. The stream gradually erased his Earth body and its memories, and a blue-white sphere implanted a different corporeal sensation.[13]

Billy saw his former wife, Ingrid, floating before him as a solar-system-like constellation. Her stars and planets told stories of the different stages of her life: a blonde baby digging in sand, a teenager dancing onstage, a young woman strung out on cocaine, a hag doing time in prison. The strands of her anger harmonized attractively at a soul level. As the two of them circled each other, he understood why he loved her in the first place.[14]

The Divine Presence called him by his soul name, a rune he recognized from before he was born.[15] He found himself staring at a beautiful woman twice his height with the look and vibe of a Hindu goddess: rings, bracelets, and precious stones around her feet, a tiara of golden light circling her head. As she rotated her hands in a mudralike dance, Billy followed in devotion until he gradually began to resemble her.[16]

Numberless other folks like himself were following their own guides up to a white building.[17] Its stones were opalescent with cosmic wisdom formulas built into them.[18] The tantric lady led him to a cave with pictures of blossoms carved around its entrance. A blossom shimmered, showing Billy his past lives, which were shaded purple or red and illuminating petals of individual lotus flowers. The guide offered him a cup of the milky nectar from a pond; it tasted sweet and pungent. He was barely ready for its deluge of wisdom. A golden dragon formed at the top of the cave, a fierce-looking entity with fiery eyes. Billy recognized it as his guardian through many lifetimes.[19]

This is a brief summary of a book that many consider the first modern narrative of the afterlife as well as historic permission to break the encryption between the living and the dead. Others dis it as New Age blarney. Another possibility is that Kagan is receiving a *different* transmission and using a literary device to communicate it. A similar defense has been offered by apologists for Carlos Castaneda regarding his encounters with shaman Juan Matus—that the events themselves were fictionalized to create a narrative out of nonlinear experiences that would otherwise have been incommunicable.

But Kagan can *only* tell the truth, as Quesalid and numerous shamans found out, so it is a matter of *which* truth: her own intimation of an afterlife projected onto Billy or Billy's cables beyond death. The universe always holds the last card, and it doesn't have to be from the deck you are dealing. Billy's messages, even if invented by Kagan, are "real."

Is Consciousness after Death a Projection?

Psychologist Matthew McKay offers a kindred account of communication with a recently deceased family member: his son Jordan, who was murdered in 2008 at age twenty-three in San Francisco. Jordan was shot by one of a group of youths trying to steal his bike as he fought them off and started to ride away. The first communication was McKay's clairaudient perception of Jordan's voice during an EMDR* session with Veterans Administration psychologist Allan Botkin. McKay soon realized that he was communicating with not only a twenty-three-year-old boy but also a soul that encompassed that boy's many incarnations, including his recent one as his own son.

McKay acknowledges that Jordan can't give us a comprehensive view of the afterlife or act as our travel guide to another reality. There is no direct speech or even a common language between the dead and the living. Meanings pass from Jordan's spiritual field, where he is now, to McKay's spiritual field, where *he* is now, then they pass through McKay's brain into language. Of course, the language is McKay's, but it is not McKay's *instead of Jordan's*. It is generated by McKay out of concepts he and his son shared even when he was alive, presum-

---

*EMDR stands for Eye Movement Desensitization and Reprocessing; it is a nontraditional psychotherapy that uses guided ocular, auditory, and somatosensory tracking to alter the way the separate hemispheres of the brain interact to lock in memories of traumatic events. Botkin modified EMDR to trigger after-death communication.

ably in other lifetimes too. Earth-like landscapes and experiences are no longer relevant where Jordan's spirit is. Jordan can only communicate a radically different situation in terms humans would understand; McKay can only translate it into terms that *he* understands. Channeling is not art or literature or ethnography; there are filters and contaminations.

The encryption between the living and the dead *can't be broken*. The notion that Billy Fingers and others communicated anything more than a pale sketch of post-embodied beingness is soporific thinking. Consider the richness, color, palpability, depth, and poignancy here, the way in which all our senses and modes of proprioception and kinesthesia have been stitched into an organism. Any afterworld, as experienced, would have to be woven at the same intensity and pitch. Yet channeling depletes the "travelogue" through its ontological permutations. We are getting esoteric information, but the files have to be, as it were, unzipped, then expanded and translated by a disciplined spiritual etiology.

Many years ago, Ellias Lonsdale, an astute querent of the mysteries as well as a psychic and astrologer, said to me,

> The big picture is right in front of us and we are missing it. Our situation, our entire world or state of being, is defined by the fact that our dead seem to disappear and we lose touch with them. Almost everywhere else in the universe, there is a swinging door between the living and the dead. The living know how to reach the dead when they need to, and the dead know how to contact the living. We have lost the tools to even see the dead or respond to their attempts to reach us. For that, we pay a huge price. The dead are not somewhere else being weird while we're here having fun. Yet that's the way most people view it.

We are out of touch with the dead not because we are out of touch *as such* but because we are out of touch with spirit and the spirit world altogether. Our reality has been reduced to one set of dimensions into which we are crammed like an imaginal prison cell. Bottoming out the universe starts with seeing beyond the cell—through the shadows of Plato's legendary cave.*

Jordan describes transitional scenes like those reported by Billy Fingers, but he is laid-back and observational, like waking up in a sensory deprivation tank with new sensations. In a sense, Jordan's voice has been added to a larger entity that was there before he was born. It remembers many prior death metamorphoses as it views the universe and its own being from a soul's perspective. It can't take Jordan's place or speak for the young man as he would have spoken if he had continued to live in his earth form; instead it picks up after he was shot and stumbling into a doorway:

> I felt cold, oddly, even though I was out of my body. And a sense of shock. I had been knocking on a door. I thought I had lost consciousness and come to again. . . . [I] couldn't figure out why I was outside my body. . . .
>
> I could hear something like wind, but probably more like breath. I was moving. No sense of direction. . . . At some point there was more light—as if the morning sun were just starting to penetrate a mist. But the light ultimately became brighter than any dawn, and shapes began to appear in the mist. Tall, vertical shadows. There was a sense of ground, although I wasn't actually standing on anything. The shadows clarified; they were souls. . . .
>
> The landing place lies at the gateway to the world of spirit. It's not an actual location, like on a map, but an energy field reserved for calming and instructing incoming souls. . . .
>
> There was a jumble of stuff around me, remnants of Jordan's life that seemed real. But they were just images made of energy. . . . I could feel a hand touching me, urging me to slow down. . . . I could also feel love bathing me, radiating from the souls around me, but

---

*In his Allegory of the Cave, Plato describes people chained to the wall of a cave onto which shadows have been projected by objects passing in front of a fire behind them. The shadows are the prisoners' reality. A philosopher, freeing himself from the cave, sees not only the fire but the sun. This allegory could be applied to the more quotidian kinetic depth effect described in chapter 2.

also from the light itself. Someone, a guide perhaps, asked me to select one image that could stabilize the scene. . . .

As the meadow stabilized and I felt more and more surrounded by this murmur of love, I relaxed. As my energy expanded, my vibrational level increased, and I could hear more and more of the sound of *all*. . . .

I was guided to a spot by a lamppost and lantern where I could meditate on the life just lived. . . . [I] was instructed that I would remain here for the review of Jordan's life. The lantern turned on.[20]

Jordan eventually entered a liminal realm of thoughtforms:

If you think of each soul as a point of light, the spirit world is a vast array of such lights. It has far more lights than the population of Earth because souls reincarnate to so many other planets and dimensions. And there are souls who have completed their incarnations, and souls who cluster to create, who are the source, who turn knowledge into matter and energy.[21]

Like Billy Fingers's afterworld, this is a more benign and healing place than most generic religious destinations. There is no hell, dismemberment, or stampede of hungry ghosts. The authoritative *Egyptian Book of the Dead* and the more graphically anecdotal Tibetan *Bardo Thodol* are reclassified by Jordan as personal death visions rather than universal paths. The Christian inferno described by Dante and painted by Hieronymus Bosch is also seen as an optional nightmare, for death is a fluid realm of imagination and invention, a landscape created entirely of consciousness. If individuals experience phenomena in life differently, in death those divergences intensify because of the heightened aspect of projection. Jordan says:

Souls who are steeped in fear project their own demons in almost the same way 3-D printing works on Earth—and then run or learn to battle with them. Souls struggling with desire and avarice keep acquiring and then losing the things they acquired. Some have confused these bardos with Hell, but there is no punishment. These are simply well designed, concentrated learning environments. These plots function like dreams do on Earth—helping to process pain and distress. And, like dreams, nothing truly bad can happen to souls in the strange dimensions. Guides add small twists to the plots so they gradually resolve, and the soul's vibrational energy will eventually move to a higher level.[22]

Some souls actually prefer a "life" without bodies because the polarities of matter overwhelm them. In the after-realm, they get to translate their thoughts into energy and objects:

[A]n average day in Paradise, because we are awake and learning, will always involve some creative form. The most common one is creating images out of energy. A house, a temple, a landscape, a garden, a complex geometric shape, a sculpture . . . [like] the Victorian house that my soul group lives in. . . . The group also creates music and new energy patterns designed to precipitate social change on earth. All souls and soul groups create like this.

Remember, thought eventually coalesces into form. Every new thought *creates*.[23]

No guarantees—except maybe that a system that teaches is not a system that punishes. "Even karma is not punishment," John Friedlander attests. "Pain for the universe is a healing, a redirection. The message when you feel pain is, 'Try something else.'"[24] After death too.

In another variant of channeling after death, Ellias Lonsdale and his partner, Sarah, collaborated on an esoteric line of communication—they named it "soul speak"—to communicate with each other during Sarah's passage through breast cancer, death, and crossing over in 1992–1993. Ellias continued to share her experiences on a subtle level as she journeyed in the afterworld. When I asked Ellias about his "Theanna" channeling in 2019 (Theanna was Sarah's "Atlantean" name after death), he described it as a form of "super telepathy." But, he added, "telepathy is external and 'soul speak' is inside, behind the scenes. We were keyed in, attuned to cosmic sources together, so we were always in hidden conversation and communion. It was not the usual situation."

Theanna reported her descent and transformation as if a phase of Eleusinian mystery rites. Her account has harrowing elements missing from the others: the ineluctable pangs of birth, death, and rebirth. She shared:

> When the time was ripe, I was guided to take the world's heaviest karmas into my body and transmute them to the point where I felt ready to embrace my innermost destiny. Just before I died, all the circuits started to click in and show me what I was to do, how I was to do it, and the exquisite rightfulness in what looked like a tragedy. Among the instructions was the core message: You are now to dive through death, sink to the bottom of the death realms, and pull up to the surface the living soul who is your own vast and limitless self awaiting you there. When you have her, bring her to the ones who sent you out upon your journey. . . .
>
> I did as I was told. The death sharks could not get any grip on me. I was far too slippery for them. I was all water. I dove far under their vigilant guard and came to the living soul, the vast one awaiting me so expectantly and joyously.[25]

No floating among party lights or traipsing along magical streams for this girl! She sank into painful soul remembering. "My surface consciousness was whittled to almost nothing, so I pierced right through it in the birth moment and became the breath of the deep. My subtle awareness bubbled to the top. My outer-mind permanently split open, and I walked onward with far clearer awareness and more open space into the unknown."[26]

Only after passing through numerous death pictures did Theanna finally confront the lord of death himself and experience how he operates: he matches each person's picture of him.[27]

A person who accepts only material reality may not even recognize his continued existence after dying. Since he expects annihilation, he vegetates in pretend nonexistence, denying his own self-awareness because beingness is impossible without a body. He corroborates his belief system by creating an alias that fools *even him.* It may require eons of Earth-time for him to notice that *something* is denying its own existence.

A confirmed skeptic (like Oliver Sacks or Stephen Hawking) has three options: one is to continue to consider himself dead until his unconscious self begins to stir under new terms; the second is to blend into a greater truth and recognize one's theory of the universe as an authentic response to his time and place on Earth; the third is to think, "Ah, did I ever sell the universe short!"

He wouldn't have to amend his belief system because conditions where he is are more fundamental. The belief that death is final and ends all experience *matches* the belief that existence is eternal and changing. The universe, once bottomed out in all its platforms, doesn't make distinctions between life and death, mind and matter, faith and doubt.

"You're all going to die," martial artist Peter Ralston told his students. "What else is there to do but grasp what life is, what you are, and what Absolute Reality is before you die? Are you satisfied with just believing you are going to go to heaven, or wherever, or become nothing? Don't be silly. Get beyond a childish relationship to this matter and become responsible for grasping it firsthand. When you die, you will know what death is."[28]

The nihilist position is not antispiritual; it is generating negative energy essential for the soul's evolution. To be mired in paradise, an inert beatitude, without possibility of creative transformation—an angelic theme park and light that casts no shadows—would be as pointless as it is unsustainable.

8

Trauma and Redemption

In 2009, I helped publish a book called *The Angel of Auschwitz* by a woman writing under the name Tarra Light, who recalled a past life as Natasza Pelinski, a prisoner in a concentration camp. I won't vouch for its authenticity. The narrative is certainly within the range of what could be improvised from a vernacular knowledge of history and a literary imagination—and there has been no lack of Holocaust memoirs, novels, and films from which one could draw characters and scenes. Light explains that a past-life regression during which she was experiencing "physical and emotional afflictions . . . became the catalyst that unlocked the floodgates of my soul memory."[1]

I take Light at her word. Yes, she could have made the whole thing up or cobbled a few arcane flashbacks into a novella. Yet the text bears an inherent credibility beyond the issue of its authenticity.

As Light plunged through her regression, multiple identities flooded into her mind. In lifetime after lifetime, she found herself locked in a Manichean battle with an ambitious, deviant soul known to the twentieth century as "Adolf Hitler." Before Atlantis, the two were rival magicians: *she* believed that the key to the universe was the force of love; *he* believed it was power generated through a blend of magic and technology.

Through his incarnations, Light tells us, the Hitler soul "studied metaphysics and the occult sciences . . . the chants of Atlantis, the mystery schools of Egypt, and the pagan rituals of the Celts and the Druids."[2] He appropriated sacraments, including ones forbidden to noninitiates. Drawing on racial memories in the Aryan bloodline, he established a creed fed by subconscious greed and envy.[3] In his recent lifetime as Adolf Hitler, he drew on what Light called his "soul memory" (perhaps his aura) as he "reformulated [ancient rites] into the new state religion . . . based on the magical properties of blood."[4]

The Nazi High Command launched their Reich in Bavaria's Black Forest, using satanic rituals and protocols of diabolism. "Like a mystical order, they donned hooded black robes and lit shining black candles. Standing side-by-side in a circle, they recited ancient incantations, then sang Atlantean chants."[5] According to Light, Hitler was not exalting the Aryan race as much as he was trying to restore a mystery school and warrior guild *from another plane.*

In her lifetime as Natasza, Light dreamed of the Führer inspecting her concentration camp in person. Natasza saw him transdimensionally and read "the magnitude of his power as an adept black magician" trying to penetrate "her shields and defenses." Banishing fear and opening her heart, she released a surge of energy within her aura. "Hitler turned to face me and pulled open the front of his trench coat, revealing the truth of his inner being. White light as bright as lightning burst out from within. The radiance of his True Self dazzled my eyes."[6]

He could have been a great teacher who served humanity; he might still be in a future lifetime. In 1930s Germany, he chose a different path.

According to Light, Hitler's successive lifetimes have nonetheless opened an underbelly of darkness in All That Is. If its tinder wasn't there, he couldn't have ignited it. If he hadn't ignited it, its energy wouldn't have begun to get redeemed. Until we admit its place in our collective psyche and start to absolve it, it will continue to incarnate, as centurions of Interahamwe, Daesh, and Boko Haram or whoever follows. It has to be dredged, experienced, and transmogrified. Otherwise, it will settle, an unknowable slag radiating sterilely through Creation down to its least particle. The soul incarnates in order to know and redeem it.

The Atlas of Auschwitz

As Light's chronology of a past life begins, fourteen-year-old Natasza is forcibly separated from her family by gendarmes of the Nazi war machine, her belongings snatched from her. On her own, the girl is placed in a gloomy building inside a large concentration camp.

Soon Natasza was contacted by a voice. "It entered my mind as a stream of pure thought with neither pitch nor timbre."[7] She used her inner sight to focus on the source and her telepathy to illuminate its words. A ghost annealed from the murk, introducing himself as Boris Brozinski, a former professor at the University of Warsaw. Boris told her that he had ignored his colleagues while they were being arrested. He did nothing to oppose the Nazis when he had a chance; now he was attached to the earth plane by the weight of his guilt. To atone and pay off a portion of his debt, he offered to serve as Natasza's guide, to teach and protect her and to enable her to aid others in their distress. He explained that he had been drawn by the lodestar of her psychic power—a bright energy in a grim landscape.

From Light's memory of her incarnation as Natasza, she reports that Boris "focused his mind and projected into my third eye simple diagrams of the organs and systems of the body"[8] to the end that she could function as the camp's unofficial nurse and medicine woman. After that, he spelled out some guerrilla tactics: "I have a repertoire of stratagems to outwit the guards."[9] These included spying on their conversations and revealing their plans to her, projecting alter egos into their minds to confuse them, and merging with her own energy field in such a way that light would pass through her and they would see but not recognize her.

Boris emitted an ectoplasmic double who could steal medical supplies from the camp infirmary. "Being transparent," he joked, "has many advantages."[10] Whenever Natasza needed his help or participation, she directed telepathic energy into the subtle body of his ghost-being and his Astral form appeared.

Later, Boris explained that he had "enlisted the aid of our airborne allies [because] they want to serve as members of the healing team."[11] He told her how to proceed. After she made twin runic patterns of stones on the ground while sending telepathic messages to the high-circling messengers ("Greetings to you, birds of the great sky"), two crows landed on either side of her rows.

One communicated telepathically through caws: "Hail, child of Light. Many animals would like to serve humans but are unable to break through the interspecies communications barrier. We are here to offer our assistance. . . . We can carry messages from one part of the camp to the other. We can spy on the Nazis and tell you their secrets." The bird then taught her flying symbols and calls by which they would transmit urgent information. Three caws in a row meant "All is well," while four followed by a pause and then four more was a general "All clear." Loud and repeated caws with pauses between them meant "Warning: danger."[12]

Upon Boris's next manifestation, Natasza was astonished to see thousands of tiny faces floating within clouds above each of his shoulders. "I looked into their eyes," she says, "and they looked back at me. My heart broke with compassion to see the faces of the fallen ones. They were the spirits of the dead who had attached themselves to Boris. He walked hunched forward because he was carrying this astral weight." These beings were "confused and disoriented . . . bound to the earthly plane by desire. At the moment of death they did not claim their freedom. They were unprepared for the journey into light. . . . They are still in shock and do not realize that they are dead."[13]

Boris's guilt attracted them to him; he was the only recognizable object to which they could fasten their otherwise blind fugues.[14] They continued to maneuver by projecting their memories of who they had been onto the karmic cloud of his remorse.

Natasza conducted many acts of espionage and rebellion, including sabotaging camp agendas and healing sick prisoners. But Boris recognized a danger incubating in her heart. The young girl was witnessing too many crimes and violations for her gentle vibration to absorb.[15] She was turning cold and bitter.

"Anger and hatred dam up the flow of your healing energy," the professor explained to her.

They lower the frequency of your transmission. . . . An angered healer is a crippled healer. These soldiers whom you hate, whom you call "enemies": do you know that their minds are programmed, that they are being controlled? They too are prisoners of the Nazi war machine. . . . They wield the power of the world; they command with muscle and might. But you have the greater power, the universal power of love. Imagine how they suffer because they do not know love.[16]

When the girl asked Boris for an explanation of the death camps, wondering why, if a soul has a choice, it would select such a life and fate, he told her, "Before a soul incarnates on Earth, it makes many choices about the nature and circumstances of its new life. . . . The soul has karma, debts to pay off before it can be free. . . . It . . . chooses the lesson to be learned that can resolve the karma. . . . Decades ago, a clarion call was sounded in the heavens. Millions of souls heard and answered the call. They lined up at the Karmic Gates, volunteering for this mission. They said, 'We will sacrifice our lives so the world will choose a higher way to live.'"[17]

His lessons clarified and enhanced her mission. She became a medicinal and spiritual guide for guards too, as well as a lover of one of them, Captain Otto. The captain initiated the relationship by bringing the still virginal girl to his room and raping her like an animal while, in her words, she was "unprepared to receive the male energy."[18]

During encounters as his lover for more than two years (age fourteen to sixteen), she gradually awakened his soul and transformed him through their ritual. "Due to the bond of our sexual union, I was empathic to his feelings, telepathic to his thoughts."[19] She called it my "pathway into womanhood . . . as moon shadows [nightly] marked my footsteps."[20] Lying in Captain Otto's sheets, she prayed that his young wife (in a bedside photograph) would forgive her.

Ultimately, Natasza emitted so much light that she came to the attention of the camp's commandant. Initially bemused by the presumptions of a girl, Herr Schuller was increasingly troubled by her fearlessness and charisma. Ordering her brought to his office, he issued an ultimatum: renounce her mission—or die. She had become, he said, a danger to security. Sending daggers of psychic luminosity from her eyes and infusing her syllables with holy power, she held her ground, telling him defiantly that she was married to the truth.[21]

"Brave words fly like sparks from the mouth of a child," he declared as he rose from behind his desk, clicked his heels, and saluted her. He was as powerless to resist his own fate as he was to refute the penetrating brightness of her presence, for "the Commandant of Auschwitz was not free. . . . Even the Führer was a prisoner of his own madness and fanaticism." Then he declared, "I admire you for your bravery, rebel child, but I am not free to let you go. . . . I am obligated to follow orders. . . . I order you to death by the firing squad."[22]

After the sentencing, Boris reached out telepathically, "This is not your first life," he promised. "It is not your last. Realize that the memory of this life is imprinted on your soul. You will be born again, to Jewish parents in the United States, before this war is over. When you awaken to your innate divinity, you will write the true story of your life."[23]

Prodded along by soldiers with rifle butts, she saw Boris at her side as he projected a blue ray of peace into her field. She heard boots crunching on ice. Her mind filled with the caws of crows gathering overhead. She descried a choir of muffled voices calling out her name, and they chanted, "We love you." Then Boris disclosed her sacred errand:

Now is the time for the full truth to be revealed to you. Thousands of lost souls saw your light like a beacon in the night and attached themselves to you. Through your grace, they hope for their own salvation. You are the Atlas of Auschwitz, carrying thousands of souls on your shoulders. . . . It takes a great soul to carry the weight of the multitudes. You would not have believed yourself capable of this noble task. Your doubt would have undone you.[24]

Aware of the greater reality in which her time on Earth had played out, Natasza stood in willing surrender. "Seven shots rang out."[25] Her life ended. As her soul flew heavenward, freed, she saw with her spirit eyes "the fallen body of a young woman, lying on the frozen ground . . . curled up in fetal position . . . a pool of blood collecting around her body.

Her abdomen was ripped open. A pair of black crows landed by her side. With tender care, they rearranged her hair, strand by strand, pulling it out of her eyes and away from her face." The Angel of Death arrived, announcing, "The moment of death is the birth of spiritual life. Now you shall know the truth of who you are."[26]

She saw a sphere of light and felt a presence within her, as she discovered that she was pregnant with Otto's child. There had been no way for her to bring its soul into the world, but it addressed her clairsentiently: "I am Meesha, spirit of your unborn child. I have come to accompany you in your last moments. I shall be with you during your time of passing. Do not fear. The love of God is with you always. The power of God is everlasting."[27]

Natasza projected the seed of her liaison with Otto into an epoch far beyond their current lifetimes. Then she crossed over:

"The celestial wind swept me along, past dreamlands and fantastic worlds, carrying me to the gate of a heavenly amusement park. A trumpet sounded, and the gate swung open. I heard the music of the spheres playing from the loudspeakers. Bears danced gaily to a lively tune, acrobats performed amazing feats, and jugglers swallowed balls of fire. A sky-blue angel with gossamer wings handed me a ticket for a ride through time. Like a revolving wheel of time, a giant Ferris wheel turned around and around. As each seat passed me, I saw an aspect of myself as I was in a previous life." She glimpsed the shape-changing shadow of an Inca healer, the incarnate disciple of the living Christ— and then an Egyptian student of metaphysics, who in one of his lives would become Adolf Hitler.[28]

Dealing with Karmic Reverberations of Trauma

In 1974 in one of his last papers, psychotherapist D. W. Winnicott wrote about patients who so dreaded their own anxiety and psychotic breakdown that their actions were driven by phobic avoidance patterns. What they needed, Winnicott proposed, was, counterphobically, to experience the events behind their fantasies and fears.[29] The inability to resolve long-forgotten ordeals led to maintaining a ritualized defense mechanism, which over the years became more painful in its bondage *than the incident instilling the trauma*. Their imagination of future danger distorted reality, as there was always a way to project some dreaded apparition onto the near horizon. Compared with such an omniscient threat, reality was a piece of cake.

One traumatized patient who was near the World Trade Center during the 9/11 attacks remarked to his therapist how calm he was, helping people cope, leading strangers to safety. As horrific as the event was, it *couldn't hold a candle* to his more gruesome fantasies. It was the first time that external reality matched what was happening *inside* him.

I accept Winnicott's contention in a conventional psychiatric context while at the same time wondering how it might apply to past (or future) lives of an individual or soul, that is, whether there is a *karmic* reverberation of trauma, a transpersonal avoidance pattern and defense mechanism too. Encountering reincarnational trauma would lead to reliving other lifetimes' painful events, including wars, massacres, plagues, death pictures, travels in bardo realms, and womb and birth memories. Humanity might also be dealing with miasmas of the species, planet, or sentient life in the greater cosmos.

Events like those at Auschwitz and Hiroshima have been multiplied by the trillions since the earliest bands of hominids or, in keeping with our DNA, since the first sea predators. These "holocausts" were mostly at smaller scales but no less poignant to those experiencing them. Who knows what waves of trauma originate elsewhere in the universe and ripple through galaxies, planes, and dimensions? Who knows where the souls of the current Earth have tarried en route to their bodies?

This model dovetails with Family Constellations, the transgenerational healing system of German psychotherapist Burt Hellinger.[30] What Hellinger proposed was that traumas transfer energy to the offspring of both the violators and their victims, which then radiates through future generations. Crises left pending in one generation return in subsequent ones as the energy tries to get itself released. Karma holds any experience that a soul cannot assimilate; it bounces back and gets reexperienced until the soul *can* assimilate it.

Ancestors are not "dead"; many are wounded and need recognition and healing. They have the capacity to heal and bless in return.

Hellinger developed group minidramas as a way to convene bygone epochs and incarnate and clear karma. Every recruit into a constellation, though unrelated to the sufferer, played a role in recovering a forebear inaccessible to ordinary memory. Each participant turned into an agent of the ancestral field, animated as if by voodoo. It wasn't acting; it was clairvoyant possession. Hellinger drew these rituals, in part, from his interactions with Zulu shamans in South Africa, but the method is not uniquely South African. Ancestor expiation is common throughout the nonindustrialized world, where burial grounds are sites of petition and communion. Hellinger's performances achieved a shamanic function similar to Asian family shrines or Navaho sand paintings, which, with their accompanying ceremonies, bring together assorted icons to specify and conduct energy.

According to Gladys Reichard, in her *Navaho Religion,* the Navaho used "the medicine bundle with its sacred contents: prayer-sticks, made of selected wood and feathers, precious stones, tobacco, water collected from sacred places, a tiny piece of cotton string; song, with its lyrical and musical complexities; sandpaintings, with intricate color, directional and impressionistic symbols; prayer, with stress on order and rhythmic unity; plants, with supernatural qualities defined and personified; body and figure painting; sweating and emetic, with purificatory functions; vigil, with emphasis on concentration and summary."[31]

Any symbol will do, as long as it stores a charge—a libidinal load—because any representation will converge with all its proxies and aliases (see chapter 2). The medicine bundle, sand mandala, chants, and so on turn secular time into mythic time while placing the trauma in a tribal and communal matrix. All its members, living and dead, participate in its ceremony.

Hellinger's reenactments mostly exhumed proximal generations and known family figures, but in some instances they took individuals back to the Middle Ages, the Stone Ages, and beyond in the form of clan matriarchs and patriarchs whose karma was still active among descendants. Whether the events were real or imaginal, they functioned therapeutically *as if real.*

Many factors we have been discussing come into play: past lives, afterlives, spirit guides, souls and group souls, agitated death pictures, voodoo, and so on. If you accept the gist of these, it is no stretch to believe that the dead have unfinished business, some of it with the living (and *vice versa*). Death is less of an absolute barrier than an alteration of the field of consciousness and relationship. It can be mediated like any other boundary as long as its terms are understood and accepted.

In a sense, every entity, like every god, is both real and imaginal. Imagination is not imaginary; it is how we participate in theogony, the power of creation. A blogger using the name Fr. D. Eosastraios writes, "The manifested dynamic cosmos, populated with myriad occult correspondences, mythic realities, and host of nonmaterial beings, exists on various levels of perception, with the senses perceiving the world, the active imagination, the soul, and the daimonic consciousness through the intellect."[32]

In modern, revised "Constellations" practices, a ceremonial field includes anything that circulates through the gestalt and needs to be healed or redeemed. Participants may play nations or national identities, religions, or tribes; forces like racism, chaos, terror, shame, secrets, or rage; and former or dormant selves or states such as refugee, bully or victim, homeless person, revolutionary, gang member, or committer of a crime. A side effect is that other participants in the ceremony not only embody the circumstance of the seeker for whom the field was fired but enact parallel dramas in their own lives (called "shared realities"), as synchronicity and overdeterminism take over. For instance, while a seeker is activating parental betrayal, a trans participant performing the seeker's father may experience gender dysphoria and exile, and an Iranian woman playing his mother may cathartically relive the execution of her relatives by the Mullah Regime.

Shamanism and psychoanalysis converge. Yet while psychoanalysis provides an emotional catalyst through doctor-patient transference, traumas can remain stuck in an inertial field of narratives. Patients and therapists go in circles for decades. The therapy, while churning up juicy material, reinforces the pathology and its avoidance cycle. It can never grasp the full picture or find the moment of traumatization because traumatic leverage is nonlinear and not rooted in any one event or place.

Furthermore, once a trauma gets transferred to the aura, it can pass between lifetimes. It is incorporated back through the fluid (Etheric) body into the physical body in current or reincarnated form, sometimes as disease, sometimes as phobias and resistance patterns. The "reincarnated" wounds described by Ian Stevenson represent another aspect of a disturbed traumatic field, which transfers replicas of itself wherever it is drawn by psychic or morphogenetic resonance (see "The Biology of Reincarnation" in chapter 3).

So where the patient might look for the fear of breakdown is in the aura rather than the mind and memory. He or she should consider any "story" legitimate, no matter how supernatural or unlikely and fantastic. That is how past-life therapies can heal present-life traumas regardless of whether the past lives are "real." The stories are real; the meanings are real; the energy is real. Authentication is up for grabs, but then authentication is always up for grabs. There are no errors, only better and or worse representations of events the conscious mind can never directly perceive.

Trauma is not only energy frozen, it also is meaning withheld. The trauma exists in *order to be released,* to disseminate its healing power into the community and universe. Trauma biologist Peter A. Levine states this axiomatically:

> We have symptoms, but really trauma isn't about just getting rid of those symptoms. It's about accessing the energy, the frozen energy, that's locked within those symptoms, and bringing that energy back into our own being. . . . I see trauma, not as a pathology, but as an opportunity, because when we meet the challenge and really access the energy, this is a hero's journey, a hero's and a heroine's journey. . . . When we uncouple the fear, the paralysis . . . the immobility opens, and there's energy. The task in transforming trauma is to learn to live with that energy, to allow it to awaken within us, and to use the energy in the forward movement of our lives, to experience joy, vitality, spontaneity . . . freedom.[33]

A psychic exercise* like dissolving pictures in the aura can perturb an old karmic pattern and convert a psychologically regressive event into *a psychically energetic one*, often instantaneously—though it may also take repetition with accrual over days, months, years, or lifetimes. Other healing methods—yoga, chi gung, guided visualization, chant, prayer, cranial osteopathy, and the like—function similarly as *enantiodromias*—ritualized reversals releasing unconscious energies.

One can also construct a shrine, medicine bundle, or other sort of altar or totemically configured object to summon and conduct energy. Even though the ritual is personal, a larger field is invoked. It may not be clear whether the field gets activated at a psychic, psychosomatic, emotional, or interdimensional level, but it doesn't matter because these converge as needed once valid terms have been set. The macrocosm's overdetermination becomes its signature or similitude in the microcosm: this is the mechanism of ritual magic, astral botany, and the homeopathic microdose.

Again, one doesn't have to locate or identify the traumatic lesion, only to provide the quantum or tug needed, as if to slip a piece of string through a single tie of a tangled energetic necklace in order to release the trauma into the direction in which it is potentiated. Each knot has too many cords to specify in a single story or configuration anyway.

Winnicott described each "underlying primitive agony" as literally "unthinkable"; that is, of such a horrific nature that it is inconceivable that one would *try* to think it. Yet thinking it is *exactly* what one needs to do in order to get past its block into the neutral cosmic energy that constitutes its core.[34]

Public rituals of truth and reconciliation that bring victimizer and victim together not only allow reliving of a traumatic event in present time but also provide a ceremony for each party to disclose to the other

---

*A version of such an exercise, one with theosophical and Rosicrucian origins, is to place an image in a rose—you needn't "see" the image; it is sufficient to feel it energetically—to move the flower to the edge of one's aura and dissolve or explode it there. In ideal circumstances, the image activates and pulls along thousands of other unseen pictures from many lifetimes. Comparable Buddhist practices use *tulpas* like lotus flowers or divine beings for conversions and releases.

what happened for them and to recognize "self" in "other." Souls try desperately to grasp the polar aspects of their own nature.

Unless given an opportunity for absolution, the energy field of the abuser—murderer, enforcer, rapist, or sadist—proceeds in a septic cloud until it bursts or forms a meteor (metaphorical or metallic) in some cosmos, to pick up its pieces and kindle again with galactic dust. Universes come into being for such reasons, though they are imperceptible to the worlds they generate.

"You do not understand the dimensions into which your own thoughts drop," Seth tells his assembled listeners, "for they continue their own existences, and others look up to them and view them like stars. I am telling you that your own dreams and thoughts and mental actions appear to the inhabitants of other systems like the stars and planets within your own; and those inhabitants do not perceive what lies within and behind the stars in their own heavens."[35]

The universe transmutes thoughtforms across timeless time. In future theaters, long-ago agonies turn into gifts, talents, even superstar skills.

Tibetan lama Ngawang Tsoknyi Gyatso proposed that even if this planet were destroyed by nuclear bombs (or by greenhouse gases), it would be re-created from its karma elsewhere in the universe, and that doesn't just mean another planet in another galaxy; it also means that the thoughtforms generating this reality will continue generating it at a frequency of All That Is, and the rest will follow. If necessary, a whole other universe will appear. Tsoknyi Rinpoche couched his "physics" in punctilious Buddhist theory:

Even hundreds of thousands of nuclear bombs detonated at the same time will not stop dualistic mind from creating more emotions. If someone were to kill every single human being in this world, dualistic mind will still continue making emotions. Through the power of karma, all these minds would take rebirth in some other world and continue in the same way as before.[36]

That's how intrinsic the primal lesion and karma are.

Some crimes lodge at a community or nation level; for instance, the genocidal acts of paramilitary groups in Rwanda, Bosnia, Iraq, Sri Lanka, the American West, and the Australian outback. Others crystallize as a clan or family artifact. That's the "big game" that ideologues miss in their self-righteous interventions.

A few years ago, in my book *2013: Raising the Earth to the Next Vibration,* I wrote "This Is How I Think the Universe Works":

> Tribal elders from Jafferabad, southwestern Baluchistan Province, Pakistan, kidnapped three young women because they planned to marry men of their choosing. Hauled to a deserted area inside a vehicle bearing provincial government plates, they were beaten and shot and, while still alive, covered with earth and stones and buried. Two older women who tried to intervene were throttled and then thrown into the grave with them, alive too. Local senator Israr Ullah Zehri defended honor killings as "our norm" and said they should "not be highlighted negatively."
>
> A thousand or maybe a hundred thousand years from now these men will not remember this act they carried out. As whomever or whatever they are then, they will be different, and they may well oppose it. They will suffer an excruciatingly profound, elusive regret that must be exorcised and sublimated in whatever state grace finds them. But it will be way, way inside, at the deepest lode of their aura and karmic pattern, and they will futilely seek its mystery and meaning, the origin of inklings they feel, that they felt in another way while carrying out their cowardly act, killing the god they claimed to uphold.
>
> The fact that they are on the opposite ideological side by then will not change the imprint on their souls. The stain is indelible, but it can be turned into something beautiful if they will allow themselves to go through the anguish and reflect deeply enough on their parts and how they got there in that ancient life on Earth. They don't have to remember what Pakistan looked like. In fact, they can't.[37]

"I contend [writes Winnicott] that clinical fear of breakdown is the fear of a breakdown *that has already been experienced.* It is a fear of the original agony which caused the defence organization which the patient displays as an illness syndrome. [italics mine] This idea may or may not prove immediately useful to the clinician. We cannot hurry up our patients. Nevertheless, we can hold up their progress because of genuinely not knowing; any little piece of our understanding may help us to keep up with a patient's needs."[38]

Perhaps this is why folks keep reincarnating—those who do. Winnicott adds:

> There are moments, according to my experience, when a patient needs to be told that the breakdown, a fear of which destroys his or her life, has already been. It is a fact that is carried round hidden away in the unconscious. The unconscious here is not exactly the repressed unconscious of psychoneurosis, nor is it the unconscious of Freud's formulation of the part of the psyche that is very close to neurophysiological functioning. Nor is it the unconscious of Jung's which I would call all those things that go on in underground caves, or (in other words) the world's mythology, in which there is collusion between the individual and the maternal inner psychic realities. In this special context, the unconscious means that the ego integration is not able to encompass something. The ego is too immature to gather all the phenomena into the area of personal omnipotence.[39]

A definition of a "young soul" is that it thinks that it has committed no sins and suffered no traumas because *it doesn't yet know what they are.* Winnicott continues:

> It must be asked here: why does the patient go on being worried by this that belongs to the past? The answer must be that the original experience of primitive agony cannot get into the past tense unless the ego can first gather it into its own present time experience and into omnipotent control now (assuming the auxiliary ego-supporting function of the mother (analyst).
>
> In other words, the patient must go on looking for the past detail which is not yet experienced.[40]

At the level of cosmogenesis, this transfers from soul to soul, universe to universe. Who knows what antecedent suffering produced a Michael Jordan or Johann Sebastian Bach. Their moves (and chords) are expiating those events.

9

Worshipping the Algorithm

An algorithm is a set of rules for a sequence of operations. If the operations are being conducted by a computer, the rules are written by a programmer to elicit a desired outcome in an efficient manner. If there is no programmer and the computer is the universe, the rules are set by thermodynamic and gravitational laws operating on the outcomes of random events. Either there is a desired outcome *or* all outcomes are pertinent and irrelevant to the same degree.

What I am coronating here as "the algorithm" is science's rules for the evolution of the universe since the Big Bang, rules that also guard against metaphysical effects or divine interference. The algorithm is not implicated otherwise; it is a neutral bystander without a dog in the hunt. Because it has no operator except the laws of physics and their application to an original hot universe and since creatures with a capacity for thought weren't in the original set of instructions, they *have to be* chance effects of gravity, thermodynamic activity, and combinations of contingent events in the universe, the Milky Way galaxy, the solar system, and on Earth. Mind cannot barge in *sui generis* and hijack the coach. That is why consciousness has no ontological standing. This is territory I have covered from many angles, but I haven't personified the algorithm until now.

While the presumption is that a programmer-less algorithm is as inefficient as it gets, the universe had limitless time, so it didn't have to be efficient. In fact, its potpourri of positive and negative feedback gave it capacity for creativity and novelty. Given that and the nearly fourteen billion years that have elapsed since the Big Bang, scientists believe that an algorithm can make just about anything out of original bosons and fermions (or out of anything else). Every object and artifact—every pebble and methane droplet, every gnat and duck-billed platypus, every sensation and thought, every feeling *about* every sensation and thought—are algorithmic effects. They have to be. The paintings on the walls of Lascaux and Chauvet, the philosophies of Parmenides, Augustine, and Einstein, Bach's organ music, and the Kabbalistic Tree of Life each arose in the infinitely reflecting grottos of a mathematical function replicating only itself. They came from heat, mass, gravity, and quantum gravity. The universe didn't have to make mice or Einsteins here, or anywhere—but as long as it did, it played by its own rules. It also didn't have to know what it was making in order to make it.

Artificial Intelligence is algorithmic intelligence because there is no irresolvable difference between it (electronic circuits and software) and us (neural circuits and DNA). Both simulate logic using symbols (see my discussion of AI in chapter 1). Terrence Deacon set the evolutionary ratio in immaculate informational terms:

> Nature itself produced minds by blind trial and error. . . . [A] theoretical understanding of the nature of mind is not an essential ingredient for producing them. . . . Mind is a physical process, and physical processes can be copied whether we understand what we are copying or not.[1]

Even the algorithm came out of the algorithm and created its own capacity for recursion. It is an algorithm's algorithm. It does everything God used to do without His imperious stagecraft or vulgar oversplash. It is the God of modernity: impersonal, minimal, microsoft.

The Cult of the Algorithm

The cult of the algorithm is imposed by social contract, ideological gendarmerie, and subliminal seepage. Everyone buys into it—long-haul truck drivers, erotic dancers, chaps crunching concrete with steam shovels and laying pipe under cracked stone—despite their honest day's labor and hard-earned victories over entropy. Politicians preach it to their constituents, no matter what else they bloviate: "Make hay while the sun is shining [meaning the local hydrogen-helium aster]. You only go around once, so grab for all the gusto you can get!"

It is taught in most schools of religion, reinforced by socioeconomic imperatives, and serviced by a pharmaceutical industry with profits from the symptomatic relief of mental and physical states caused by—what else?—a sense of meaninglessness and loss of identity. Worship of the algorithm is broadcast openly and telepathically from the capital control centers of our species, calls to prayer from invisible temples, decoy ideologies, and admen-perpetrated façades.

The algorithm is even disseminated by those whose beliefs refute it. Mainstream religious authorities reinforce its hegemony by ideologically challenging it while otherwise behaving *in full and complete compliance.* That's how locked down the paradigm is.

Anyone who doubts it is considered a wimp, a fool, or a jerk. According to Larry Dossey, in *What Is Consciousness?* modern folks "actually prefer annihilation with physical death to any sort of survival. Longing for immortality is seen as a defect of character or a philosophical sellout in people too weak-willed to face their impending doom. In the face of certain extermination, one should simply man up and go quietly, proudly, and gravely into that dark night."[2]

Mortality is modernity's boot camp and initiation rite.

A college friend, Sidney Schwab, spoke eloquently on behalf of "blind trial and error" in an Amherst class chatroom debate:

Nowadays I barely have a concept of yesterday. Who can grok billions of years? I can't, but I'm pretty sure it's enough time for evolution to make a brain. It can make MRSA overnight, after all. There are billions of planets in billions of galaxies. There may or may not be life somewhere else; and if there is, it may or may not resemble ours. That we are who we are is remarkable, but demands some sort of nonphysical explanation only to the extent that we're unable to see ourselves as a very unlikely result of random happenings. The chances are one in who knows how many billions of billions that life (whatever it is) happened here, of all places? But it did, and here we are. If it hadn't, we wouldn't be. That's the least and most of what there is to it. That there are, presumably, countless non-life-bearing galaxies serves to confirm that, rather than a result of intent, we're a happy accident. All the more reason we need to enjoy it while we can, in whatever way we can, without adding more mystery. Unless it's what you need. In which case it's cool. Part of the mystery.[3]

The algorithm turns everything into a numbers game. After all, that's what *it* is. The *coup de grace* is to assign every event or structure or whim to three billion years of feedback by natural selection.

Intelligent Design and Creationism are no match for the algorithm. Claims that living systems are *too* complex to be the work of mindless selection impose architecture on a calculus that doesn't require it. Evolutionists have the mathematics and molecules to back their position up, with margin to spare. If the algorithm can make MRSA overnight, it can make an autogene in three billion years. It can flip phenomena into phenomenology and replicate them in DNA-differentiating blastulas billions of times a second on any suitable planet. It can create the master theater on Earth—the "first" person ("*je*," "I," "*ich*," "*yo*," "*nuy*"), what the bloke-in-the-street calls "me-self."

In his next post, Sidney dismissed nonlocal mind with a spree of unassailable logic:

Why, for example, if past lives/reincarnation are a thing, do so few people—mere handfuls, compared to all the lives lived and living— think they know of them? Why only under "hypnosis?" What would be "the point," if there's no recollection? I watch my grandson discover the world and find it wondrous; but I see no evidence of influence of a prior life. (Why not, at least, be born knowing how to use a toilet?) If everything must be relived and re-acquired and re-learned, is there a point to it? Doesn't seem like part of a larger truth. And I can't help but be tied to the notions of self and brain function. I suppose reincarnation is a gift given only to a few. Do all of those have access to their prior lives? What distinguishes them from the billions and billions who don't and didn't? If my mom's in heaven, did she go there in her final state of dementia? Or did she unwind to a certain point? Age 60? 20? Did she get to choose? If not, how does it work? And what of children who die agonizing and premature deaths at the hand of our loving god? Do they stay three years old? Or do they age like bottles of wine? It's pretty clear, neurophysiologically, that who we are is intimately related to what goes on in our brains. Does metabolism have a heavenly form? If our souls are that which is independent of such matters, in what way do we relate, in heaven or wherever people like me will find themselves, to who we were? If it's an entirely different existence lasting for all of eternity, what's the point of this immeasurably brief time in physical form? If it's a test-run to determine our level of reward, isn't it a little disproportionate? It'd be like having my two-year-old grandson take the SAT and determine the rest of his life from that. Only a billion trillion zillion times more unfair. If god has a plan for us all, why not just plunk us into heaven and get it over with? Less than the single vibration of an electron, in cosmic time, to determine all eternity?[4]

All reasonable points by an astute retired surgeon. But in presuming that these are the right questions to ask of the universe, Sidney also assumes the universe is following the "logic" he expects it to follow. What if the universe is running deeper algorithms?

Sidney is playing possum, bottoming out the universe short of itself—and the universe is who he is debating, not the guys in the chatroom.

Whether life can arise from a dynamic disequilibrium of billiard-ball effects is *both* an epistemological and ontological riddle. Science and religion are finally metanarratives that give rise to each other, for an algorithm generating galaxies and roses, cobras and tardigrades out of quarks and baling wire could be a god generating them out of divine intelligence or a nonlinear gyre writing the flap of every butterfly's wings on an ineffable hard drive. Since we can't source the algorithm's dawn kōan in our psyche or read it in the universe at large, we don't see where gods and gravities trade hats or what mandate put a flower in a crannied wall.*

Beyond the paradigmatic crunch of fundamentalist biblicism and fundamentalist scientism lie the actual vastness and complexity of nature, from nebulae and tides to the orbits of electrons and dives of jellyfish—what Alfred North Whitehead called "process and reality," a network of interrelated subprocesses that feed back into each other and give form and expression to information, creating "planes of existence" as far as they extend.

The only map of the territory *is* the territory, and the territory is infinite.

Novelty and Complexity

As we hiked together in Maine, I asked another college classmate, Jeffrey Hoffman, a retired NASA astronaut and now a space scientist at MIT, if he accepted his guild's premise of a Big Bang occurring "in the middle of nowhere for no reason."

I was citing entheogenic philosopher Terrence McKenna's 1998 brief: "Let's look at what the competition is peddling. What the competition would have you believe is that the universe sprang from nothing in a single moment for no reason. . . . That is the limit case for credulity. If you can believe that, you can believe anything. I challenge you to top it. I know that the scientologists think that God is a clam on another planet, but I don't think that tops this idea."[5]

Jeff objected to the phrase "for no reason." "'Reason' is anthropomorphic," he reminded me, "and the universe doesn't operate on human terms." Later, he added,

As science progresses from generation to generation, its view of the universe changes. A hundred or five hundred years from now, our current paradigm may look as dated as the universe before Copernicus

---

*In 1863, British poet Alfred Tennyson wrote that if he could understand the tiny blossom he had plucked, *"root and all, and all in all,"* he could *"know what God and man is."*

and Newton does to us now. Scientists used epicycles then to describe position and motion without a sense of the forces that would organize those epicycles. We're in the same position today. How can anyone believe they have a complete description of the universe when they are missing most of it: dark matter and dark energy? There may not be a "reason," but one thing is clear, the universe goes from very simple and lacking much structure in the hot environment after the Big Bang to increasing complexity: molecules, chemical compounds, life, and then consciousness.[6]

McKenna agreed, nineteen years earlier:

Why doesn't science take on board, as a major problem in the description of nature, the emergence of complexity? You ask a scientist, and they say, "Well, these are separate domains of nature. How atoms become molecules has nothing to do with how animals become human beings." This is bullshit. . . . The understanding of the fractal ordering of nature now makes it clear that voting patterns in Orange County, distribution of anemones on the Great Barrier Reef, and the cratering of Europa all follow the same power laws. . . .

The second thing that science has staring it in the face and has refused to take on board is that this process of complexification . . . as you approach the place in time called the present, happens faster and faster. . . . Since these processes have been running since the Big Bang, there is no argument to be maintained that they will reverse themselves suddenly. No, they're not going to reverse themselves after thirteen billion years—duh! . . .

The universe is under the influence of a strange attractor* . . . pulled toward an ultimate denouement as well as pushed by the unfolding of causal necessity. It's an engine for the generation of complexity, and it preserves complexity, [as] it builds on complexity to ever higher levels. If you entertain this, guess what happens? It's like a light comes on on the human condition. . . .

*Strange attractors have a fractal structure and organize chaotic systems.

Who are we in my story? In science's story, we are nobody; we are lucky to be here; we are a cosmic accident; we exist on an ordinary star at the edge of a typical galaxy in an ordinary part of space and time, and essentially our existence is without meaning, or you have to perform one of those existential pas de deux where you confirm meaning—one of these postmodern soft shoes.

But if I'm right that the universe has an appetite for novelty, then we are the apple of its eye. Suddenly cosmic purpose is restored to us. People matter, you are the cutting edge of a thirteen-billion-year-old process of defining novelty. Your acts matter, your thoughts matter.

Your purpose? To add to the complexity.

Your enemy? Disorder, entropy, stupidity, and tastelessness.

Suddenly you have a morality, you have an ethical arrow, you have contextualization in the processes of nature, you have meaning. You have authenticity, you have hope. You have the cancellation of existentialism and positivism and all that late-twentieth-century crapola.[7]

We can still hope for that—that consciousness, having come so far through matter, has ballast and momentum beyond the imperative of its reptile brain. Our fate is going to be a cliffhanger, though, for a "reign of quantity"* has been reenforced by the algorithm, giving positivists their ultimate Molten Calf.

The Corporate Takeover of Reality

This is a book about consciousness, but it is consciousness under capitalism. I can't change that fact, no matter what I write. We "sell" our ideas, our literary styles, our words. We don't intend to, but persuasion is built into language and tone. Under the circumstances, I have tried to make *Bottoming Out* sell-neutral, but it is of its time and there are only so many voices available. I am trying to say that science is *not* sell-neutral, not anymore. Electrons, quarks, quanta, and the like are products, intellectual

---

*French metaphysical philosopher Réné Guénon coined this term during World War II to depict the essential hollowness of the modern world (its metaphysics, by the way, as well).

currency. Their value vanishes at the burning of the Amazon and the suicides of Native American youths.

What scientistic liberals miss is the subtext with which they have saddled themselves. Rationalism and empiricism mask a marriage of science and capitalism for the crony takeover of reality. The algorithm has been blackmailed into converting everything into commodities and cash flow, hiding the theft in its own quantitative depth. I say "everything" because even parsecs of space and zettagrams of meteor dust are used to inflate the algorithm and make its hegemony inviolable.

When twenty-six individuals hold more wealth than the poorer half of humanity—almost four billion people—and displaced carbon imposes an accelerating greenhouse, the algorithm is no longer a neutral bystander. Its ledgers are protected by mercenary armies and bought politicians using industrial ordnance, programmed assassinations, redaction of whistleblowers and reporters, and incitement of populist envy and rage. The privileged, as journalist Chris Hedges prophetically put it, are engaged in "a mad scramble . . . to survive at the expense of the poor."[8]

Charles Stein, a mathematician as well as a poet, nails the root deception:

> Today's financial sphere already has manifested ten times as much money as is required to buy everything in the world; but in principle an infinite amount of money is available because no limit can control the infinite production of numbers. You need the numbers in excess of everything that you need to count it for. But then, you need infinite numbers to count the numbers, and you need money to measure the possible price of money forever. "That one man must eventually have all the money" (Ed Dorn*) used to be called a proof of the existence of god. . . .
>
> *until the bottom in reality falls out and there is nothing*
> *but number, nothing but information, nothing*

---

*American poet, 1929–1999, author of *Idaho Out, Some Business Recently Transacted in the White World, Gunslinger,* and others.

but MONEY
computers in vacuo
having discovered how to provide themselves
with the minimal hardware and electricity
to keep them computing . . . and the entire informable universe
decrypted as a database

simultaneously transparent and unhackable
a non-duality of clarity and opacity

when consciousness disappears into computability

and the stone of the wise
degrades.[9]

Marrying the algorithm to an international market has decimated villages, towns, and cities, transferring mercados and shops to the internet while furbishing communities into ghost towns of opiates and trifles. Capital flows to where it gets its greatest return; the algorithm sets no limit on that. If you want to know why there are homeless encampments in First World cities and nationless fugitives adrift between worlds, look to the algorithm. In its personalized march from the terror of its own infinitude, it discards the weak, the old, the luckless, the lame, and finally the rest until no one and nothing are left. Under the banner of "let freedom ring," capital shoves everything into its great maw.

A bizarre twist has been put on things. Modernity's mirror has gone flat and noncongruent, but that doesn't mean there's nothing there. We are living in a diminishment of the actual world, outside a vastness that is running parallel to us, sweeping us up.

Hyperobjects

According to the term's innovator, literary philosopher Timothy Morton, *hyperobjects* are "entities that are massively distributed in time and space, at least relative to human scales. . . . [They] are viscous, molten, nonlocal, phased, and inter-objective. . . . They appear in the human world as products of our thinking through the ecological crisis we have entered. . . . [T]his is the moment at which massive nonhuman, nonsentient entities make decisive contact with humans, ending various human concepts such as world, horizon, nature, and even environment."[10]

So hypnotized are we by smart phones and social media that we don't fully register the real world anymore, let alone the hyperobjects all around us, from climate and failed states, favelas and warlords and mass displacement of people, to nuclear arsenals, radioactive waste, and plastic. Each is too bewilderingly vast to be comprehended as what it is, so we know it in fragments, proxies, or copacetic imitations. Hyperobjects are not only too large and discontinuous for comprehension, their cultural and natural aspects also continually displace each other, sabotaging common identity.

We try to antidote each hyperobject by another, and it isn't working, even with high technologies, because the algorithm is itself a hyperobject. You can't move an entire sun-star, let alone one you can't see.

Waves of fragmentation and depersonalization have splintered our civilization to near unrecognizability. Craft and mastery have been sucked out of governance and culture as they are regurgitated by a fiber-optic maze of forged and rhetorical substitutes.

Yes, artificial intelligence will replace us if we cede it our lien. Twentieth-century occultist P. D. Ouspensky foresaw as much when he warned that for every new power a machine grants us, a human power is taken away. The rise of artificial intelligence has made human intelligence more and more artificial and human reality less and less real.

We are giving up the freedom and capacity to create our own thoughtforms, transferring it to robots, which are of course created by thoughtforms too, but strictured ones that take no prisoners and give no exemptions nor know the meaning of grace, nor could.

Worshipping the algorithm in lieu of God or Spirit has diminished mystery, texture, honor, and creativity and introduced a synthetic era, the Anthropocene, with *Homo sapiens* its defining geological and meteorological force.

The algorithm's viscosity means there is no evasion: the more one tries to dodge or resist it, the deeper one's entrapment becomes. The algorithm's massive distribution in time and space distorts both X and Y axes, melting their previously infinite containers; its bottomless configurations appear everywhere and nowhere—and elsewhere. Assignment to security number and password is followed by adware, remarketing, encryption blackmail, ghosting, identity theft, and finally deportation or incarceration (figurative or actual). There is no constabulary to turn to: mad kings and priests occupy the thrones and pulpits, deputizing graft, hypocrisy, and doublespeak, not because they want to (even though they do), but because algorithm worship has made alternatives lame and spurious. Might as well look for an igloo or island without video surveillance or facial-recognition software; industrial fallout and methane follow. "We find ourselves," Morton warns, "unable to achieve epistemological escape velocity from ontological density."[11]

The algorithm's distribution produces a nonsentient, nonlocal "configuration space"—a "mesh" in which there are only hyperobjective imprints on other objects. The algorithm's strange attractors spawn virally recombining conspiracies, "inverting," Morton notes "what is real and what is only appearance."[12]

Fidelity is obscured by a flood of information backing up at least three centuries. We can't absorb its testimony or underwrite its debt at anything like the rate at which it is being produced, so we can't sort our way to what it means. Most of it is meaningless anyway—algorithmic overrun, spurious rumor, data debris.

The Hardy Boys placed a Sinister Signpost in the fifties, but we hardly saw it or knew it for what it was. They tried to say: *The Broken Blade . . . The Melting Coins . . . The Secret Panel . . . The Phantom Freighter . . . The Hidden Harbor . . . The Tower Treasure . . . The Clue in the Embers*. . . . Those names made it across Y2K with deconsecrated editions of the books, but the titles meant something occult and magical that the words no longer say. As a host of cyborgs, superheroes, and Harry Potters captured Middle Earth, Narnia, and Earthsea, the great Sphinx was scaled and desecrated without its mystery being solved.

While culture and nature are collaborating on hyperobjects, spirit guides, angels, and souls are collaborating on meta-objects—hypersubjectivities. These *are* sentient; they are also nonlocal, phased, and too vast to be grasped by humans. *Listen!* Life and consciousness are resilient and inscrutable; that's algorithmic depth too. Even climate is subject to latent human capacities and subtle energies in nature.

The world may have shrunk from its context, but the rest is still there and advancing. We live in a self-imposed exile that keeps everyone in meager ambitions and acts, the rich with their goods and recreations as circumscribed and destitute as the poor. Meanwhile reality is creating unknown realms we have already entered. It's time to pause and consider—not anything in particular but the whole shebang.

Is matter the only merchandise, capital its sole measure? Is the algorithm a map or an antimap, the path or the maze?

Ask *the universe* what's happening, guys! Don't *tell* the universe what it's doing. *Ask it!* There's no downside. We are doing it all the time anyway.

PART THREE

Simulations

All those impulses of love return to the love that made them. Even memory is not necessary for love. There is a land of the living and the land of the dead and the bridge is love, the only survival, the only meaning.

THORNTON WILDER,
THE BRIDGE OF SAN LUIS REY

10

Personal Identity

Shadow Selves: An Editorial as Prologue

On December 14, 2012, twenty-year-old Adam Lanza took a Bushmaster rifle and three hundred rounds of ammunition to Sandy Hook Elementary School, where he killed as many first-graders (twenty) and affiliated adults (six) as he could in the time allotted. Reality was a video game to him, and he was competing against a Norwegian sociopath's score. Afterward, he turned a Glock on himself. His way out of Dodge was to end the game.

Like many who are depressed and suicidal, he wanted to be (to cite Andrew Solomon in *The Noonday Demon*) "null, beyond sorrow . . . freed from the affliction of consciousness . . ."[1] He deemed that beingness turned into nothingness without an intervening state, for what could exist on the other side of death if, as Solomon wrote, "the human spirit is no more than a temporary chemical arrangement"?[2]

He expected to disappear—in essence and sum—to get released from the assorted fixes he was in, the legendary nightmare from which we cannot awake.*

It isn't that far from "a light goes on, a light goes off, but it wasn't even a light" to "they're not real people, so who gives a shit!" Lanza didn't think that, but it was in the air he breathed, the electrons he sucked off

---

*An oft-quoted reference found in James Joyce's *Ulysses:* "History, Stephen said, is a nightmare from which I am trying to awake."

the internet. Regarding his self as a toss of cosmic dice, he had no basis for personal morality. He assumed that the oil slick known to him as "Adam Lanza"—its misery as well as responsibility for his crime—would be eradicated for good. What would happen to him was what he told himself would happen: *Nothing happens. Nothing happens forever.*

But the notion that personhood can be discontinued is little more than a throw of dice when neither physicists nor priests *know what consciousness is*—what turns on its light, what happens after its synapses are disconnected.

What if, with the light off, each person sinks to the propensity of *what he or she is*? Perhaps death snaps the narrative but not the vortex from which it is arising. What if willful interference with a karmic pattern breaks critical links, leaving one in some sort of purgatory?

In choosing suicide, mass murderers Eric Harris, Dylan Klebold, Adam Lanza, Seung-Hui Cho, Stephen Paddock, and others of their ilk meant to raze their social identities and everything that could be identified as them or traced to them, but not *themselves.* My guess is, they did not believe in their own nonexistence, and they could not "conceive of not being"; they could "conceive of the absence of experience but not of absence itself."[3]

Islamic jihadists assume they are punching their tickets to paradise. Same deal as Lanza and Harris: you woke up one place, you'll wake up another—or not.

Women volunteering for explosive vests before boarding a bus in Tel Aviv or Colombo City are taught that the moment will be over before neurons can deliver the unhappy message to their brain. Any discomfort is as fleeting and minimal as a pinprick. Then nothing—or bliss!

Thenmozhi Rajaratnam, Mohammed Atta, Sana'a Mehaidi, Wafa Idris Arafat, and countless others weaponized themselves to dissolve death pictures of the transnational state. From their view, the West was a fair target: a heresy zone of corpses in mimetic life.

These were neither lone-wolf acts nor calculated strikes of asymmetrical warfare. They were ancestral fields seeking to equilibrate or discharge eons of violence and theft.

Contrary to their intents, recreational killers and jihadists are giving voice to a deeper terror: "Something is happening. It's really big and it's really real, and I can't stop it. You don't believe me? You won't listen? *Well then, let me show you!*"

Would that the next jihad, a hundred or a hundred thousand years from now, tips the clash of tribes into a rainbow body joining the living and dead in one community, conscious death its calling card.

The Relation between Consciousness and Personal Identity

Where primal biological energy—Freud called it the id—encounters an epigenetically emerging membrane, a provisional identity forms. The nascent ego contacts a world (its environment) through its own primitive sensations. As it matures, a habitat and society impose rules and mores, grafting a superego—a juridicial "self."

In traditional psychology, self is the biodynamic charge of the id individuated by the ego and civilized by the superego.

In psychospiritual terms, a dimensionless spirit-soul contacts the microcosmic realm. Through its karmic predispositions, the positioning of the cosmos at its conception and birth, and various archetypes, it molds a transient psyche. During fetal and social development, the psyche-soul projects a "self."

We are also hatched in a hierarchical system of orbs generated by molecules under gravity's curvature: Earth . . . Sol . . . Solar System . . . Milky Way . . . Laniakea supercluster (100,000 galaxies stretching over 500 million light years) . . . Universe. Our bodies are orbs too: blastulas emerging from prior blastulas going back to jellyfish.

Consciousness is at once an illusion and the only thing that is *not* an illusion.

Personal identity is the turnkey; it differs from consciousness in that it recognizes itself *as itself*. It is how consciousness inserts itself into a universe that does not otherwise express agency. When the self experiences *its own* existence, things seem to happen to it as an individual, divorced from all other individuals. That is a radical situation, even in as simple an entity as a worm.

Consciousness can run on autopilot—a robot has artificial intelligence—but *personal identity is what makes consciousness conscious,* able to represent itself *consciously.* It is how individual beingness comes to know that it exists. Otherwise, consciousness doesn't notice itself or its plight.

The surprise is how creatures take to it like ducks to water. According to Seth, "[T]he miracle of physical materialization is performed so smoothly and automatically that consciously you are not aware of your part in it. . . . Nature is created from within."[4]

Personal identity is where the ladle of being scrapes its other absolute bottom—the fully rinsed gravel of matter. A worm is *chemotactically* aware of its surroundings and agency. A fox or swordfish is *cognitively* aware of both but doesn't distinguish its subjective beingness from external reality. A human not only differentiates its state of being from nature but also is aware that *it* is what is aware—and that transforms the universe.

As biologist George Wald put it, "A physicist is the atom's way of knowing about atoms."[5]

Quantum Entanglement and Consciousness

Painter Charles Rasmussen, a keen observer, noticed a bumblebee tumbling in the pollen of a wild rose, seeming to enjoy itself. A spider who had made his web in the same rugosa was perturbed by the intruder's entitlement. He jabbed at it with one of his legs.

As the spider's pokes disturbed its rapture, the bee became agitated. It interrupted its nectar bath, shot out of the stamens buzzing, got a flying start of a few yards, and dive-bombed, whacking the spider so hard he was nearly plunked out of his own web.

If that's not personal identity and road rage, what is it? Mindless reflex? Chemicals under protolibidinal charge hitting tipping points via trillionfold quantum switches? Atomic strings synapsing through their own uncertainty states into microtubules and ganglionic webs?

There are not enough neurons in a spider or bee to achieve "I," let alone affect and volition, so who is poking and who is having its reverie disturbed? That is science's ultimate riddle: not only *what* is consciousness but also *who* is conscious and how does "who" become "I"? Beyond neuroscientific gerrymanders of nerve nets and ganglia, the lone candidate is quantum effects inside neurons.

Yet quantum superposition and entanglement* only translate across zones of very tiny things into *other* quantum states. You can't quantum-entangle bees or horses; meteors never get entangled. Paradoxically, you don't have to quantum-entangle horses for them to be quantum-entangled. The quantum universe is not stowed behind subatomic barriers where it safely spins away without impact on thermodynamics or animal behavior. Its quantum aspect is intrinsic and takes place at every instant in every atom in every molecule. It is essential to the makeup and bonding of molecules and cells because it is essential to the makeup of atoms.

"The quintessential quantum effect, entanglement," avows physicist Vlatko Vedral, "can occur in large systems as well as warm ones—including living organisms . . . those effects are camouflaged by their own sheer complexity. They are there if you know how to look . . . and are more pervasive than anyone ever suspected. They may operate in the cells of our body."[6]

If horses weren't quantum-entangled, they wouldn't be conscious (they wouldn't even have mass). But I suspect that, contrary to the "wave function collapse" of Hameroff and Penrose, they are not conscious because they are entangled; rather, they are entangled because they are conscious. The physical realm expresses quantum entanglement not because of its subatomic particles but because of an underlying entangled state that gives rise to *both*. Mind permeates matter at a much subtler rung than the Penrose-Hameroff induction, so what we interpret as particle activity—information, relationship, spin—may be an afterburn of swarms as infinitesimally remote in scale from quarks as quarks are from molecules (or perhaps galaxies—who can know?).

In any case, quantum fluctuations are what made the Newtonian uni-

---

*Quantum entanglement is a phenomenon whereby two or more subatomic particles are generated, interact, or stay connected to each other in ways such that the quantum state of each cannot be described independently of the state of the others, even if the particles get separated by a great distance. In principle, they could end up in different galaxies without becoming "disinformationed" or unentangled.

verse Newtonian, albeit a specter in Newton's time. Newton the alchemist may have intuited occult forces behind celestial movement, but he had no way of sounding the Philosopher's Stone at its minuteness of scale.

There is another wrinkle: material reality seems to need the intervention of consciousness to *become* material or to exist *at all*. Without the view of an observer, reference points in the quantum realm disintegrate into probabilities and alternate realities. But an observer must be made of atoms made of entangled particles and quantum computers too. How do objective and subjective views of the "same" circumstance resolve this paradox? There may be no *physical* solution except in the nature of measurement, the vector spaces themselves.

In the transactional interpretation of quantum mechanics, teleological directives collide and combine as sources simultaneously emit waves forward and backward in time. Recipient points, ahead of them in time, emit their own pair: an advanced wave (backward) and a usual wave (forward). When a "handshake" of waves occurs, it triggers a quantum event, a transaction in which energy, momentum, and angular momentum are transferred.

Each particle is not so much a wave wrapped up into a ball as the front of a wave, a one-dimensional point moving through a "possibility" space that, as it becomes observed, unfolds into a particle whose physical tendencies materialize from interference patterns in its field.

The primary particles—muons, gluons, protons, mesons, electrons, and so on—might not be distinctly different things but rather the same formation at successive frequencies of time. They differ *ex post facto* by phase, charge, spin, and as vibrations in a quantum field. They may not even exist apart from the mirroring of the observer, in which their mirages fuse, dissipate, revert, and turn into each other. A universe that collapses its own wave function to arrive at definitiveness of property and locale is a universe that *arises from the collapse of a wave function* as mind continuously unlocks and relocks the lock that imbeds it into nature.

According to historian of magic Robert Podgurski, "Physicists can only theorize and work on probabilities in quantum research, whereas magicians, whether they have known it or not, manipulate the quanta themselves in practice . . . with the mind's nonphysical eye."[7]

Intention doesn't (and can't) generate form directly, so it sends sigils and similitudes into quantum fields. The occult universe and the physical universe conduct their own handshake by which we are all magicians, initiated at birth. Seth posited the handshake's origination:

> All That Is, before the beginning, contained within itself the infinite thrust of all <u>possible</u> creations. All That Is possessed a creativity of such magnificence that its slightest imaginings, dreams, thoughts, feelings or moods attained a kind of reality, a vividness, an intensity, that almost demanded freedom. . . .
>
> The experience, the subjective universe, the "mind" of All That Is, was so brilliant, so distinct, that All That Is almost became lost, mentally wandering within this ever-flourishing, ever-growing interior landscape. Each thought, feeling, dream, or mood was itself indelibly marked with all the attributes of this infinite subjectivity. Each glowed and quivered with its own creativity, its own desire to create as it had been created. . . .
>
> Thoughts of such magnificent vigor began to <u>think their own</u> thoughts—and their thoughts thought thoughts. As if in divine astonishment and surprise, All That Is began to listen, and began to respond to these "generations" of thoughts and dreams. . . .
>
> It is very difficult to try to assign anything like human motivation to All That Is. I can only say that it is possessed by the "need" to . . . lovingly transform its own reality in such a way that each most slight probable consciousness can come to be . . .[8]

We originated with the first thoughts, but we didn't know ourselves yet; it took a universe to accomplish that.

A mystery remains: How? Why? What is the nature of our own presence as well as presence itself? When materialists say, "I didn't exist before I was imprinted from DNA," the issue becomes, Where were you? "Who" wasn't you? Or as a Looney Tunes cartoon put it, "How'd ya get in the tub, bub?"

And once in, how do you get out?

Death

Back then I was a teenager holding a plastic skull; now I'm an old man holding my own skull."

My childhood friend Philip Wohlstetter,
who played Hamlet in college at Columbia

In Woody Allen's movie *Café Society,* a husband tells his wife he's not afraid of death. The wife says, "You're too stupid to understand the implications."

Allen's joke has two meanings: one (his), the husband is too stupid to realize that his identity vanishes for good. In the words of another movie character (Clint Eastwood as William Munny in *Unforgiven*), "Death takes away everything you have and everything you're going to have." The second (mine) is that death opens you to your greater being. It *gives* you everything you have and everything you are going to have. (That would have been even *further* above the husband's pay grade.)

It rarely occurs to people in an ordinary way that this vivid emanation ends, always in death. Contrary to each dawn's early light, no one stays here forever, nor do Earth and sun.

Immortality may sound attractive, but it's impractical, psychologically as well as ecologically. To be any single thing forever would lead to dementia or running out of bandwidth. Plus, for some creatures, death is the only release from servitude or pain. Jane Roberts notes that it is "the way out of what would otherwise be a dimensional dilemma in which further development would be impossible."[9] Life would become a "life" sentence without hope of reprieve or parole. Instead, mortality is a welcome annulment of the soul's marriage to the body. For the ego, the universe goes black, but the ego was one form of the soul. "[I]ts inviolate nature is not betrayed," Seth consoles "It is simply no longer physical. . . . [It] knows it exists beyond its form."[10]

In insect metamorphosis, a larval form is melted down and a new set of genetic instructions is introduced, leading to a moth or butterfly. In human metamorphosis, the transition takes place in another dimension, so we don't see the intervening stage or dormant phase.

At each death, the source "I" reemerges from its ego-self as the recently lived life melds with the Atman, the fractal monad of Divine Consciousness and sum of all its incarnations. The soul gains access to all its lifetimes. By Roberts's trope, "[C]onsciousness is condensed [like a Black Hole] and 'born back' into the same probable system."[11] She knights "consciousness," but she deems "identity." When personal identity is condensed, it becomes transparent, first to its just-completed lifetime and paling mind, then to its God or gods, then to the terror of its own profundity (including sins, regrets, and presumptive hell realms)—then to itself *as itself*. Everything that has gotten (or gets) in the way *becomes the way*. What other compass is there?

The soul sometimes chooses to live multiple lives at once or to keep parts of itself in spirit while others manifest in bodies. A woman I heard speak at a 2019 consciousness conference recalled a dream portraying the rebirth of her recently deceased husband. Eventually, she met the woman identified as his new mother. Her daughter, now five, showed striking resemblances of style and behavior to the speaker's late spouse. Yet "he" was still appearing to her in other guises, plus their friends described moments when his persona imbued a room. As a soul, s/he was already many selves and possible selves, able to incarnate or visit from outside of time according to summons and intent.

Once we consider death in terms of the heterogeneity of the soul, possible past and present lives align for, as we saw with Katie and Nogorigatu, our larger beings are not marionettes in an irreversible flow. Each life is not only a future of any past lifetime, it also is a past of any future life it will have. James Huston is a past self of James Leininger; James Leininger is a future self of James Huston. What would it feel like to have a future self of yours show up? You would be alive again only because *you were already dead.*

The ambiguity of this situation asserts itself when we try to contact the dead. They adopt semblances—ghosts, spirits, ectoplasm, and so on—like the holographic recording left by Princess Leia for Obi-Wan Kenobi in *Star Wars*. That fictional technology was at least time-stamped. The relationship of a dead person to someone still alive is chronologically indeterminate in *both* their auras.

When psychic medium Salicrow did a reading for me in Montpelier, Vermont (August 22, 2016), she began by inviting any being who wanted to come in peace, love, and healing. Then she told me that a woman had been seated behind me the whole time.

We were not meeting for mediumship but to talk about a prospective book by her. After our publishing discussion, I asked her to show me the sort of thing she did, so she obliged. Eyes closed, lips moving, she silently channeled the visitor. Following each exchange with it, she put into words what she had received—a mix, she said, of the spirit's thoughts and pictures. In the process, she brought to life a believable representation of my mother, Martha Rothkrug, who had committed suicide by jumping from her window in New York City forty-two years earlier.

Sali relayed accurate facts from my mother's life. More profoundly, she captured my mother's personality and way of presenting herself. The "ghost" filled in details of Martha's youth unknown to me and spoke of events that had occurred since her death. It expressed pride in my daughter Miranda, identifying her as a woman in her lineage who had transcended the traumas of the family.

Though the visitation was compelling, it didn't change my mother's thread for me; instead, it created a new thread, that of my mother's ghost. The ghost apologized for things that my mother had done and thanked me for turning her damage into healing. It moved me to tears.

When I discussed the episode with John Friedlander, he offered his own interpretation—that the spirit, though real, was not a continuation of my mother. It was a medley of things. First, it was Sali's telepathic scanning of my own aura. My mother's aura had unconsciously deposited information there while she was alive, stuff from the future as well as the past. The karmic thread of our relationship, flowing across incarnations outside space-time, could be read by a necromancer without my mother's contemporaneous beingness. In fact, Sali had hooked into an inner dimension of my mother that had more awareness and wisdom than the woman I knew.

Sali also consulted spirit guides familiar with my mother and her situation; she read Martha Rothkrug's "bio" in the Akashic records. All these vectors came together psychically in the spirit's intersection with Sali.

The entity was a piece left behind, real in that it could communicate to me and address aspects of my mother's and my relationship. It was created by human existence but incapable of new action. It "knew" about my daughter's life and career but could not discuss them in the way a living grandmother would. It could only rehearse its own notes like an opera singer performing an aria.

Of less spiritually cohesive ghosts, John said, "I believe they're debris from beings who have died with unresolved stuff. They're thoughtforms. They don't have their own mobility. All their mobility is derivative." They are the Etheric or Astral equivalent of brain-dead bodies that keep moving as though still alive.

Later, he provided a broader context:

Your conscious mind needs to understand, or at least open to the fact, that you're not meant to get the full picture. You're meant to focus very sharply on certain contrasting modalities. The full picture comes to you every night in the dream state. You may not bring it back, but it's there. And it comes to your self-understanding at some point after death. It might come very quickly after death if you're pretty aware and not in resistance. It might come after a thousand years more experience, or ten thousand or ten million, but it comes to everyone, no matter how sacred their life is, no matter how impeccable or how horrible it is. If someone's really evil and does torture and murder, it might take them twenty million years on another planet, but everyone gets there and eventually finds that place in the Monadic plane where they become the Atman. Every portion of the universe is ultimately redeemed in something approaching self-identity, but your self-identity does not happen in that part of your self that has pat answers. It happens in a part that's a little bit bigger, or even a lot bigger, but it is still part of your personal self. When people have near-death experiences, so many of them report that everything made sense. *Everything made sense.*[12]

Six decades earlier, Jack Kerouac wrote to his ex-wife after a similar revelation:

I have lots of things to share now, in case we ever meet, concerning the message that was transmitted to me under a pine tree in North Carolina on a cold winter moonlit night. It said that Nothing Ever Happened, so don't worry. It's all like a dream. Everything is ecstasy, inside. We just don't know it because of our thinking-minds. But in our true blissful essence of mind is known that everything is alright forever and forever and forever. We were never really born, we will never really die. It has nothing to do with the imaginary idea of a personal self, other selfs, many selves everywhere: Self is only an idea, a mortal idea. . . . There's nothing to be afraid of and nothing to be glad about. Close your eyes, let your hands and nerve-ends drop, stop breathing for 3 seconds, listen to the silence inside the illusion of the world, and you will remember the lesson you forgot, which was taught in immense milky way soft cloud innumerable worlds long ago and not even at all. It is all one vast awakened thing. I call it the golden eternity. It is perfect.[13]

Like a dream, after which you will dream a different dream, and then another, and then another. But who is the dreamer? And who undreams the final dream?

The Fallacy of Life Extension

An egoic identity seems short, as even a Big Bang universe does; anything less than eternity is short. Some Silicon Valley billionaires don't fancy death's breach of their lucky sprees. Larry Ellison (Oracle), Pierre Omidyar (eBay), Larry Page and Sergey Brin (Google), and Mark Zuckerberg (Facebook) are funding cryonics: freezing and storing bodies to be defrosted in a far future epoch when cures have been concocted, if not for death, then at least for the major fatal diseases.

Freezing a brain or body for later defrosting not only depends on a hypothetical industry's capacity to preserve, recover, and reconstruct personal identity without terminal damage from frost and thawing but also to reboot it with a memory of itself.

Transhumanists, as these guys are called, believe that machine intelligence will eventually match and surpass the human equivalent, a tipping-point milestone they hail as "Consciousness Singularity." Since they also believe that our experiences and feelings are outputs of data points—neural imprints—if the majority of such points can be identified and captured, personal identity can be simulated down to the minutest detail: what it is and how it runs.

In a digital world, self and experience are commodities, and they are no *more* than that. Like other algorithms and operating systems, they follow the rules of their source codes and software; they tabulate and abridge extrinsically. Freezing may not even be needed at Singularity; existence will be bluetoothed directly onto a hard drive.

Computer scientists set the current data expenditure of one brain at about half the world's current digital storage capacity—an insurmountable obstacle for copying whole minds. They do cite continued miniaturization with exponential increases in computing power, a process that has gone from room-size mainframes to personal cell phones in less than a generation. As this ratio continues to improve, it will (they assume) allow a cost-effective mapping of all the connections in a person's brain—they sanguinely dubbed it a Connectome—which can then be copied, archived, and used to rekindle selfhood in another body or, if extra bodies are not available or viable, without a body. Just like that!

One ambitious plan is to inject nanobots (nanorobots) into bloodstreams to scan folks' brains and wirelessly upload the electrical patterning. Robotic transfer is predicated on keeping the mind's holograph intact so that it can be 3-D–copied and then resurrected. But how? How do you even find the holograph?

Nanobot copying infers that "mind" is what the brain is computing—that digital content is concomitant with "being." But if personal identity cannot be captured in a Connectome, cybernetic resurrection is of no use. At best, it will produce zombies. Nanobots can't replicate cliques and cavities, let alone auras and ground luminosity. And they can't tat chimeras onto silicon, iridium, and tin.

The idea of transferring selves or souls between hardware units combines machine worship with idolatry of the real, a Silicon Valley substitute for reincarnation. World identification is so strong that local technology presumes to rival All That Is.

Even predicating success at these tasks—an unwarranted concession—there remain significant hurdles. For instance, a personality that can be copied is, by definition, not unique. While its clones may have the memories of the original to the point of transfer, each new entity would continue as its own separate identity. Each person would sever into a number of separate people.

Plus, what would you "do" in a world in which "you" were a computer file—certainly not Pilates or yoga. All you could do would be think-think-think and drive yourself nuts.

Aside from countless other problems, some scientists believe that miniaturization has reached its limit; we can no longer manipulate quantum fields and entangled qubits to reduce software further or streamline computational agendas. We have crossed from our world into theirs, which has different rules. In fact, we may have reached the limits of our entire Stone Age technology. If so, biosphere recovery is what we need, not artificial immortality for the wealthy.

Cryopreservation is a death cult posing as a technology of life. Immortality is already imbedded in the "hard drive" of the aura. Consciousness Singularity exists in shamanic journeying, rainbow bodies, energy medicine, and *phowa*. We were uploaded (or downloaded) by a technology so gossamer and elegant as to make cybernetic replicas clumsy to the point of absurd.

It is worth noting that no one, even cryopreserved or nanocopied, will be around when the sun novas or the Milky Way and Andromeda collide. You may say that that's a long way off, but why develop an all-time tactic that will someday be obsolete? Even if members of our species construct ships to get our descendants to another solar system or galaxy—an unlikely venture—we're still up shit creek without a paddle when the universe collapses in a blue shift, terminating all business. Better to rethink the equation.

Hundreds of billions of years is a very long time, but it is not forever. Long before that, wannabe immortals will be subject to highway accidents, rattlesnake bites, murders, and the daily spinning of Atropos,

Lachesis, and Clotho, those ancient Hellenic fates. The universe doesn't want us hanging around forever.

Transhumanists trick themselves by a volte-face of illusion and reality, like trying to stay in a dream. We key books and laws into electrons, create cities of vibrating strings. Our cosmologies, religions, bank accounts, and databases are written in quarks. None of it will, can, or should last—neither the most indomitable cyclotron or cathedral nor the most impeccable sonnet of Shakespeare or sculpture of Michelangelo. If it can be tossed into a fire, let alone conflagrations trillions of times the size of our sun-star, it will get razed to less than a neutrino, and then not even that.

Erasure is liberation. The heat deaths of temporal fires like the sun, even the supergalaxy, mean nada to self-arising radiance. When the physical plane has been liquidated, crushed, or cremated, its energies redound to other planes. The only things that escape the obliteration of the universe epitomize their own identities. Everything else—everything that can be located—goes into the garbage disposal. But if it's outside the continuum, it can't get tossed into a compacter or macerated in a blueshift.*

Personal identity can't be found unless it is ransomed to an output of neurons and synapses. Otherwise, it is unconditioned, self-arising, self-illuminating—the background against which a landscape unfolds.

Is This Reality a Computer Simulation?

What about the proposition that the universe is a computer simulation in which we have been invented and programmed by super-beings in another universe (a "real" one)? Their screen saver is starry night, a faux Milky Way against an imaginary dome. As the program hums along, a tree rustles in an ocean breeze. Erosion and tattering of the display—unraveling atomic debris at the edges—suggest spots where the technicians failed to tie down the edges. Elon Musk lays the baseline trope:

---

*A blueshift is a decrease in the wavelength of electromagnetic fields with an increase in their frequency and energy: a cosmic contraction. The current, predominantly redshift of galaxies in relation to the Milky Way indicates that the universe is still expanding from the Big Bang. A blueshift will return the contents and energy of the Big Bang to a pinhead, what physicists euphemize as the Big Crunch.

So given that we're clearly on a trajectory to have games that are indistinguishable from reality, and those games could be played on any set-top box or on a PC or whatever, and there would probably be billions of such computers or set-top boxes, it would seem to follow that the odds that we're in base reality is one in billions. Tell me what's wrong with that argument. Is there a flaw in that argument?[14]

It's a wild exaggeration of a one-way trope. Its flaws are provinciality of scale, misplaced concreteness, unexamined anthropomorphism, and overly ardent gamesmanship. If the distances of our universe are real as perceived rather than simulated, then the game is too large to fit. If the game is scaled to its display screen, then we (and everything else) would have to be programmed not to find that out.

Astronomer Neil deGrasse Tyson concurs with Musk: "I think the likelihood may be very high." Citing the gap between human and chimpanzee intelligence (while sharing more than 98 percent DNA), he proposes that somewhere in the cosmos are beings whose intelligence is as much greater than ours along the same scale. "We would be drooling, blithering idiots in their presence," he adds. "If that's the case, it is easy for me to imagine that everything in our lives is just a creation of some other entity for their entertainment."[15]

He means his own astrophysics too, for he would not only be scanning other planets and faraway pulsars, quasars, and black holes but also looking across a monitor at simulations of them.

"If I were a character in a computer game," observes MIT cosmologist Max Tegmark, "I would also discover eventually that the rules seemed completely rigid and mathematical. That just reflects the computer code in which it was written."[16]

Some cybernetic philosophers have warned against continuing this inquiry. They worry that if we discovered our simulation, its creators would terminate it. But why should discernment be a dilemma rather than a dividend for the simulators? And why should termination be of concern to cartoon rabbits?

Reality as a computer artifact—an algorithm generating our world in a scalar facsimile—presupposes that something along the lines of the present technological trajectory could have proven itself sustainable both politically and ecologically and that the intelligence imbedded in computers could have transcended a reality in which computers are props. It assumes, possibly because Sol is a relatively new star, that we're not the first horse across the finish line, but that would have to have been programmed into the simulation.

This digital-age kōan is less an epistemological riddle than a symptom of a technology on such a fantastic run that its overseers have lost any sense of their own context or proportion. I mean, we can't even keep radiation and plastic out of our oceans or Roundup out of our fields. The world that a supposedly limitless technology has created is discarding whales, parrots, and bees while it forges ahead with higher and higher pixel replacements *as if these were tit for tat*. The algorithm has bewitched us into thinking that there are *only* algorithms and that we or our cyber-creators can write them (or write them off) quite as well as the universe.

In any case, the challenge for the hypothetical super-beings remains personal identity: theirs first, then ours. How did the simulation's creators acquire *their* identity? Where in relation to the simulation are they situated? Around an X-box as large as the universe (or a projection of a universe)? Is their origin moleculo-atomic? If not, what made them? How did they get into their own universe? How did they get us into ours? Did they write us in quarks and molecules, or did they write the codes for those too? Did they copy their own template or design a new one?

Is our awareness of ourselves, including our capacity to contemplate our reality as a simulation, built into the software by the designers? If so, is personal identity a by-product of codes or does it ensue once the simulation is activated? This is the same question (by the way) to ask of test-tube-generated life forms or AI robots: How (and when) do they know that they exist? Or is it "turtles all the way down (and up)?"

The concept of reality as a computer simulation intuits a truth without recognizing its substance. Our reality *is* a simulation. How can you tell a simulation from a program written in atoms and molecules? When scientists turn their instruments on a dab of matter and peer inside it, they find gateways to realms that are at once incomprehensibly vast and impenetrably tiny. Space, time, and matter vanish into energy, curvature, and uncertainty states.

Matter only *looks* like matter. That's a simulation all right.*

Why Is There Something Rather than Nothing?

In a legendary, perhaps apocryphal final exam for a Harvard philosophy course, a professor asked his class a single question: "Why?"

A student grabbed a test, scribbled in his bluebook for a few seconds, and vamoosed. He got an *A*.

He wrote, "Why not?"

I heard that story in high school and never liked it. The answer is too wise-guy, and if the exam wasn't apocryphal, the professor was rewarding *his own* nihilism with an equally nihilistic *A*.

I prefer the "answer" of my philosopher friend Andy Lugg: "I figure things have to work some way and I could care less which way they do."[17]

Why do they have to work? Why did the universe allow an Aristotle and a Wittgenstein to scribe treatises here? Why is there *anything anywhere* rather than *nothing everywhere*?

The general premise of modernity (remember) is that all this rigmarole—the universe *(creatio)* of gravity, stars, and cities—arose *ex nihilo* for no apparent reason. Subjective experience—personal identity—accrued from emergent effects of molecular compounds. As Robert Butts put it (in his notes on the worldview contravened by Seth), life owes its "physical existence to the chance conglomeration of certain atoms and molecules in the thickening scum of a primordial pond or ocean . . . atoms and molecules scattered by chance through the universe."[18] Basically nothing, *or nothing much*.

What the ancient Greeks called theogony—the desire or will of gods like Aether and Eros—is, to modern science, a feckless nascence.

---

*Orwellian spins and imaginary conspiracies are based on the same logic as computer simulations. But the illusionary basis of reality is not the same as its intentional falsification. Ideological and political narratives pretend that truth is relative and situational; yet even if reality's design makes it manipulable, it is never fake or falsifiable.

There as likely could have been nothing, nothing anywhere, or a very different sort of universe—and may well have been both of these for countless epochs. Forget simulations. Stuff concatenates not because nature has *intrinsic* intelligent complexity but because it has *extrinsic* algorithmic complexity. "Why" is not on the drawing board—shit just is.

That there is something rather than nothing is not even the *basis* of science's inquiry into what "something" is. Most cosmologists consider our cosmos a routine break of particles or fields, probably one of a termless series that transfuses new universes out of the debris of dismembered ones: quotidian business for a cycle that runs solely because it can. Our day in a sunny plaza is a rare, unscheduled event among the snap, crackle, pop of untended waves.

What began as a blind pool shot will dissipate when the energy behind it has subsided. The entire starry landscape will ooze back into a speck. There was no agenda for it, so its tchotchkes are circumstantial, in effect nothing too. The script went: Nothing—Nothing—Nothing—Big Bang—bosons, fermions, atoms—molecules—tchotchkes—algorithm, algorithm, algorithm—more tchotchkes. It will go: algorithm, algorithm—different bling (or nothing, perhaps forever).

Our situation is so inadvertent, our beingness so ephemeral and systemically hollow, that modernity chooses to celebrate *non*meaning—sublime irrelevance—against the bogus pieties of prior chantries. For twentieth-century existentialists, context had to be reinvented or bluffed in order to make existence worth the struggle and fuss. Samuel Beckett staged *Waiting for Godot* as the *Hamlet* of his generation, turning "not to be" into a spare street celebration. Beckett also wrote, with the grace of a fugitive ghost, "But what matter whether I was born or not, have lived or not, am dead or merely dying. I shall go on doing as I always have done, not knowing what it is I do, nor who I am, nor where I am, nor if I am."[19] This is the canticle of the dispossessed, awaking from a long delusional dream in the West of self-importance, divine appointment, and a final Judgment of consequence. Now we find only "slings and arrows of outrageous fortune" (*Hamlet*, Act 3, Scene 1, line 58): sun-stars, meteors, and quasar dust.

Nothing

In order to grok "something," you first have to grok "nothing." Nothing means *nothing:* nothing now, nothing ever—no time, no space, no intimation of time or space, no things or events. No in, no out; no light, no darkness; no dimensions, no directions, no gravity, no mass.

It is hard to wrap your mind around. You first have to shut everything down and unmake it into not just nothing but also the fact that it couldn't have existed in the first place, nor could anything. A universe of nothing can never be tainted by "something." It brushes incipience away like gnats on a rhino's ass.

Ex post facto erasure doesn't count because if none of this had come into being, there should be nothing to delete or, for that matter, no difference between nothing and something. (I realize that this is beginning to sound like Abbot and Costello's "Who's on First?" routine,* but you know what? They were talking about why there is something rather than nothing too.)

In any case, it is impossible to arrive at "nothing forever" once there is something, for "something" continually ponders its narrow escape. Nonexistence has to settle for a provisional derivation, that this pavilion got designed by happenstance collisions of explanation-less particles and fields. A difference separated itself; black chips off a black pot. The universe was (and remains), at core, empty.

Once "something" began scuttling about, it placed its lien in the form of heat, gravity, mass, and so on, or their predecessors. Each new force and property arose from the propensity of a prior one. But how is *anything* prior or intrinsic? Most physicists say "for a reason we don't understand" or "nature chose" or "it's a mystery of the universe."

Why a muon and tau particle instead of just an electron? Why strange and charmed, up and down quarks? Might as well ask why the cow jumped over the moon.

An algorithmic hen squats on eternity laying quantum-entangled

---

*The baseball-comedy riff eventually devolves into "Who picks up the ball and throws it to What. What throws it to I Don't Know. I Don't Know throws it back to Tomorrow, triple play."

particles and will until an underlying tension exhausts itself. Then it will vamoose too.

Where did the Big Bang get its inventory from, let alone enough that it could dilate spontaneously from a little jujube to two trillion galaxies filled with stars (and counting)? Scientists have no idea, but (like Andy) they don't care. "Because there is a law such as gravity," wrote Stephen Hawking, "the universe can and will create itself from nothing."[20] He meant (I assume), that gravity was the original intrinsic propensity, thereby granting it permission to exist without a forerunner or account. By this calculation, "nothing" was naturally heavy.

Painter/rock climber James Moore dissents (in due modesty).

> How can we get a universe as vast (millions of billions of galaxies) as this one arising in an instant from one point from nothing . . . all because of the laws of gravity? I'm no physicist but how can you have all that mass/energy exist the moment after a Big Bang, but not before? Gravity can explain the actions/reactions of that kind of mass but not its creation (gravity is what happens in the interaction between two objects having mass, and may well exist as a force without mass, but not without energy, and still the fundamental question of the cause of this gravity remains).[21]
>
> Why should nothing have had *any* weight, motion, mass, or curvature? And why should it have been "attracted" to *something*?

"Spontaneous creation," Hawking counters, "is the reason there is something rather than nothing, why the universe exists, why we exist." He suspects that M-theory, an offshoot of string theory, will lead to an explanation, that is, a unified field that does not require prior intelligence:

> What has convinced many people, including myself, that one should take models with extra dimensions seriously is that there is a web of unexpected relationships, called dualities, between the models. These dualities show that the models are all essentially equivalent; that is, they are just different aspects of the same underlying theory, which has been given the name M-theory. Not to take this web of dualities

as a sign that we are on the right track would be a bit like believing that God put fossils into the rocks in order to mislead Darwin about the evolution of life.[22]

"Sorry Stephen," says Moore, "but to try and explain the cause of the Big Bang as causeless spontaneous creation sounds like 'blind faith' to me."[23]

How are dimensions and dualities ultimately different from an Atmic plane or a yellow-and-white disk in midair? For the Athapascan First Nation peoples of southern Oregon, spontaneous creation came from five mudcakes tossed by two tobacco smokers into the unformed depths (aided by the tobacco smoke). I understand that extra dimensions and their relationships are more challenging than mudcakes. They hew to centuries of underlying mathematics, but they still don't explain what causes gravity (or what causes what causes gravity). Plus, mudcakes and tobacco smoke are "quanta" too and took centuries to become ontological. (As for the smokers, where they came from is equivalent to how the makers of our computer simulation originated.)

Protean club member Freeman Dyson brought out the larger console:

Nobody can be sure of anything. Stephen Hawking doesn't know the difference between a model and the real thing. That's an occupational disease of theoretical physicists. Theories don't actually help a great deal; the world is much stranger than we imagined. Even in the hard parts of science we're not even close to understanding what's going on. If you look at anything that seems plain and obvious and look at it in detail, we find we don't understand it. The people at CERN* are in the position of a horse wearing blinkers and only able to see a very small patch of the road in front of them. They are constrained by their machines to look at very narrow questions.[24]

If Stephen Hawking doesn't know the difference between a model and the real thing, then algebra and geometric topology are little more than think-tank send-ups.

---

*European Organization for Nuclear Research

Statisticians infer countless "failed" universes in a time frame dwarfing the event that set the present clock ticking a tad under fourteen billion years ago. We happen to be in a spot and time where the "right" criteria converged, making "something" out of "nothing," but ontologically, it is still "nothing" and could have remained nothing forever.

Even "failed universes" are "something," so we have to ask where they came from and how they broke the silence.

"Nothing's" universe is the one in a trillion trillion tries that "took," and the fact that there *is* something (here or anywhere) is a forgery and will redound to nothingness, which is what was meant to be in the first place. Darkness again will rule the abyss.

Or it will turn into something else—same thing.

Something

Now let's evaluate "something." For there to be something, the Big Bang must be rooted in *something else,* not just what-you-see-is-what-you-get. In Buddhist liturgy, that "something" is primordial luminosity. It, not matter, is the fundamental substance, the ground of being. From our vista, matter slams into it like the broad side of a barn.

In Genesis 1:2, the earth *(Eretz),* that is, the universe, was without form and void. "Darkness was upon the face of the deep." The King James's "void" was derived from the Hebrew *tohu wa-bohu*: *tohu,* a "wasteness" or "vanity," and *wa-bohu,* "reflected in itself." It emulated or reverberated its own shadowless cipher for eternity. Then "the Spirit of God moved upon the face of the waters."

If the Spirit of God, or whatever it was, could enter unopposed, then the void without form was an imposter universe, pretending to be *tohu wa-bohu* when differentiation (and script) were waiting in the wings. Spirit said, "Let there be light." A multidimensional reflection imbued and supplanted the void.

That darkness upon the face of the deep wasn't nothing. It was the profundity, fabric, and passion of the universe—a vestal murk about to be sprouted and born.

A wasps' nest hung on a tree. Only there were no wasps, there was no tree, and it wasn't a nest. It was the inherence of the universe that hung from a crooked branch, unrealized for eternity. As long as Spirit was authorized to open it, the universe (All That Is) was never "nothing" nor could it have remained nothing forever. It could never bottom out as shallowly as materialists propose.

Intrinsic luminosity yokes conditional reality to the unconditioned basis of there being anything. An actual universe cancels all hypothetical ones.

"Something" means that the universe bottoms out at consciousness rather than matter—or that it doesn't bottom out. "Something" means that the specified can never be unspecified, but neither can the unspecified be specified. As Seth put it, "Consciousness is always conscious of itself, and of its validity and integrity, and in those terms there is no unconsciousness."[25] He also said, "Physical matter by itself could never produce consciousness."[26]

This kōan flips back and forth: Is the universe something that is really nothing, as scientists claim, or is it nothing that is really something, as Seth (and others) interpret? Or is it nothing that became something that is really nothing, a Buddhist view?

Dreadful Powers

Let's look at the science again. Was the Big Bang a random implosion that spun gold out of straw? Or was the straw an interiorized string packed with sacred information and star systems? Either the universe sprang from nothing for no reason and there is no bigger picture—just soap operas among rocks, winds, and thermonuclear cauldrons—or the bigger picture is *our* becoming and its charmed, inviolable dance through the engines of destruction.

"More than 200 parameters [of the universe] are exactly right for life to exist," notes biologist Robert Lanza. "If [the Big Bang] was one part in a millionth more powerful, it would have rushed out too fast for galaxies and worlds to be here. If the strong nuclear force were decreased by 2 percent, atomic nuclei would not hold together . . . hydrogen would be the only element in the universe. If the gravitational constant were decreased just [slightly] . . . just a hair, stars, including the sun, wouldn't ignite."[27]

Juggle a few variables and quarks would not have hatched or their stars would not have incubated elements for molecular life.

Accident of matter and energy or cosmic blueprint? One in a trillion trillion or the residue of ground luminosity and design?

How can there even be a spot where "right criteria converge"? Can a whirlpool or formless cloud spin in the middle of nowhere for no reason? For then the issue becomes which "nowhere" and for what "no reason"? Sixth-century BCE Greek philosopher Parmenides reasoned similarly: "Out of nothing nothing comes. . . . And, if it came from nothing, what need could have made it arise later rather than sooner . . . ? For there is no nothing that could keep it from reaching out equally, nor can aught that is be more here and less there than what is, since it is all inviolable. For the point from which it is equal in every direction tends equally to the limits."[28]

In other words, how can something come from nothing (and launch time) unless existence itself is eternal? Why construct self-aware creatures and proxy habitats from incidental and spare parts? Why make blue jays, eels, and catfish out of mudcakes?

I can see how a random whirligig might centrifuge atoms out of quantum scrap—maybe, maybe even forever. I get that formal and efficient causes can ricochet molecules, even without a primary "uncaused" cause, though *even* that seems extravagant and clunky. What I *can't* see is how this entire temple complex with its priests, wishing wells, and gamelans was created by the equivalent of Ping-Pong balls bouncing into one another.

"Something" blows "nothing" out of the water by splitting the proposition into a teeming latency that underlies it. No entity could emerge from that depth unless it bottomed out at the same depth. No sentient being could exist in a universe unless it bottomed out *with that universe*. (When I named this book, I was, of course, bluffing. I was proposing the impossible in order to say that our possibility, meaning "us," was already and only bottomless. I know that that doesn't do it, but nothing will.)

Mind arises from matter *because* matter was already arising from mind, not because a hundred monkeys typing away on their machines found Shakespeare. As Jeffrey Kripal puts it, consciousness is "the fundamental ground of all that we know, or will ever know. . . . [Its] presence is entirely *sui generis* . . . its own thing. We know of nothing else like it in the universe, and anything we would know later we would only know in, through, and because of this same consciousness."[29]

If a single particle that could fit on a pinhead (with room to spare) gave rise to this entire cosmos, it wasn't a mote and it wasn't just spat by an ogre void. It was a shadow, the kinetic umbra of an object of illimitable dimensions.

"Something" was present, not just something but *everything:* an alphabet wading in its own permutations. The Primal Flaring Forth (as cosmologist Brian Thomas Swimme retagged the Big Bang) was a white hole, a puncture in a higher dimension, a gateway and shape-shifter.

Naturalist philosopher Loren Eiseley cast the sphinx (like Sophocles) into his own *Oedipus at Colonus:* "If 'dead' matter has reared up this curious landscape of fiddling crickets, song sparrows, and wondering men, it must be plain even to the most devoted materialists that the matter of which he speaks contains amazing, if not dreadful, powers."[30] Eiseley probably didn't mean "dreadful" in the Old English sense of "causing apprehension" or "foreboding" but in the Late Medieval sense of "inspiring awe and reverence." Yet there is a fretful undertone to his knell. For a materialist (and Eiseley has one foot in), the shameless concatenations of nature are as terrible as they are spooky.

The problem for physics is, *a universe that has consciousness in it is a conscious universe. Everything that isn't conscious is incipiently conscious.* On Earth, life forms replace three-quarters of their atoms every sixteen days, as they must for their morphologies to survive. Surrogates from nature enter their biological fields and become alive. Dreadful powers indeed! Every molecule on Ceres, Chiron, and Makemake screams it: "Consciousness unites us. We are vibrating at a single reality."

Scientists *assume* that there will be some form of life—microbial, viral, or protist if not actual "jellyfish" and "fish"—on Europa, Titan, Callisto, Enceladus, and under the poles of Mars (maybe Titan and Jupiter too) because there are hydrogen, oxygen, nitrogen, silicon, and other elementals: no basis beyond atomic charge, molecular bonding, phase states, and selective survival—no existential gap between matter itself and life itself.

Terrence Deacon's account of how mind arose from matter isn't magical or foreboding, but it doesn't have to be. Intrinsic semiology supplants dreadful powers. Deacon concludes his book *The Symbolic Species* with an impish riddle meant to discombobulate biologists and theologians alike:

Unmasking the source of subjective experience behind human consciousness is less likely to demonstrate how mental processes can be eliminated from material explanations than to demonstrate how they are implicit in them. And this may help us recognize that the universe isn't, after all, the soulless, blindly spinning clockwork we fear we are a part of, but is, instead, nascent heart and mind.[31]

"Nascence" implies that we are here—or anywhere, or that anything is anywhere—because some *other* thing is framing it. Teleodynamic feedback becomes fiddling crickets and song sparrows (wherever it doesn't get lost in its own noise).

Likewise, consecutive universes are not random, flawed, or cataclysmic; they are lesson plans, works of cosmic art. Through his father, Jordan McKay speaks of concluded creations as palettes for fresh universes:

When everything has been learned from the Universe we now occupy, it will be archived—like a beautiful, but already read book—and the next one will begin to form from the primordial energy of collective consciousness. . . . [T]he creation of each universe sparks unimaginable growth and learning by spirit. . . .

Beyond the spirit world and the universes it has created, lies the dark unknown. The dark unknown is both something and nothing at the same time. It is whatever collective consciousness . . . thinks that it is, and then it transforms to something else as it gradually becomes light and seen. But there is a paradox here: if the unknown can be anything, then it is nothing. The great unknown is like a dream landscape that you can project and make into anything, yet it becomes something else, wholly unexpected as you take a closer look.

[T]he spirit world is a vast array of consciousness, of light, bordered by something and nothing—all that is not yet held in conscious thought. As thought expands, as consciousness and the spirit world grows, the dark unknown recedes. As far as we can tell, there are no limits to the dark unknown, because we expect consciousness will continue to evolve and expand into it forever.

The dark, where there is no consciousness, exists in the physical universe, as well as the space that surrounds spirit. We cannot travel into these regions, so even inside a physical universe that was created by the whole, by *All,* are areas devoid of consciousness and essentially unknown.[32]

Something and nothing are not a zero-sum game. They are a cardinal dialectic, redeemed by spirit—by us—from the dark prolific unknown.

An Esoteric Teaching

After reading an early draft of this book, scholar of religion William Stranger confided that his guru, radical nondual teacher Adi Da, once set "nothing" and "something" before his students in a reverse of the originary paradox: "For you the mystery is, Why there is something rather than nothing? For me the mystery is, Why there is nothing rather than something?"[33]

I heard this at two levels. One is the traditional Buddhist view that reality is an illusion, hence *nothing* rather than *something.* The other is my outsider's view of Adi Da's teaching, that the Divine Illumination—the ultimate "something"—is present in our very beings but most of us are cut off from it by the mediocrity and addictions of our lifestyles.

I thought the kōan was perfect for my book and asked Bill if there was a citable source. He said he'd check but a few days later changed his mind, objecting that this was a privileged communication between a guru and his devotees. It would be misunderstood and desanctified if used elsewhere.

I acknowledged "sacred words" and "private transmission" but argued that esoteric texts had secular meanings too—also that, once they were published, they were no longer unutterable.

He reconsidered on *one* condition. He wanted to frame it.

"Of course."

Bill was in for a surprise. Once he found the obscure transcript, he saw that he had morphed his teacher's words dramatically. He meant to discard his own "heretical" version, but to my mind, the esoteric nature of the original was *confirmed* by how a hidden ray had deepened in Bill's mind. I believe that *any* true existential proposition fissions into seminal offshoots. Bill had produced a succinct, ironical couplet *without even trying to adulterate the orthodoxy he was safeguarding.* Here is what Adi Da actually said:

A Daist is someone whose hair if he has any at all, the full fleshy follicles, stands up on the back of his neck and head when he thinks about the fact that anything exists at all.

Why should anything at all exist—anything at all? How could anything at all exist—at all! Even more mysterious, from my point of view, is to consider how there could <u>not</u> be anything at all—but that is an expression of My unique position. Looking at the possibility of a Divine Way of life, a Spiritual Way of life, it is much more awesome for you to consider how anything could exist. Really, how could anything at all exist! [34]

Bill added, "Science's causal thinking ends in an endless regress that utterly fails to account for its own origins." That matches my diagnosis throughout this book.

Adi Da continued:

We look only at manifest forms, we can see that each of them is related to an ordinary cause. But a much more awesome question is, How did the possibility of such causing and effecting ever occur? What would have been the motive in nothing for all of this nothingness to cause all of these secondary, arbitrary, limited causes to have effects? How did they get their opportunity to be causes, to make effects, to be effects? Why should it have happened? Having accepted the fact of the manifest universe, we can see all these arbitraries, these secondary or limited causes, having their effects. But why should they have been given the opportunity? How does such an opportunity arise? If all that is is basically nothingness, arbitraries creating arbitraries, how, out of nothingness, could such a possibility ever have appeared? Where was the motivation? [35]

This question, as you know, stretches from Parmenides of Elea to Steven Hawking of Cambridge—and probably from artists of the Chauvet caves to philosophers in the Pleiades too.

Bill went on to describe playing hooky from an Adidam retreat three years later. He and his wife were at a Mexican restaurant and she was talking about something else when it hit him like a flash; he felt as though he "fell off the universe."

The sheer inexplicability of everything utterly took my mind, my self. It was absolutely awesome. And it was also clearly an ultimate, unsurpassable intuition not <u>about</u> reality, but <u>of</u> and <u>in</u> reality. It's not that suddenly I knew "my identity." The whole issue of egoic identity instantly became utterly beside the point. *Everything is simply this Mystery.* It was a moment of perfect decompression, of liberation from the implications of my presumed separate, mortal life.[36]

Adi Da's answer to his own question had triggered him:

From My view, as I suggested to you, it is more remarkable to consider how there could possibly not be anything, because to Me the Power of Being, Self-Radiant, is the most Obvious Condition of all. It is the only thing Obvious. Everything else, seen by itself, is just flashing, a puzzle, maya. All there is, at the level of manifestation, is Light, Energy. Where do all these forms come from? Impulses, changes, motions occurring within that Force, have produced forms. Yet only one Force exists. $E=mc^2$ is another way of saying it. And yet all these forms exist. Countless causes have arisen in Light. How did the Energy that is modified in all these forms come into existence? Why does anything exist? Because Energy Is, and that is it! That is IT![37]

Not gravity, Mr. Hawking. Not springing "from nothing in a single moment for no reason," thank you, Mr. McKenna. Not an imploding singularity or particle acceleration. The source energy

is not just a buzz. It is Infinitely Conscious Being, God. There never was nothing. There has always been God, Self-Radiant Being, Infinite, Absolute, Perfect Love-Bliss. That is What Is. There could not possibly be nothing. That always Is. The possibility of forms arises in That. Once that possibility is established, then the possibility for an infinite variety of causes and effects, positive and negative, occurs spontaneously. . . . How could there not be anything!

All there is, at the level of manifestation, is Light, Energy. Where do all these forms come from? . . . Why does anything exist? Because Energy Is, and that is it! That is IT![38]

"Perfect Love-Bliss" transcends all language(s) used to define it. To call it God is the same as to call it Nothing. It is so far beyond everything It manifests as to transcend Yahweh, Allah, Zeus, Kali, and more. This whole crunchy, fiery, cascading manifestation is waves of divine light—a gentle breath from the dream of creation.

Bill concluded:

This brings to an end of all theosophical musing about multiple lives and parallel selves. Obviously, the well-established fact of reincarnation provides a certain validity to these speculations. From within the viewpoint of manifest, self-identified and self-bound beings, there is a mechanics of existence that belies our usual conceit that we are merely a skin-bound, mortal creature and that points to a process of evolution to higher states, perhaps even culminating in Enlightenment. The mistake is in attributing a causal <u>necessity</u> to the process of experience itself, and in attributing "self" or subjective being to the experiencer. Once intuition or realization of the Mystery of existence becomes full and the Radiant Bliss of Being Itself is known, the presumed necessities of evolutionary experience are seen to be illusions. Reality is not unreal; it's just *unnecessary*.[39]

He closed by quoting Adi Da from a prior text:

There is the tacit Realization that there is nothing serious whatsoever about experiential existence. It could end in this moment, casually, and that cessation in itself would not have the slightest significance. Or, it could continue for infinite eons of time, through infinite permutations and transformations of experience, and its continuing would not have any significance whatsoever. This is the Disposition of Enlightenment—Realization of the non-necessity of everything. Absolutely nothing is of serious consequence or of ultimate necessity—absolutely nothing.[40]

That is because all of these interim "somethings" and "nothings" oscillate around the unmistakable *self*-radiance—"what Adi Da calls the 'Zero-Point' intuition in which all lives and destinies and worlds dissolve. What is left over?"[41]

Astonishment at the wonder of existence *is* existence.

A Trillion Trillion Trillion Eyes

Physics and neuroscience are the wrong tools for locating the source of *either* consciousness or matter. An externalized universe is a hollow chassis, an accelerating carousel of objects and effects, toys and gimmicks that turn heavens and seas into elective scenery: it is a simulation that comes to its own cul-de-sac, leaving "nothing" to preside over a charade of infinite distraction. Liberal scientists may deplore a Trumpian idiocracy that has run roughshod over their rationalism and dreams of progress, but they unwittingly helped create it by casting the shadow from which it sprang. Having eaten the forbidden apple and opened Pandora's jar, they have released a meaning they are incapable of comprehending and left us in the middle of nowhere with no rationale beyond hedonistic consumption, technocratic fascination, and material titillation.
"Something" turns into "nothing" wherever they bottom it out.

But the universe of nothing is not wrong; it is the fiber and negative capability holding together reality, the stable joy underlying Creation. Its emptiness is not even a bullet dodged; it is the ground from which everything is born and continues to arise. For the attack against consciousness, modernity's jeremiad, is an attempt to root it deeply enough that it can never be excoriated from future universes, to draw it out of fascination with its own abstraction into the stipe grounding it.

Finally, there is *only* consciousness—conscious consciousness and unconscious consciousness. The universe is not only a trillion trillion trillion atoms but also a trillion trillion trillion eyes opening like spiders, and they are the same eye. You can no more shut it than you can extinguish a biblical burning bush.

"Why?"

"Why not?" Now take your A and leave.

11

Multipersonhood

Multipersonhood is an umbrella term for the concept that every sentient being in the universe is part of a multidimensional web of consciousness, an ever-deepening subjectivity that continues to expand and differentiate at multiple levels while exploring something larger. Each separate entity is receiving meanings from other entities elsewhere. Its participation as them is every bit as real as its awareness of itself, though it knows them not as what *they* are but *what it is*. Our world is *fundamentally* nonlocal. Pleiadians and Andromedans are as present on Earth as gophers and snails or the thoughts of mountains and organelles, but these exist at their own frequencies, contributing to a subliminal choir.

Multipersonhood was systematized by John Friedlander through a series of meditations, spirit communications, and classes across more than three decades after he experienced its lineaments in Jane Roberts's 1974 channeling of Seth. John puts it this way:

Our spiritual project grows out of the work of Jane Roberts and Lewis Bostwick and, before them, people like Alice Bailey, Sri Aurobindo, and Madame Blavatsky. . . . My benefactors, as Castaneda would say, were Lewis Bostwick, who founded the Berkeley Psychic Institute, and Jane, who channeled Seth—each gave me freedom from the other. They each had their significant blind spots, so I was fortunate to study with both of them.

Regarding Seth, he added:

Alfred Whitehead said that all Western philosophy is a footnote to Plato. What he meant is that Plato set up twenty-five hundred years of subsequent human exploration. I think that the next twenty-five hundred will be a footnote, or expansion, or exploration of what Jane channeled from Seth. It's that vast and eloquent and mystically radiant.[1]

In this chapter and the next, I rely on John, Jane Roberts, and her Seth channeling. Since I am mainly their emissary, I use their words, including text I transcribed and rephrased from audios of John's classes (for a different project). Putting these many voices into a single connected flow is impossible, especially when combining my edits, rewordings, and amplifications of John's ideas with his own verbatim expressions (they are different styles and weights). This chapter is more of a montage than a commentary or exegesis.

Plus, Multipersonhood may seem extravagant, hyperbolic, and weird, but instead of trying to prove or disprove it, see if it resonates with your inner landscape. See if it expands your personal freedom and sense of who you are—if it provides hope and meaning as you confront climate change, nihilism, and mortality, if it makes you more resilient and kind. I can't deliver Multipersonhood. I can only give you (and me) a glimmer of an unknown future. It may not turn out to be Multipersonhood, but it is not nothing. As the poet Robert Kelly said to me in 1970, "We are living in the darkest West, in the dark that does not precede the dawn but the birth of a radically different order of things."

What the Universe Is

At its core, Multipersonhood proposes that all knowledge and beingness supports all other knowledge and beingness—interdimensionally as well as intergalactically. That limns neither a supercommune nor a cosmic Burning Man. It is meant to describe generically how the universe works—what, in fact, the universe *is:* information and identity. Jane Roberts states this in Sethian terms:

The conscious self is only one aspect of our greater reality . . . the part that springs into earthknowing . . . because through it we perceive our three-dimensional life. It contains within it, however, traces of the unknown or "source self" out of which it constantly emerges.[2]

Elsewhere, she adds:

Since the focus personality can only handle so much data in its time system, it chooses from the field of the unconscious only those perceptions it wants to accept in line with its beliefs about its own reality.[3]

The focus personality defines one incarnational phase: an ego-self and world—everything it considers real. At the same time, as Jane explains, its source personality is "fully engaged as that consciousness knowing itself simultaneously as each of the others. . . . You are unconsciously aware of the experiences of 'your' counterparts, as they are of yours, and you use that information to round out your own."[4]

Members of a Multipersonhood can be buddies, infantrymen in opposing armies, predator and prey, rivals for the same romantic partner—or romantic partners. Opposition supplies the greater entity with comprehensive knowledge toward becoming whole.

Transpersonal Matrices

If Multipersonhoods are a real thing, they are cached in subconscious matrices. Since I don't want to impose metaphysical constructs on subtle awarenesses, the following membership is best regarded as placeholders for a *different* collegium meeting at transpersonal levels.

Taking into account Buddhic, Atmic, and Monadic planes, our Multipersonhood includes other human beings, either individually or as parts of group souls; life forms in other solar systems; consciousnesses in other planes and dimensions; entire orbs like the earth and the sun; other terrestrial zooids; nature spirits and dream-time bodies; one-celled mites in ponds and water droplets; psychoids (elves, leprechauns, mermaids, yetis, faeries, fire salamanders); differently vibrating entities like plants and stones; and disembodied forces of nature like thunderstorms, mountains, forests, and so on. Each of these, or the intelligences and energies they represent, vibrates somewhere in your aura. Being human is just one dimension of incarnation.

Here are a few addenda:

- Nature spirits are said to exist simultaneously on multiple planets and planes. A kangaroo, dolphin, or echidna here may be one of many dream bodies of an entity elsewhere.
- Rocks have nascent modes of consciousness insofar as they are composed of "intelligently" organized atomic states. Their "minds" are not our kind of minds; they don't use thought patterns we would recognize. They have other versions of "hearing" and "taste."
- As large as the sun is (1,300,000 times the size of the earth), it is no more or less autonomous than a beetle. It supports our lives with neutrality, wisdom, and empathy. "What's in it for the sun?" John Friedlander asks. "What is the sun getting out of this? Everything in the universe is a collaboration between various consciousnesses. The sun gets at least as much pleasure shining down on you, as you get from it shining down. So see if you can feel the sun's pleasure when it shines on you."[5]

The key to the cosmology of French mid-twentieth-century Jesuit philosopher Pierre Teilhard de Chardin is that this system, the literal solar system, once a spiraling stellar cloud, *is the local physicalization of consciousness itself*, concentrated in the sun and radiating out of the earth's braid of the helix from every sentient being, in and out of time, like trans-Etheric vapor. It forms our noosphere, which is not an exospheric tier or a mere psychically ionized layer but a field of multidimensional clairsentience encompassing the *whole* planetary atmosphere and oscillating like gravity with the supergalactic field.

- Every Gaian organism is made up of free-living cells, themselves composites of the organelles that conduct their metabolism. Seth clarifies that these "are not simply minute, handy, unseen particles that happen to compose (our) organs." They maintain their own vibration and the intelligence of their lineage. "There is no need to . . . think of them as little people, but each of them possesses a highly focused consciousness,

<u>and</u> a consciousness of self. . . . There are different kinds of selfhood, and an infinite variety of ways to experience self-awareness."[6]

Our cells scan other dimensions according to their own parameters of time, directionality, and intentionality. Feel their innate intelligence. Perceive how "consciousness unites all physical matter."[7] Intuit the biological field as a psychic field. Extend it clairsentiently and then multidimensionally.

Time and Probabilities

Multipersonhood also includes our own prior and future selves, in *this* lifetime as well as others. From infancy through childhood into adolescence and through adult life, we are not the same individual, yet we have a uniquely intimate relationship to our earlier and later phases. Jane Roberts muses poignantly:

> [W]e savor our memories, secret from all others; recall in old age, for example, the endless lost Mondays and Tuesdays when we tucked our children (now grown) into bed, or talked through a thousand separate suppers. . . .
>
> The mother may envision the future man or woman in the child who sits in the highchair; and the old woman may see in the face of her grown son or daughter the child that was. In greater terms, each exists at once—young, old, born, dying—in an "at once" or spacious present that happens to be large enough to contain our lives.[8]

She describes consciousness-like particles

> . . . flowing from the source self into physical materialization. Each source self forms many such particles or "aspect selves" that impinge upon three-dimensional reality, striking our space-time continuum. Others are not physical at all, but have their existences in completely different systems of reality. Each aspect self is connected to the other, however, through the common experience of the source self, and can to some degree draw on the knowledge, abilities, and perceptions of the other aspects.[9]

Though a cosmological constant for us, time is not the same sort of organizing factor elsewhere. In our local continuum, we have singular pasts with solo futures—one probability, three dimensions of space and one of time determining our mode of experience. Yet, according to Seth, there are realms with more than one dimension of time and more than three of space. More than one dimension of time is unimaginable to us, as parallel realities would branch off every moment. Even in our cozy domain, potentiated events, things that never happened, persist as "concentrations of energy formed unconsciously by us adjacent to our living areas."[10] Each path *not* taken has karmic potential and gets expressed *somewhere*. "Each of your thoughts and actions," Seth adds, "exist not only in the manner with which you are familiar with them, but also in many other forms that you do not perceive: forms that may appear as natural events in a different dimension than your own, as dream images, and even as self-propelling energy. No energy is ever lost. The energy within your own thoughts, then, does not dissipate even when you yourself have finished with them. Their energy has reality in other worlds."[11]

Each vibration we trigger sends scenarios across space and time. Jane Roberts offers a rudimentary key:

[E]ach present action changes the past, for those past events were only the mountain tops or three-dimensional tips of far greater happenings. Each act causes the surface crust of time and space to shift slightly. Probable events are the psychological pre-acts from which physical events emerge: the creative inner stuff from which actions take earth form. . . . We come from within, not from above. We also seed other earths with our probable selves; these never happen at our intersection point, though they may spring off it.[12]

They generate "alternate earth histories still happening, and as real as our own. Any number of consecutive years, say, from 1900 to 1980 are experienced in infinite ways;" for instance, the *Titanic* missing the iceberg or Hitler never coming to power in Germany. They are "endlessly growing out of the medium of the system itself,"[13] creating a multiverse.

The inhabitants of each probable world remain unaware of their "neighbors" because their event horizons are discrete. As Seth puts it:

> Each self is free to program its own journey, choose [its] dimensional spot—the time and place of [its] growth . . . seeds of which we are usually unaware, dreams and thoughts that escape from us as easily as leaves from an autumn tree. These live in dimensions apart from our being, yet they are aspects of us and carry our potentials within them. Perhaps they are future ghosts of ourselves, mental patterns that will some day be filled with form and walk this earth or a different one, in a space and time that will be theirs, not ours.[14]

Parallel universes give rise to a popular trope; for example, in another universe you are your mother's mother, in another you are boyfriend and girlfriend, in yet another you and your mother "meet" only once, as strangers seated beside each other on a train, and so on.

It's a population explosion, but All That Is never gets overcrowded because it creates its own space-time.

Roberts herself is "convinced that in some probable earth-like world, I am not writing this book. I may not be a writer at all or I may live in a civilization where reading is unknown. My potential as a writer, there, would remain latent."[15]

Likewise, in this "earth" world, many of *our* talents and powers stay dormant.

A Shamanic Perspective

Anthropologist Michael Harner describes how guides encountered on shamanic journeys in other worlds or dimensions can be spirits of plants, animals, ancestors, devas, gods, or ancestors here. These entities do not even have to know that they are serving as spiritual teachers, for Multipersonhood lets them be in many places at once. When persons are conflated or combined with one another, in life as in dreams, it may also be that they *are* one another.

Seemingly chance events may draw a person to his or her teacher. Harner provides instances from the archives of his Shamanic Institute in which guides both *are* and *are not* the historic entities they resemble and can also be aspects of presently living people unknown to the journeyer. In one such account, a seeker regularly received dream instruction from "an old man in the Upper World who inhabited a cabin in an unknown countryside." In his wakeful life, the aspiring shaman was driving along a road in California when he came to a beautiful canyon and pulled over there on impulse. Drawn to follow a path, he "arrived at a cabin almost identical to the Upper World one of my spirit teacher. There was even a similar fence around it."

He felt compelled to knock on the door. The young man who answered graciously invited him in. After entering, the traveler saw "in the dim light an elderly man half-reclining on a couch. He turned his head toward me and smiled. . . . I recognized him as being my teacher in the Upper World or, rather, being an aging ordinary-reality version of my teacher in the Upper World."

They talked for a while, and the visitor discovered that this version of his guide was a landscape painter who had been forced to halt his work because of an incurable illness. Furthermore, he had been suffering from the illness for almost exactly the time period in which the initiate had known him as his teacher.

"I did not tell him about my teacher, but on some level he seemed to know something. He said that I seemed familiar to him, and he gave me a print of one of his paintings haltingly inscribed, "To My Old Friend." After the painter died two years later, he continued to serve as an Upper World guide.[16]

Interdependent Origination

Multipersonhood can devolve into a New Age confabulation or a trailer for the Aquarian Age. Four contexts discriminate it:

1. Multipersonhood is a thought experiment for a universe that features conscious existence, interdependence, and polarities.
2. If and when humans recognize Multipersonhood, it will feel like its own thing. By John Friedlander's diagnosis, "No human can

experience Multipersonhood with any sort of vividness at this point because we just don't have the Etheric or nervous-system flexibility."[17]

3. Multipersonhood is incompatible with duality (because it requires group awareness beyond a self-reflective ego), but it is irreconcilable with nonduality (because it validates singular identity, in fact, forever). Instead, it is a bridge between an original sacred nonduality and a secular version that incorporates dual experience (see chapter 5). Even more than a bridge, it is an alembic, enriching and deepening both.

4. Reincarnation is no longer sequential lives. If James Huston dies and is reborn as James Leininger, he goes on as James Huston while participating in James Leininger as a new center of his own experience. James Leininger continues to expand from a different center.

When Seth began to refer to Multipersonhood in his later downloads, he inverted two of Buddhism's central constructs, "interdependent origination" and "impermanence." By extending interdependent origination to multicentric participation in a sense of self while broadening felt experience to entities considered nonsentient in Buddhism (such as rocks, plants, and stars), Seth flipped interdependent origination into multiple beingness while heretically privileging all experience as a "play of desire in which each and every desire is *already* fulfilled in its richest form."[18]

In John's further interpretation:

The exploration of Multipersonhood leaves the apparent duality of one part of your multiplicity, which is your conscious, awake human self, in place, and opens to the fact that each person is always and already flourishing at multiple other levels. It is about being somewhat more comfortable with the flow of your awareness and more able to value both your uniqueness with its pleasure and the fact that you are bigger experiences too with *their* pleasure and pain.

Even though we cannot now know our Multipersonhood while embodied, each of our personalities, with further training after death, will know ourselves to be both nondual and multiply-centered gestalts simultaneously conscious in multiple perspectives. But the truth is that you are nondual right now and already, though you don't experience that as a fully existential phenomenon.[19]

Most of our ordinary feelings and thoughts would be impossible without Multipersonhood. The universe creates emotions, and bigger things than emotions that feel like emotions—healings, ways of being—that solely having an assumption of oneself as a separate individual closes out. It doesn't just close them out consciously; it closes them out unconsciously and in the dream state. In Multipersonhood, one's own experiences are enhanced through access to those of other consciousnesses. Each life is sacred and meaningful in its own terms and for its own self, though always and also for others, and always in conversation with everything that is.[20]

Multipersonhood is, in a sense, a family constellation with the whole universe—or All That Is—its field. Once the field was activated (long ago), everything resonated as a shared reality across space, time, and dimension.

The soul is incarnating as you even while it does all sorts of other things simultaneously. It is not constrained in time and space. While you explore time in a linear fashion, it explores time underneath your conscious awareness, flowing across multiple times and spaces—and even in no time. It knows you as a baby; it knows you as other incarnations. In some ways you were always part of it and in some ways you were always separate of it as a personality. It integrates all your experience which you're having today, all your experience that you've had in other lifetimes, and across probabilities, even while it gives exquisite support and nurturing to you in your experience of linear time. Imagine, just to experience a consciousness that's larger than a star while being intimately involved in the act of sipping your tea.[21]

That's the bigness we feel: all consciousness expanding in all directions. John posits that a cat may be better organized neurologically to experience it than a human:

The cat knows itself as multiple, innumerable consciousnesses that flow gracefully. It never thinks, "Oh, I'm a cat, I'll have to incarnate another thousands of years before I can individuate and become a human, and then I can become enlightened." Cats don't need enlightenment. . . . The cat always knows itself as that cat, but also as the deva, and also as the storm that's happening or the sunshine that's happening and as the emotional aspect of the family it lives with, and as part of the earth, as beings on the moons of Jupiter, as All That Is, as the star system. It knows itself as all of these things. And not with the sort of cognitive schema that humans use but as itself. It grasps them in absolute unity with its individual identity. So who is more evolved?[22]

While the soul's separate forms come and go in innumerable dimensions, the Atman gathers them across lifetimes. Each time we live and die, we gather experience until we come from the Atman in multiple times and spaces at once. Even when the universe itself disappears, we do not, because, as Atman, we are outside as well as inside of time. Our separate body and self will disappear, but they are merely the part that we track in this phase of human history.[23]

Though the Atman overrides the individual soul, that doesn't mean there's no such thing as a self or soul subjectively, only that there's no such thing *objectively* (even as there is no such thing as "consciousness" *objectively* in the composition of neural tissue). There is no *separate* entity functioning as your personality, and yet you know yourself as yourself, and its subjectivity continues to grow and change. If it didn't grow and change, it wouldn't be eternal. In one direction it grows into your soul; in other dimensions it grows into different probabilities. It also knows itself as other people, spirit forms, and devas, in both waking and dream states, and experiences their lives intermittently from its own view: *its* version of *them*. Even though we are collectively interdependent, our individual subjectivity is eternal.

There's no grand enlightenment. There's no transcendence of your ordinary humanity. If you really understand Multipersonhood, you wouldn't want to become enlightened because your soul has questions and it created you to answer those. Your soul has a lot of good information and a lot of great support, but you're the one that's here, providing your unique opinions, attitudes, experience, back to the soul. When you die, you don't get gobbled up by the soul. This personality is eternal.

I know that this completely disagrees with mystics for the last twenty-five hundred years, but they were only looking in linear time. In linear time, the soul *does* gobble you up. It spits out the bones and they form the next lifetime. But in Multipersonhood— Multidirectionality—you're eternal. You go through changes. I like to say, "Death changes people." But you are very recognizably yourself. And eventually you move into Multipersonhood.[24]

John told a later class, "A hundred thousand years from now, Ed will be very different from the 'Ed' here, but if you ask that 'Ed,' or if you go into other dimensions and encounter some six-dimensional being and find that 'Ed,' and say, 'Do you feel cheated? Have you lost Ed here, who was born in the twentieth century and lived well into the twenty-first century?' his answer will be *his recognition of your question.*"[25]

When the Hubble-disclosed trillion-galaxy cosmos vanishes at one level, at another it continues to evolve, perhaps as quantum waves with their own epigenetic probabilities. One day, believe it or not, everything about the universe—*everything*—will be walk-out-the-door different, only there will be no door, no "where." Yet the part of you that knows itself as you will be there.

12

The Superconscious Source

Seth and like entities describe themselves as composites of individual and group souls who have completed many cycles of incarnation on one or more worlds. Other aggregate beings who have contacted mediums on this plane include "Michael," "the Pleiadian Council," "Kryon," "Babaji," and the author of *The Course in Miracles*. Countless others are not well-known or known at all.

The phenomenon of composite intelligences is related to Multipersonhood, but the "hive" has advanced from a nonlocal background field of entities to a conscious melding of experiences and knowledge. Souls come together and compress their collective lifetimes of discovery into a transdimensional library that they beam for use on temporal worlds. Channeling from these beams does not entail transfer of information or language in an ordinary sense; it is instantaneous dissemination by a compound entity into coherent energy patterns that transcend space-time and the speed of light—transmission *without transmission*.

According to Seth, the superconscious source doesn't have a voice in an anatomical sense, but the voice the medium adopts is "much like the one" that the intelligence would have if it were human.[1] The medium never receives the whole transmission, just the portion she can understand as it converts clairaudiently into her own language. As noted in chapter 7, there are many filters and distortions—ontological, cosmological, neurological, and syntactic—between the originating intelligence and the receiving entity, and these all have to be accounted for, discounted, and reconciled for a message to have any authenticity or point, let alone a mission of spirit guidance and cosmic evolution. The translation is less like Hittite into German than "whale" or "dove" (or the microwave background of Saturn's rings) into "human."

The entity appropriates the channel's language and vocabulary,[2] since it must operate at his or her level of knowledge and phase of development. As Seth explains, it "cannot force from him, from his speech mechanism, concepts with which he is <u>entirely</u> unfamiliar."[3] It also must "introduce [new material] step by step," and the recipient must consent to the concepts as he or she interprets them speechwise with the entity's assistance, using his or her own associations to get to "the proper subject or image."[4] Sometimes the medium inserts a word or phrase that, by logic, is wrong but carries the correct meaning.

Words store energy. The essence behind them is altering atoms, changing their charges and pulsation rates in both the medium and the consciousnesses that receive the message, not only during its broadcast but also in all its printed and spoken versions throughout time. The emphasis is on vibrational as well as semantic meaning.[5] John Friedlander notes that "Seth's books are literally different now than they were forty-five years ago. The words are the same, but the energy connected to those words has changed."[6]

When an intelligence calling itself Seth manifested to Jane Roberts in Elmira, New York, in 1963—initially through a Ouija board—she was tapping into a higher-dimensional intelligence field whose name at her frequency was "Seth." She described Seth as but "one multidimensional aspect of many; one characteristic . . . of a kind of entity we can hardly comprehend."[7] "He" was a "laser" beam of spatially coherent information. When presented with Jane's personality and Earth's stage of civilization, the beam attuned itself to that level of listening while taking on a personality.

Jane's initial sense may have been of a person who went through a series of incarnations and was finished, but that was too linear for the scope or diversity of the sending mechanism. In "his" last lifetime, Seth told her, he was a sea captain who got high by smoking oregano. But that wasn't who he was. He didn't experience himself as just that or as that apart from countless other identities. It was one story line of a multi-dimensional being, a portion of its identity that resonated with Jane and her husband. Seth also mentioned taking a hundred-year "vacation" as a tree. At other times he talks about how he and a few others created Earth itself. Each is a layer of Seth, and Seth knows himself to be all these different selves simultaneously.

When (or if) another person (not Jane) channels the same energy, it might or might not identify itself as Seth. (For instance, John Friedlander channels the same energy field under another name.) A different entity and its body of knowledge might also be conflated by another channeler with Jane's "Seth," as "Seth" has become a proprietary name for a general range of channeling.

In 2019, I asked John to clarify his nomenclature of channeled guides. He spoke from his experience with Jane Roberts and afterward:

> I channel several entities around the Seth project. I used to call it "Seth," but Seth people get very prissy about other people channeling Seth. Seth had said he would only come through Jane in her lifetime, but it's not as though he just goes away. He was almost certainly who was talking to Alice Bailey earlier, though she thought she was talking to a Tibetan. Seth also doesn't have a single memory bank. He uses information in different ways depending on who channels him. He blends with the personality. For instance, the Dalai Lama is an emanation of something much larger, but he is not the *only* emanation of that bodhisattva. Jane Roberts likewise interacts with an emanation of a much larger being, and her channeling of it will never be repeated because no one will interact with that being in the same way.

Seth insisted that he and Jane were independent beings. "[I do not] use Ruburt as a puppet, and stuff his mouth with tapes as a recorder . . . I am not some spooky Big Brother experiencing his reality for him!"[8] (Ruburt is Seth's name for Jane, "the closest translation, in your terms, for the name of the whole self or entity of which (Jane) is now a self-conscious part."[9])

Seth also described himself as a facet of Jane's Multipersonhood, an aspect not accessible to her ego in its present configuration. He was already matching her vibration. Jane was becoming Seth, or was already Seth in another probability or future state, so she was contacting a dormant, evolving aspect of herself broadcasting to her present identity, drawing "plain Jane" into a network of which she was already part. Seth was so vast that he encompassed many probabilities of each of them.

Seth was also a form of Jane returning from a future incarnation to address a phase of himself. Roberts considers, "Would a Seth, experiencing a Jane, think of her as a lesser developed personality . . . ? He would be me in my present time, developing abilities that would later let him be him."[10]

Seth's answer: "Ruburt is not myself now, in his present life; he is nevertheless an extension and materialization of the Seth that I was at one time. . . . Ruburt was myself, Seth, many centuries ago, but he grew, evolved and expanded in terms of a particular, personal set of value fulfillments. He is now an actual gestalt, a personality that was one of the probable personalities into which Seth could grow. I represent another. I am another."[11]

Seth is, conversely, Jane's "higher dimensionalized ghost . . . drawn from the earth's entire existence . . . [including] other earths, probable to us, with different intersections with space and time; other living areas and other historic pasts than our own. . . ."[12] Jane says, "[H]is psychological reality straddled worlds in a way I couldn't understand. I sensed a multidimensionality of personality that I couldn't define . . . a deep part of the structure of my psyche, but also a definite personification of a multi-world or multi-reality consciousness that may well be beyond our present ideas of personhood."[13]

It is impossible to distinguish what is coming from a latent aspect of Jane as opposed to what is coming from an exogenous intelligence. Seth may be a future incarnation of Jane, but not exclusively; he may also be a future incarnation of her husband, Robert Butts. And when Jane gets into that future, she will be herself too (as Robert will be *him*self). The system is so labyrinthine that a future "Seth" and "Jane," while fixed at this moment, are also continuously changing, creating multiple futures simultaneously. Each falls under a different probability, yet each is pre-ordained in a different sense. Identities are continually transmogrifying, undulating both forward and backward from their local times.

"I am a part of your unknown reality," Seth inserts, "and you are a part of mine. . . . I am what I call a bridge personality, composed of a composite self—Ruburt and I meeting and merging to form a personality that is not truly <u>either</u> of us, but a new one that exists between dimensions. . . .[14] a 'trans-world' entity, a personagram—an actual personality formed in the psyche at the intersection point of [her] focus personality with another aspect[15] [with] separate existence in his own dimensions and as it is reflected in her psyche."[16]

"Seth is what I am, and yet I am more than Seth is. Seth is, however, independent, and continues to develop as I do."[17] "I was, in those terms, <u>not</u> the Ruburt that Ruburt <u>is</u>. My experiences as Ruburt were different, and Ruburt's experiences as Seth, in those terms, will be different. Ruburt will be a different Seth than I am."[18]

Does that mean that Seth is not a persona, even a composite one, but a phase of evolution in which "his" configurations fluctuate? Is he a way of knowing oneself in Multipersonhood, a stream of ones's aggregate identities? John Friedlander addressed these paradoxes:

> In a meaningful way Seth is a future incarnation of Jane, but in a meaningful way when Jane gets into that future . . . she'll be her own Seth and not the one who talked to us. Seth is not merely Jane's future, and Jane is not merely Seth's past. Each is utterly the center of an ever-expanding world. When Seth talks to Jane, Jane is new even though she's his past. In the moment he's talking to her, newness is being born, though how could newness be born out of his past . . . ? It's just as much a sort of made-up phenomenon, drawing from energies and speaking to us. But "made up" doesn't mean unreal, because Seth was as real as any of us.[19]

When Jane channeled messages from a seemingly different source, Seth told her that she had contacted a higher-dimensional form of himself. He named it Seth 2. She later channeled other very high frequencies, one of which (the Sumari) Seth described as "a psychic family or . . . guild of consciousnesses who worked together through the centuries."[20] He went on to explain that the Sumari is one of many information sets transmitted telepathically in signal form, but it "is not a language, since it was not spoken verbally by any group of people. . . . [I]t is a language that is at the base of all languages, and from which all languages spring. . . . The living vitality of the cordella rises out of the universe's need to express and understand itself, to form in ever-changing patterns and take itself by surprise."[21] (*Cordella,* Seth added, is the Sumari word for Multipersonhood.)

Seth deconstructed his own identity in speeches to Jane's classes (April 17, 1973, and January 29, 1974). In his words, his identity engages Jane, Robert, his listeners, me, now you, changing its energy pattern at each "stop." He is speaking to all of us *individually,* so we are each receiving individualized "atoms," vibrational units of Jane's phonemes. Even that aspect continues to change over time.

There is no need to search for extraterrestrial intelligence. Long after Earth itself has vanished from the universe, Seth will be broadcasting and guiding us:

So I ask you: "What is your name, each of you?" <u>My</u> name is nameless. I have no name. I give you the name of Seth because it is a name and you want names. . . . You believe that you cannot speak to me unless I have a name, so I am Seth. I told Ruburt from our earliest sessions that he could call me Seth. I never said, "My name is Seth."

Who is Seth? . . . On the one hand I am someone you do not know, lost before the annals of time as you understand it. . . .

On the other hand, I am yourself . . . so through me do you view and meet the selves that you are, and so I rise, in your terms, from the power and antiquity and glory of your own being, projected outward into the world of time from a universe in which time is meaningless. . . .

Each of you . . . project upon me those characteristics that are your own in other terms, and so I am a multidimensional being as *you* are multidimensional beings. . . .

I speak with the voices that, in your terms, come from centuries yet unborn. Yet these are the voices that you, yourselves, have whispered from the fossils of your being, when you were (in your terms now) unthinking selves on sunlit cliffs in worlds unknowing. And projected by your desire, these voices then speak to you and urge you to your own fulfillment. . . .

For there (in the deepest reaches of your being), is a greater reality that knows your present existence and looks upon it with the fondest, the dearest, the most familiar of memories; a reality that has grown, in your terms, into entities indescribably vast; realities that form worlds more complex than the one in which you now dwell.

And yet also, through that channel of being you will also find fossil cells that are not yet selves, that have not yet grouped into complex organisms, but that lie filled with the desire of being, filled with the desire of God, for fulfillment and thought and complexity . . . selves that will become entities; fossils of yourselves that still, in certain terms, contain memories of the selves that you are.

As they wander in what seems to you to be a dark world; as they seek toward a sun that is your brain; as they journey over unknown cliffs, seeking recognition; so do you wander within worlds of greater selves that you are, seeking for the rays of other suns that are the brains of your own greater being. So are you all one, and so is my voice speaking from your own greater being—from which you are forever born and always reborn. . . .

The smallest cell in your toe dreams of your reality and helps to create it, as you dream of the smallest cell's reality and help create it. . . .

You move your hand and touch your face, and what realities do you stir, and what seasons do you cause to fall upon other worlds—and how, as you lift your finger and touch your face—do you stir ponds of reality? What frogs sit by the ponds that you have stirred, and what winds blow with the power of your thoughts? . . . Your lips curve and tremble, and the muscles move across your face, and as they do the wind blows in other universes.[22]

Pretty beautiful, no? And mysterious. It suggests the immensity of our situation, the enigma of personhood. This reality is running so close to our beingness arising in relation to it that we do not experience our heft or how vast and neutral it is. While the universe is creating our reality, we are creating its. *We* are because *it* is. But *it* is because *we* are. This paradox goes all the way to the bottom—whatever that turns out to be, whoever we turn out to be when we get there.

Pick any song you want, and it begins to sound like Sumari after a few bars. I'll take Jo Stafford singing *Poor Wayfarin' Stranger*:

> *I know dark clouds will gather round me,*
> *I know my way is rough and steep,*
> *But beauteous fields lie just before me,*
> *Where men redeemed their vigils keep.*

13

Undumbing the Universe

The Heavens

To put humans, or human surrogates, in other solar systems or galaxies is impossible with current technology and, more to the point, according to the laws of physics and biology that set speed and time caps on all activities in the universe—and very limited ones on metabolizing organisms. Our current methods not only take too long by factors in the billions but also require a fuel tank the size of a planet!

In the foreseeable future, no currently operating spacecraft of NASA, Russia, China, Richard Branson, Elon Musk, or Jeff Bezos is going to deliver a humanoid object even to Alpha Centauri in the neighboring system. (Solar-wind-blown sails are conflations of current gadgets with hypothetical systems—gaming solutions rather than likely missions.)

If our goal is to travel in space, we have to figure out how to get *into* space, and it isn't by internal combustion engines, cold gas thrusters, and gravity-well acceleration. Movies like *Avatar* aside, those won't ferry us to Centauri in less than forty or fifty thousand years or carry sufficient propellant for the unlikely venture.

Even the relatively feasible colonization of Mars is beyond our current capacity. We can't be confident that astronauts will survive the 1,200-day journey. Mars's lack of breathable air, food, or shelter from subzero temperatures, solar radiation, and sandstorms is not just an incidental set of problems to be solved by on-site tinkering or a science-fiction trilogy. It is a module-by-module, molecule-by-molecule undertaking. It would make more sense to get the macro-plastics and micro-beads out of the Pacific Ocean than to pump oxygen from the Martian pole into a sealed dome—a somewhat comparable enterprise. Mars still doesn't get us very far.

If we accept the general literature of UFO sightings and contact, from the ancient Dogon and recent Ariel School incidents in Africa to Betty and Barney Hill and Whitley Strieber in present-day North America, then spaceships (if that is, in fact, what they were) got into Earth's atmosphere in a different manner from how we sent *New Horizons* to Pluto/Charon or plan to deliver explorers to Mars.

How else do we explain six reptilelike humanoids unearthed from an ancient tomb in Nazca, Peru? The mummies have elongated skulls and three anomalously elongated digits on each hand and foot. They either came here by a mode of interstellar or interdimensional travel we can't conceptualize or they are elaborate hoaxes like the Piltdown and Cardiff "men" or the "doll" dissected in the alien-autopsy film.

To break our interstellar deadlock, something fundamental has to change, not just criteria of time and space but also scaling between quantum and Newtonian fields. That means re-engineering propulsion from some combination of superposition, wormholes, negative space (or time), quantum vacuums, inertial fields, zero-point energies, and miniscule repulsion merry-go-rounds. Instigations of very small objects and forces might transfer effects from nanospaces into either human-size vehicles or miniature equivalents that can transport body-minds or their information faster than photons and then presumably return them to human form and scale, but I wouldn't count on it, even if our civilization lasts another millennium.

In Seth's view, NASA is designing for a camouflage universe. The starry piñata is "there" all right, but it is also generating a thoughtform that makes it look like *its own gospel geography*. In truth, we have no idea what the Hubble telescope is capturing: matter, intelligence, a mirage, or the inability of the human mind to comprehend the intricacy of Creation.

"Your idea of space travel," Seth explains, "is to journey over the 'skin of your universe.' You do not understand that your system is expanding within itself, bringing forth new creativity and energy."[1]

What does he mean? Where is the inner expansion that matches the expansion of hydrogen and helium under gravity? Ellias Lonsdale was sitting at Sarah's bedside when she passed, and he glimpsed her transition. "She didn't go *out*," he told me, "as I expected, but *in*."

Where is "in"? Is it shamanic, psychogenic, or incarnational? Does it require *not* having a spaceship?

But if it is only shamanic, how does the shaman traveler re-embody on another continent or planet? How did those E.T.'s get their carapaces here? Is there a lost physics of "in," trapped somewhere at the dawn of Western civilization, as the Egyptian "astronomy" of transformation and dimensional travel diverged from the oceanic astronomy of Homer, Aristotle, and Magellan? Where does the native Hopi vibratory landscape, the heart of nature behind forms and appearances, cross quantum entanglement in establishing interstellar or cosmological travel? What if the Hopi were Earth's first physicists?

Given the daunting scope of the astrophysical universe, the Native American "in" may lead "out" more than "out" does, perhaps into dilated scalar fields. Portals to multiverses or multidimensional domains may be disguised in domains too tortile for the most powerful microscopes. In string theory, entire universes are folded into one another based on their inherent topological structure; dimensions that come into being as degrees of freedom resolve their dynamical tensions, whatever that means under game conditions. Our own landscape arises from the behavior of quark-scale "objects" in spaces now lost to inquiry or passage. By the same rationale of disproportion, the Big Bang pulled this whole cosmos out of a clown car tinier than a flea.

By another view, the universe's internal expansion may be a matter of consciousness as well as topology. When Albert Einstein put space and time into a continuum, he was mapping the human brain as much as stars and galaxies. Relativity is mind observing nature as they wrap around each other. Masses, shapes, and motions construe into observers and relationships of complex objects. There is no universe otherwise—no matter without mind, no mind without matter, no matter or mind except by interdependent origination. More than 90 percent of the model is AWOL anyway, in galactic rotation, scalar fields or whatever. Seth continues:

Your own coordinates close you off from recognizing that there are indeed other intelligences alive even <u>within</u> your own solar system. You will never meet them in your exterior reality, however, for you are not focused in the time period of their existence. You may physically visit the "very same planet" on which they reside, but to <u>you</u> the planet will appear barren, or not able to support life.

In the same way, others can visit your planet with the same results. . . . Some intelligent beings have visited your planet, finding not the world you know but a probable one. . . .

Effective space travel, creative space travel on your part, will not occur until you learn that your space-time system is one focus. Otherwise you will seem to visit one dead world after another, blind to civilizations that may exist on any of them. Some of these difficulties could be transcended if you learned to understand the . . . multidimensionality of even your own physical structure. . . .

[U]ntil you <u>understand</u> that, you will not . . . be able to thoroughly explore any planet—or any reality, including your own.[2]

In other words, the trajectory of science from Anaximander and Thales to Carl Sagan and Neil deGrasse Tyson has narrow-banded one aspect of cosmology and intelligent life. If we want to do a "star trek" for real, then we need a warp drive for real—a completely different type of ship.

Alternate Cosmology

The ostensible channeled transmissions from the *Challenger* astronauts, which began soon after their shuttle exploded in January 1986, speak to an alternate cosmology shadowing us, whether you believe in their authenticity or not. Traumatized in the aftermath of their plunge into the ocean, they apparently tried and failed to contact NASA by a psychic-messaging protocol in which one astronaut on each mission had been trained. The crew did succeed in contacting several mediums, including Jeanne Love, in Adrian, Michigan, and Regina Ochoa, based in Northern California.[3]

All seven astronauts reportedly have been reaching out to humanity through them, trying to tell us that their own fate is a clue to our collective situation: only when we have learned how to exteriorize interior space will we enter the cosmos. (According to Love and Ochoa, the main reason the public message was delayed until 2017 was a series of personal threats against them if they disclosed the exchanges. If true, this would seem to support the validity of at least some of the more controversial information received: it is a danger to the reigning paradigm and governing order.)

The message may not be what it seems (or from whom it purports to come), but it is not to be dismissed out of hand as a stunt or fake news either.

Interplanetary Expansion

Deploying an algorithm on the internet, Amazon's Jeff Bezos has amassed more money than he can deploy in his lifetime, so he hopes to use it to trademark the future. A sci-fi junkie and transhumanist, he considers interplanetary expansion the solution to humanity's present crises: building cities on other worlds in the solar system, which means faster rockets, durable domes, and synthetic ecosystems. He makes an educated argument:

> [I]f you take baseline energy usage globally across the whole world and compound it at just a few percent a year for just a few hundred years, you have to cover the entire surface of the Earth in solar cells. That's the real energy crisis. And it's happening soon. And by soon, I mean within just a few hundred years. . . .
>
> Now take the scenario, where you move out into the Solar System. The Solar System can easily support a trillion humans. And if we had a trillion humans, we would have a thousand Einsteins and a thousand Mozarts and unlimited (for all practical purposes) resources and solar power unlimited for all practical purposes. That's the world I want my great-grandchildren's great-grandchildren to live in.[4]

A trillion humans! Remember, there's no breathable air on any other planet or moon. There's also no food, shelter, or liquid water. Except for a few borderline regions of Mars, any rocky surface in the solar system other than Gaia would freeze or fry a visiting mammal in less than a minute. The rest of the orbs are frigid balls of gas. We cannot bring back the New World or Oceania with their aboriginal fertility and cornucopia by contriving pseudoreplicas on other orbs. Even Amazon Prime has limitations. It's back to the drawing board, Jeff.

The Moral Dimension

Perhaps the universe *is* bleak, impenetrable, and (mostly) uninhabitable, except (thus far) for Earth, because it is only our dream and we have not yet dreamed the rest, not filled its vacancy with anything but paranoid, apocalyptic reflections. Perhaps that's what's keeping us out of interstellar space.

I don't mean this in a simple or facile sense. Stars and planets and comets are solid as resolved through Galileo's and William Herschel's lenses and elsewise assayed, but their preponderance hides other celestial skies, cluttering our view of Middle and Upper Worlds, which have their own prairies and Milky Ways. I have no fallback for the violence and sheer scope of interstellar space or to pace gravity. I can't justify the vacuums, thermonuclear fires, absolute-zero cold, and novas, but they must be necessary for this manifestation.

In January 2019, I was invited to join a Lockheed Martin engineer, a CERN physicist, and several other scientists at a forum at MIT; this section of the book is a rewrite of the talk I gave there. My colleagues believed in some sort of psychoid transport or not only wouldn't I have been their guest, there wouldn't have been a conference. Time travel, levitation, crop circles, and dimension hopping were on the table, and not from me.

Crop circles speak in mathematical and alphabetic ciphers, perhaps because they are trying to tell us something about their makers, ourselves, and the universe.

In 1974, Carl Sagan designed a different sort of cipher: an interstellar radio message (IRM), giving pertinent information about *Homo sapiens* (average height, DNA structure, location at Sol 3 in the Milky Way, plus our recognition of decimals, chemical elements, and prime numbers). It was broadcast by SETI from the Arecibo Observatory in Puerto Rico on November 16.

On August 19, 2001, a matching bar code–like design appeared as flattened grain stalks in a field in Chilbolton, Hampshire, beside the largest radio telescope in England and regional SETI headquarters. Using the same format as Sagan, it described silicon-based (not carbon-based) creatures, four feet tall, with an extra string in their genetic molecules, occupying the fourth, fifth, and sixth planets of their solar system. This could have been a brilliant prank. But my hosts at MIT cited their high security clearances when insisting that a paraphysical Skunk Works was a prerequisite for interstellar travel.

It is possible that our capacity for distant flight, like our capacity for remote viewing and telekinesis, is related to our current spiritual development and that we are encountering systems that are not value-neutral or objectifiable in the way that scientific experiments and their technologies are. After all, anyone can build a hydrogen bomb or laser, for good or evil, by their own definition. Dan Drasin, a journalist and media producer who has traversed the space-science/metaphysical borderline since the 1970s, spoke directly to this in a 2019 email answering mine that described the MIT event:

> Any venturing into psychic phenomena and other supraphysical arenas surely puts us into territory where, as the first order of business, we need to understand our own natures and motives far more deeply than we do now. Pushing boundaries within the constraints of 3-D reality (however naïve, mischievous, or misguided) would seem to be relatively harmless in the grand scheme of things. When one ventures out into higher dimensions without first becoming intimate with them on an inner level (which presupposes becoming familiar with *oneself* on an inner level, and how one projects the reality one perceives) one may be playing with fire on thin ice.
>
> I have no idea to what extent the lore surrounding the putatively catastrophic Philadelphia and Montauk Experiments is true [sailors imbedded wholly and partially in their ship's metal or transported into the future in muddled states of mind], but even viewed as fic-

tion in the vein of *The Sorcerer's Apprentice,* these stories do provide sobering food for thought, and should be taken to heart by anyone considering exploring in these directions.

I think most of our collective assumptions about space travel have been formed more by the shallow glamor and veiled machismo of twentieth-century sci-fi than by much genuine understanding or deep perception.

We forget how much we are taking for granted in proposing to go far away in machines. The settlement of the indigenous Americas and Australia, allegorized in *Avatar* and the more recent *Shape of Water,* which is not even interplanetary, serve as cautionary tales. Scientific curiosity and the terrestrial benefits of space technology are fair values, but going somewhere else in ways that challenge the basic nature of matter and mind has psychospiritual and ethical implications.

To talk about moving folks among worlds far apart, much more needs to be understood about the nature of the touring entities, the worlds themselves, and the universe's modes of transport and transfer. Going to an Earth-like planet in the Crab Nebula 6,500 light years away, or even Kepler-452b in Cygnus, 1,400 light years from here, confronts not only the topology of space-time and range of quantum fields but the stability of selfhood, the nature of mortality, and the distinction between inner and outer space. We may have to meld advanced propulsion with our psychic and moral development. To solve the physics may be inseparable from where we want to go and what we want to do when we arrive there.

To advance from quantum fields to intergalactic space flight requires an ontological transformation at the level of basic identity. Perhaps one reaches the Pleiadian system most cost-effectively by being reborn there. The whispers of the dead may be what get us from the Hardy Boys' crooked arrow to the clue in the hydrogen atom to the inverted complexity of the Big Bang.

It is possible that we can't figure out how to bend relativistic fields of space-time or conduct instantaneous morphic-resonance transport until we have gone into the empty spaces around our hearts and explored our local planes of consciousness. Then our sense of planet, matter, locale, and distance might change enough for us to figure out how to build a radical machine. At that level, every interstellar "ship" would have tele-kinetic aspects, and the journey would also be across frequencies, turning astronomical into dimensional space.

Astrophysical subplanes vibrate at the frequency of their atoms and molecules, making it a slow trek. A different type of life flows through the Astro-Etheric—its own life, maintaining separate contracts with the earth and stars and ignoring the mere speed limit of photons. Plus, the zone itself is conscious. Parts of it are independently conscious, smaller consciousness that collect in pools and eddies and redistribute space-time while instigating probability jumps.[5] If we could turn physical thrust into Etheric propulsion, we might travel between galaxies on lei lines—cosmic nadis—as smooth as butter (no meteors, dust, novas, or black holes). But that requires a coup of mind, technology, and resources. A psychically cyborged vessel can be designed only after a neurological shift of our action-reaction physics and psychology.

The Astral plane is a consciousness too, and it transports objects even faster than the Etheric. That's one reason it's called Astral (or Astrum); it has *its own* astronomy, populated by flying saucers, faeries, and hyper-spatial humanoids.[6]

Can we bypass the astrophysical corridor in swifter planes and then return to a physical vibration? Is that how those Peruvian humanoids and legendary "grey" Zeta Reticulans got here? Are the saucer-shaped waves we call UFOs Etheric or Astral "ships"?

In the Flower of Life yoga of sacred-geometry maven Drunvalo Melchizedek, interstellar "aeronautics" involves breathing a *merkaba* (a divine light vessel) around oneself into a personal vehicle. The space-craft is created by a spiraling sequence of sixteen or seventeen connected breaths, each fused with and energized by affirmations and an image of three star tetrahedrons made from sigils or supersonic runes. Drunvalo's *merkabas* can go anywhere in the universe, propelled by love. According to rebirther Bob Frissell, "The highest frequencies of the heart chakra emit a force like gravity, the purest energy ever created, and inexhaustible. It is the meta-substance that accelerates saucers above the speed of light."[7]

You don't have to believe in love propellant, sacred geometry, or *merkabas* to ponder the implications of a *prānāyāma** trope commuted into aerospace terms. Something major is missing, and we don't know what it is, so we have to approach it by metaphor, analogy, and proxy trainings at our level. They won't get us into the stars, but neither will rocket ships and guns.

Everything

Most citizens of modernity believe that the universe hits an absolute horizon at the Theory of Everything (give or take a pint) and needs no undumbing.

Yet science is looking for a new Rosetta stone. It took it centuries to put galaxies, mosquitos, and electrons veridically onto the same scale—that is beyond dare. But it leads to no consummate paradigm. Physics phenomenologist Nima Arkani-Hamed calls the cosmic bluff: "The ascension to the tenth level of intellectual heaven would be if we find the question to which the universe is the answer."[8] Everything has been running backward for at least three hundred years, pulling even relativity and quantum physics under a reverse shank. The result: multiple levels of causation and meaning continue to camouflage whatever is camouflaging them. Science writer Natalie Wolchover puts the impasse in context:

> It's as though physics has been turned inside out. It now appears that the answers already surround us. It's the question we don't know. [That is because] there are multiple valid ways of describing so many physical phenomena. But an even stranger fact is that, when there are competing descriptions, one often turns out to be more true than the others, because it extends to a deeper or more general description of reality. . . .
>
> When there are many possible descriptions of a physical situation—all making equivalent predictions, yet all wildly different in premise—one will turn out to be preferable, because it extends to an underlying

---

*Prānāyāma is a Sanskrit couplet describing expansion by breath; in particular, the translation of individual energy into cosmic energy, whatever that means or could someday mean.

reality, seeming to account for more of the universe at once. And yet this new description might, in turn, have multiple formulations—and one of those alternatives may apply even more broadly. It's as though physicists are playing a modified telephone game in which, with each whisper, the message is translated into a different language.[9]

If you keep asking fundamental questions of the universe and getting "correct" answers that are different in premise, you might start wondering about the assumptions behind your initial premise.

Of course, physicists, microbiologists, and neuroscientists "bottom out" their perspectives more fully than I can—no contest there. But they have not clawed fastidiously at their own contradictions and systemic oxymorons. As methodical as their delving has been, they have not considered that they are tilting at a refraction of their own mindedness as well as the self-*re*-reconciling intricacy with which it is enmeshed in an apparition. Matter is irreducible to any algebra.

The main thing that modern physicists have proved is that the universe was not created in the way *they* would make a universe. The provisional answers of physics shape-change because they are answers to different questions from those the universe is posing.

"The long sought after Theory of Everything is really merely just missing one important component that was too close for us to have noticed," states Robert Lanza. "Science hasn't confronted the one thing that's most familiar and most mysterious—and that is consciousness."[10]

It was missing in my introduction and it is still unaccounted for, despite tortuous attempts to wrest it from the algorithm, despite a fierce counter-campaign to exclude it from empirical immunity. Consciousness won't vest a fair squire to joust on its behalf, yet it keeps reflecting its maze through every equation and assessment. The truth remains as unutterable as the secret name of God: consciousness is its own thing. Richard Conn Henry, a physics and astronomy professor at Johns Hopkins University, remarks, "What Lanza says in his book is not new. Then why does Robert have to say it at all? It is because we, the physicists, do not say it—or if we do say it, we only whisper it, and in private—furiously blushing as we mouth the words. True, yes; politically correct . . . no!"[11] Lanza is amused by the response, which, he says, "has been much how you'd expect priests to respond to stem cell research."[12]

In the view of George Wald, "Mind, rather than emerging as a late outgrowth in the evolution of life, has existed always . . . the source and condition of physical reality."[13] Sir James Jeans, a physicist who calculated the radius of an interstellar cloud in space dependent on the temperature and density of that cloud, famously concluded that the universe is "more like a great thought than a great machine. Mind no longer appears to be an accidental intruder into the realm of matter . . . we ought rather hail it as the creator and governor of the realm of matter."[14] Interstellar clouds included.

Physicist Max Planck joined his verdict:

As a man who has devoted his whole life to the most clear-headed science, to the study of matter, I can tell you as a result of my research about the atoms this much: There is no matter as such! All matter originates and exists only by virtue of a force which brings the particles of an atom to vibration and holds this most minute solar system of the atom together.

We must assume behind this force the existence of a conscious and intelligent Mind. This Mind is the matrix of all matter.[15]

He looked as directly at vibrating atoms as possible and came to a nonmaterial recognition.

I ran this quote by a materialist admirer of Planck. He attributed it to dotage and human fallibility, comparing it to Newton's belief in alchemy. Yet panpsychism is no longer ridiculed or rare among biologists. In the twenty-first century, even atheistic scientists are proposing that matter might contain some form of primitive mind or be predisposed to consciousness. It needn't be numinous; particle oscillation, glycolic lava melt, or phase states with attractors are good enough. Aristotle called it *hyle,* a primary substance that continually converts its intrinsic nature into extrinsic form. Astrophysicist Gregory L. Matloff proffered a "proto-consciousness field" extending through all of space, adding, "The entire cosmos may be self-aware."[16] It is not a case of figuring out how the mind and matter are entangled and which is the progenitor; it is a single field emanating as mind at one level, matter at another.

That's the elephant in the room, but not everyone recognizes the same pachyderm. Prague-based philosopher Peter Wilborg emailed a critique of an early draft of this book to a mutual friend in Ljubljana: "Grossinger's own 'philosophy' remains stuck in an old-new form of 'panpsychism' which holds on to the matter-mind dualism. No, the universe is not conscious in the way he and other panpsychists think. Instead, the universe is *nothing but consciousness*."

I am not a panpsychist, new or old, so the import of Wilborg's words lies outside their first meaning; it goes something like: "Grossinger says that mind came before matter, but that is a copout. There *never was* matter. What we are experiencing is an expansion of conscious energy taking form in pseudo-material mirages."

I agree. "The universe *is* consciousness." But look at how it billows into a woodland onto which sunlight is pouring, as squirrels bound and birds alight, or illumines an urban thoroughfare packed with vehicles, people, and shops. The mystery of *physical manifestation must be explained*. Our bodies are not virtual-reality wardrobes; they express a depth that could not be ventured, a journey that would never be taken, without them. Their unforgiving density and rivalry may be the only way for the universe to experience its inherent dialectic. Otherwise, it would consume its own radiance.

The fact that the Big Bang expressed itself in gravity, quarks, and ecosystems says what consciousness *is trying to get at*. If matter arose from mind, mind likewise arose from matter. Reality was designed simultaneously inside out as consciousness and outside in as matter. Matter can't arise independently because then the field itself wouldn't exist, and that's not possible.

Meaning

Medieval theologians proposed that God re-creates the world from moment to moment. John Friedlander put this in contemporary terms:

No matter who you are or when you are, the whole universe wraps itself around you and re-wraps itself around you each moment. The whole universe changes its address to you each moment. No matter how small a change you make, the whole universe—and all universes—instantly change in a way that wraps around you. Not just you of course; you as part of the whole universe and every other subjectivity in the universe. . . .

The universe is always listening to you; it never goes unconscious. I might gather wool for a minute or two, but the universe never does that. This world is so cool that everybody, through their Causal soul and the interplay between themselves and other beings, has an individualized dharma,* depending on what's up for them. And moment by moment, your individualized dharma changes. No matter what decision you make and no matter how horrible a decision you make, at that moment the universe immediately reconstructs itself to optimize your chance of developing spiritual freedom or spiritual meaningfulness. The ground of manifestation is biased in your favor. I'm not saying it makes it easier because you may have made enough bad decisions that it's really pretty hard, but given the context you have created, the universe always changes every aspect of itself to optimize your ability to make meaning in that moment. If you make great decisions, the universe immediately recalculates and is available in the next moment. All experience is sacred and eternal, and nothing is ever lost.[17]

We should be so lucky, when God threw the dice and drew our card—I mean, our universe. It takes no siestas and leaves no slack. Each time an eagle snares a gull or a fisher cat claws open a squealing chipmunk, the universe is maximizing meaningfulness and spiritual freedom *for both.* Imagine a system complex enough to optimize spiritual freedom and meaning simultaneously for the executioner and his victim. That is the unified field—reality collapsed in upon itself by an invisible

---

*"Individualized dharma" means that every sentient being is subject to its own cosmic order and law.

expanding wave. Herman Melville glimpsed its reflection in the aftermath of a whale's breach: "Silence reigned over the before tumultuous but now deserted deck. An intense copper calm, like a universal yellow lotus, was more and more unfolding its noiseless measureless leaves upon the sea."[18]

The wave is quantum entanglement, Multipersonhood, over-determination, and even that doesn't begin to undumb what's going on. Anything less *wouldn't justify the manifestation*. A given crow on a tele-phone line looking down at you may be you or an associate in a past or future life, and that is why it is looking and you are noticing it. Or not. At the heart of things it doesn't matter. Nothing is incidental, just as everything is *only incidental*. Meaning and randomness intersect at every juncture. After all, there are a lot of crows and beetles to account for.

You and that crow—or that gopher darting out of its burrow and back—exchange Etheric energy. Seth calls attention to "the countless times counterparts [have] unwittingly gathered . . . and what sorts of numberless exchanges [take] place on unconscious levels between those who [are] psychically related in some fashion."[19]

As an osprey tries to hoist a giant trout out of a stream, but the fish spirals the bird down into gorging waters. A hawk descends from on high and rips a prairie dog off the ground. There is a blood price, but the deed is not irreconcilable, nor is it an obliteration of the prairie dog's poten-tial for future happiness and spiritual growth. Likewise, the zebra cut down by a pack of jackals, the water buffalo felled by a pride of leopards. Probabilities are mixing with dimensions of time and energies we don't begin to track. In the greater system, each Etheric body converts its own agony within a system of birth, death, and knowledge. Seth points out that animals "understand the nature of the life-energy they share, and are not—in those terms—jealous for their own individuality."[20] There is intimacy and value in absorbing the Physical-Etheric field of another creature. "The slain animal [knows that it will] look out through its slay-er's eyes—attaining a newer, different kind of consciousness."[21]

The cat tormenting the mouse is playing with the universe, as is the mouse. They are teaching the universe who they are and who it is. They couldn't be teaching the universe unless the universe *were teaching them the same thing*. They will work it out in the vastness of All That Is.

Consciousness cannot act against itself. There is only curiosity of an untold force staring deeply and wondrously into its own nature and capacity to mirror itself to near-infinite depth. Philosopher Jean-Paul Sartre dead-reckoned it in France in the midst of World War II:

A vast entity, a planet, in a space of a hundred million dimensions; three-dimensional beings could not so much as imagine it. And yet each dimension was an autonomous consciousness. Try to look directly at that planet, it would disintegrate into tiny fragments, and nothing but consciousness would be left. A hundred million free consciousnesses, each aware of walls, the glowing stump of a cigar, familiar faces, and each constructing its destiny on its own responsibility. And yet each of those consciousnesses, by imperceptible contacts and insensible changes, realizes its existence as a cell in a gigantic and invisible coral. War: everyone is free, and yet the die is cast. It is there, it is everywhere, it is the totality of all my thoughts, of all Hitler's words, of all Gomez's acts; but no one is there to add it up. It exists solely for God. But God does not exist. And yet the war exists.[22]

Sartre took a default existential position; he was confronting a horrific war. I do not want to sound namby-pamby or holistically facile either. The universe is unfinished; a look at the night sky gives us the scale of what is at stake and how much needs to be done for individualized dharmas to claim the ground of their own embodiment. In post-Daesh Iraq, innocent people get accused of jihadist collaboration, then, without a trial, are maimed, imprisoned, and beheaded or set on fire while alive. In Honduras and El Salvador, gangs conduct indiscriminate theft, blackmail, rape, mutilation, and torture. In the Amazon, tribes are being slaughtered and driven or burned out of their homelands for resource looting. In Gaza, Yemen, Syria—aerial bombing, poison gas. In North Korea, in the Australian outback, in the Xinjian Uygur Autonomous Region, at Guantánamo Bay Detention Camp . . . on Earth—slavery, imprisonment of the innocent, identity erasure, starvation, inquisition, institutionalized humiliation.

All those people in bad situations aren't doomed any more than

people in good situations are home free or spared the woes of *samsara*.*
A single vibration encompasses our sphere and touches everyone, from
TGIF partygoers and executives in private jets to the downtrodden in
prisons or refugee boats and caravans.

This hell realm grants no pardons or exemptions. But it is *our* world,
the world of jackals, spiders, and hawks, and its arraignments are not limited regionally or confined to any particular chamber of space or time.
There is no wall or shelter to be built or portfolio in which to hide. It
is us and who we are, so if the universe is to work, we have to end our
charade. Otherwise, we are as stalemated as a John Deere tractor in a
three-year-deep mudhole.

Look around; there are lots of demolished cities, panting fangs, and
gluttons seeking requital and peace—in their hearts and our hearts.
Leaving aside a science and species mind unable to solve the problems
it has created, we have a depletion of meaning and context that itself is
unsustainable. That there are no easy answers is the *true depth* of All
That Is. Undumbing the universe begins with the *nonrenouncability* of
our own situation.

Bottom it out, folks! And it starts with getting that tractor out of
the mud.

Thoughtforms

In conclusion, the reason that physics can't corral its own catechism or
justify and make congruent its manifestation—and these are just words
applied to an estate of words—is at least threefold:

1. It applies itself only to a physical vibration and its sources. It sets
   "reality" above "existence."
2. It doesn't recognize the provenance or range of thoughtforms governing it, so it tries to top out nature and extract secrets instead of
   bottoming out its own latency.

---

*This Sanskrit term meaning "wandering" or "world" describes the cyclical or circuitous
nature of life, matter, and existence.

3. It takes the space-time continuum at face value while space and time are being generated at different frequencies of *each other*.

Considering these matters together, I think that physics is trying to bottom out an epiphenomenon. By identifying the basis of mind incontestably in matter, it has neglected the transparency of mindedness while trapping itself in a maze of minded projections onto *its own* relativistic outcomes. This recalls the fable of trying to repair a clock with a hammer, only the clock is an electron and the hammer a cyclotron. Materialists are so dazzled—and rightly—by the forces and forms of extenuation that they do not recognize that internalization is an equal function.

All of us—Lady Gaga, Vladimir Putin, Sacha Baron Cohen, Pema Chödrön, Jennifer Doudna, Angela Merkel, Donald Trump, the Pope, Joseph Kony, Abu Musab al-Zarqawi, Kevin Durant, Bill Gates, Malala Yousafzai—are matching the same picture. We are not just matching; we are also creating it, as is every other creature. Birds surfing between rooftops share not only our DNA but also our thoughtform. The thoughtform determines that they are birds rather than humans (or beetles or whales), that their picture is a bird one. Like fireflies in temporary unison, our pictures are creating—well, reality. There is no exception. If you're here, you're matching pictures.

John Friedlander provides a defining instance:

Everyone on this planet creates reality according to their beliefs, so if the Dalai Lama is on this planet—and he is—then he plays some part in the movement to world peace, but there are aspects in his aura that match—not in the normal English sense of the word "match" but in the psychic sense—that get lit up in the same way as terrorists because there couldn't be terrorists if he didn't have some match. It's not like if all of a sudden he cleared that match, all terrorists would disappear from this earth. *He* would disappear from this probability.[23]

In Seven Planes cosmology, we are converting Etheric, Astral, and Causal energy into molecules while the Buddhic plane figures out instant by instant how to cast a single reality that works for everyone. Otherwise, this universe and thoughtform *don't exist.*

But how is this possible if each personal reality is discrete and subjective and if the world itself—the universe—is made of objective, inanimate particles? It should be a train wreck out of the gate because people can't agree absolutely on anything, let alone blend realities so they match and also create and corroborate a concrete world.

This is where the universe's real complexity sets in. Atoms and quarks are in reciprocity with thoughtforms, as Atmic energies descend and materialize according to the laws of physics—except that this is only a metaphor. There is no descent. Everything manifests at its own frequency, and the frequencies cohere with one another and with everything else. Thoughtforms become atoms and molecules, as atoms and molecules transform their quantum states into phenomena and phenomenology. Reality is a plasma-like matrix of thoughtforms, energy fields, and dimensionalities, creating and transforming information. The "starry vacuum" astrophysical universe is astrophysical at one frequency, Astral at another, Atmic at another, and so on. Countless other planes and tiers of planes, each of them subtler and more informationally complex, radiate through the field, shimmering, transmitting, converting. *That sets the parameters of the universe we are in.*

The reason the universe doesn't read like a thoughtform is that so many entities, living and dead, are projecting it through the physics of its *own* manifestation. It's impossible to see behind such a screen or ruffle its mirage. The conundrum is how consciousness in the form of individual personal identities, each known subjectively only to itself, gets inserted into a collective thoughtform such that the awareness of reality becomes identical to the physics of that reality.

Each individual mind, rooted like a flowering mycelium in All That Is, breathes in the Buddhic dream. The landscape of meadows, seas, and stars holds unshatterably because the plane is summarizing all the planes and nests of planes existential to it.

That doesn't mean that the entire Creation is a mirage or chimera—though of course it is—it means that there are *only* chimeras, and they are *all* real. They are individuations and give rise to subjective experience, which is what reality is—and nothing is *more* real.

A fluctuation of thoughtforms can never come to a conclusive denomination within an atom or quark because the atom and quark are *within* the thoughtform and dissolve into curvature at its actual arc and into energy at par with its output. That is how a quantum particle can be physical while possessing only potential existence and why "the so-called measurement problem in quantum physics [as neurobiologist David Presti reminds us] has no agreed-upon even metaphysical interpretation."[24]

Change the scintillation of the thoughtforms and different universes and life forms spring into being, ones that take place beyond the frequency of matter and vibrate into representations with their own quark- and string-like particles. Each specific parameter value gives rise to its own conditions for existence.

The way to understand how Seth and a few others created the earth is to presume that they generated the *thoughtform* behind its planetary manifestation. They didn't raise a clay firmament in the middle of waters or divide the waters or gather an atmosphere. They set a frequency and dimensionality; the rest followed by natural and karmic law. If you read Genesis 1–31 closely, that is what God did too, not clay and nuclear fusion (light) but mudcakes and Atmic fields.

The Crisis of Consciousness

Humanity's noblest endeavor—not its crossbows and siege towers—up to the scientific revolution was to decipher thoughtforms and nature in tandem and make provisional holy books and keys. Once technocracy took over, the thoughtforms were not so much banished as put under their *own* lockdown thoughtform, which stripped them of rights, power, and their true nature. The result has been an outburst of violence, cruelty, and madness, because you can't hide a whole universe in a porcelain pitcher or a safe-deposit box. Of course, these same crimes and deliria took place in earlier times, but on a smaller scale and under different rubrics of society and selfhood.

Enormous thoughtforms are gathering now like thunderclouds across our planet, crying out for recognition: *"We are creating this. Recognize us. Absolve us. Recognize yourselves."* As long as we are mesmerized, we cannot act. We don't realize that materiality with its wonders is *both* inexhaustible and binding. Meanwhile the so-called "real" is burgeoning with crises of fixation, from opiate addiction to hyperconsumption, from industrial pollution to nuclear proliferation to mass shootings and executions, from human trafficking and sexual enslavement to savagery against children and animals. These cannot be derailed by rules or good intentions or even remedial acts; they can only be changed by the thoughtforms creating them.

The good news is, they are thoughtforms, so we *can* change them. If we change ourselves, we change the universe. That's a tall order, but it's the only order.

The crisis of consciousness is to recognize that its very existence *is* a crisis, for while its rational capacity has driven the evolution of culture and technology, that capacity has also decimated the environment—oceans, forests, soils, atmosphere—on which it depends for its survival. The only remedy is for consciousness to recognize its own depth, imaginative range, and capacity to transform from within.

As in any yoga, there is a hitch. When Seth proposed, "You create your own reality," he was widely misunderstood to have meant that we can control reality, and, if we do it well, we can get what we want. But we know we can't control reality. What he meant was, "You engage the outside world because it *is* you."[25] A little-recognized hinge, at the juncture of cosmography and epistemology, is: the world is the universe. We know no other, inside looking out or outside looking in. The Latin word *mundus* captured this meaning in all its mystery, hope, and homing.

The trick is that existence is not a mere fantasy; it can't be molded or finessed to suit our desires. The more we try to force events, the further we get from our actual agency. There are no guarantees or sure paths; entheogens and spiritual retreats provide openings but no warrant. That's how Creation works; finding its sweet spot is trying to remove a treble-barbed hook while eating a slice of watermelon or drinking a cold beer. The hook is self-inflicted and metaphorical, but sweetness is also a hook, as wind through trees and calls of gulls adorn a planet (or plane) of first love, a child's loneliness, a midsummer swim, and the loss of a loved one.

To truly bottom out All That Is is to recognize our presence flowing through a palpable but incomprehensible event *and that event*.

What Is Happening

What lies at the basis of this reality? Is it a presemantic intelligence? Or is it a thing, a mottle behind the evaporating materiality that underlies matter (or the predisposition toward matter imposed by gravity)? How did raw particles cobble thought? Did they ignite emergent properties of atoms and star systems or *invent* it for the first time ever out of innate complexity and system flow?

This is serious business for the lion as well as the goat because everything has to pass through its gate. In one universe, you're a "dead man walking" (or dead woman or being or beast). In the other, you were there at the beginning and you exist in some form forever.

Look again at "origin by Big Bang." Did a wee pinball pop out of a breach in nowhere and start ricocheting and agglomerating in gravity, as it fissioned into a measureless cosmos? Was the pinball packed with blueprints for alphabets, oceans, clouds, hogs, and evening gowns, or are they reverberations of a lucky bounce?

If intelligence was antecedent to the Big Bang—the only competing option in a space-time continuum—then the implosion was a shift of reflection in something already present, a *fata morgana* of dimensional tilt. There was no sequence of universes or multiverses nor quietudes between them—no intermission for cosmogenesis. Sacred sigils flowed through timeless catacombs as dark energy, dark matter—dark knowledge.

Gravity, heat, light, fission, and fusion—the expanding dispersion of energy and matter—emerge out of our collective intelligence along with nebulae in deep space, breezes off seas, schools of fish, and deer passing between copses. That means not only our *conscious* intelligence but also the unconscious intelligence of all beings in cosmic and spiritual planes, and the core universe itself—the translation of All That Is *into* All That Is, as each dimension expresses itself in the parameters of another.

In this scenario, the "Big Bang" is false "shock and awe" imposed by Earth's guardians, who have lost hope in their civilization or in the inherent repair of Creation. If it is rebranded as a Primal Flaring Forth, then the candle was sacred, votive, and wise. Its billion-plus-degree fire, malgré the slag it shed, was a Ground Luminosity, not an Improvised Explosive

Device. Maybe it was a hypnagogic onset, trillions of souls surging to a psychic commons to tell their tales.

Consciousness can effect just about anything, even a material universe that behaves materially.

What is happening is what *it looks like is happening*. Starry night is not only a mirage but also *a perfect mirage*: a phantasmagoria by its ephemeral nature, a spell because of its prolongation, an altar because of its capacity for transference, and an inertial field so powerful that it drives more proximal fields and galaxies by its zodiac. The universe knows that. Of course, it doesn't; it simply *is*, which is a more profoundly bottoming-out state.

The thoughtform visible through the Hubble telescope as myriad galaxies is being generated and transmuted this very moment by sentient beings, ourselves included; it is a residue of the creation and destruction of trillions of *tulpas* emanating from All That Is at the frequency and collective intelligence of spirits everywhere.

If the universe were real, it would be exactly the same as it is, so it *is* real and looks exactly like this, but *in a totally other way*. I'll leave Seth 2 the last words because he can bracket this matter from where he is, and I can't:

> [T]his dimension [e.g., source realm] nurses your own world, reaching down into your system. These realities are still only those at the edge of the one in which you have your present existence. Far beyond are others, so alien to you that I could not explain them. Yet they are connected with your own life, and they find expression even within the smallest cells of your flesh. . . .
>
> We do not understand the nature of the reality you are creating, even though the seeds were given to you by us. We respect it and revere it. Do not let the weak sounds of this voice confuse you. The strength behind it would form the world as you know it and sustain it for centuries.[26]

Amen.

Notes

Introduction

1. Question asked by Will Cloughley in "Quantum Physics and the Hard Problem," email posting, November, 13, 2018.
2. Robert Butts, quoted in Roberts, *The "Unknown" Reality, Volume Two,* p. 811.
3. Robert Butts, quoted in Roberts, *The "Unknown" Reality, Volume Two,* p. 812.

Chapter One
The Hole in the Materialists' Universe

1. Deacon, *The Symbolic Species,* p. 23.
2. Shteyngart, *Absurdistan,* p. viii.
3. Robert Butts, quoted in Roberts, *Dreams, "Evolution," and Value Fulfillment, Volume One,* p. 206.
4. Torres, *We the Animals,* p. 99.
5. Nagel, "Is Consciousness an Illusion?" p. 34.
6. Harris, "Opinionator."
7. Max Planck, quoted in Sullivan, "Interviews with Great Scientists VI: Max Planck," p. 17.
8. Deacon, *Incomplete Nature,* pp. 483–84.
9. Deacon, *Incomplete Nature,* p. 492.
10. Dennett, *Consciousness Explained,* p. 406.
11. Daniel C. Dennett, quoted by Nagel in "Is Consciousness an Illusion?" p. 32.
12. Larry Dossey, quoted in Laszlo, Houston, and Dossey, *What Is Consciousness,* p. 60.
13. Arnold, "Dover Beach," in *Dover Beach and Other Poems,* pp. 86–87.

14. Moffitt, *Awakening through the Nine Bodies,* p. 25.

15. Needleman, *The Heart of Philosophy,* p. 198.

16. Moffitt, *Awakening through the Nine Bodies,* p. 82.

17. Roberts, *Dreams, "Evolution," and Value Fulfillment, Volume One,* p. 206.

18. McClure, "Wolf Net," pp. 146–47.

19. Roberts, *Adventures in Consciousness,* p. 194.

20. Friedlander, "Interconnected Ecological and Etheric Body Workshop," 2012.

21. Staletovich, "Outrage over Shark-Dragging Video Deepens as New Pictures Surface."

22. Solomon, *The Noonday Demon,* pp. 21 and 20.

23. Darling, "Supposing Something Different," p. 4.

24. Robert Butts, quoted in Roberts, *The "Unknown" Reality, Volume One,* p. 92.

25. Orr, in a review of *Mind and Cosmos* by Nagel, p. 28.

26. Eccles, *The Human Psyche,* pp. 19–20.

27. McGinn, "Neuroscience and Philosophy," pp. 82–83.

28. Heisenberg, *Physics and Beyond,* p. 114.

29. Pinker, *How the Mind Works,* p. 146.

30. Penfield, *The Mystery of the Mind,* pp. 79–81.

31. Charles Richet, quoted in Kean, *Surviving Death,* p. 310.

32. Kean, *Surviving Death,* pp. 312.

33. Theodore Johannes Haarhoff, quoted in Kean, *Surviving Death,* p. 313.

34. Kean, *Surviving Death,* p. 313.

35. Maurice Barbanell, quoted in Kean, *Surviving Death,* 313.

36. Kean, *Surviving Death,* pp. 87–88.

Chapter Two
Reincarnation and Past Lives

1. Bernstein, *The Search for Bridey Murphy,* p. 133.

2. Bernstein, *The Search for Bridey Murphy,* p. 134.

3. Bernstein, *The Search for Bridey Murphy,* p 134.

4. Bernstein, *The Search for Bridey Murphy,* p. 134.

5. Bernstein, *The Search for Bridey Murphy,* p. 252.

6. Shroder, *Old Souls,* p. 22.

7. Bernstein, *The Search for Bridey Murphy,* pp. 43–44.

8. Bernstein, *The Search for Bridey Murphy,* pp. 143–44.

9. Bernstein, *The Search for Bridey Murphy,* p. 171.

10. Bernstein, *The Search for Bridey Murphy,* pp. 181–82.

11. Bernstein, *The Search for Bridey Murphy,* p. 183.

12. Shroder, *Old Souls,* p. 16.

13. Shroder, *Old Souls,* p. 17.

14. Shroder, *Old Souls,* p. 20.

15. Shroder, *Old Souls,* p. 89.

16. Shroder, *Old Souls,* p. 21.

17. Shroder, *Old Souls,* p. 21.

18. Shroder, *Old Souls,* p. 21.

19. Shroder, *Old Souls,* p. 22.

20. Shroder, *Old Souls,* pp. 15 and 89.

21. Shroder, *Old Souls,* pp. 102–3.

22. Bowman, "Why Don't Most People Consciously Remember Past Lives?"

23. Tucker, *Life before Life,* p. 149.

24. Stevenson, *Twenty Cases Suggestive of Reincarnation,* pp. 231–34

25. Tucker, *Life before Life,* p. 55.

26. Tucker, *Life before Life,* pp. 55–56.

27. Tucker, *Life before Life,* p. 58; Grayson, "Near-Death Experiences," p. 36.

28. Tucker, *Life before Life,* p. 57.

29. Tucker, *Life before Life,* p. 58.

30. Stevenson, *Twenty Cases Suggestive of Reincarnation,* p. 79.

31. Stevenson, *Twenty Cases Suggestive of Reincarnation,* p. 80.

32. Shroder, *Old Souls,* pp. 163–64.

33. Shroder, *Old Souls,* p. 163.

34. Shroder, *Old Souls,* p. 74.

35. Shroder, *Old Souls,* p. 50.

36. Shroder, *Old Souls,* p. 74.

37. Shroder, *Old Souls,* p. 70.

38. Shroder, *Old Souls,* pp. 56–57.

39. Shroder, *Old Souls,* p. 82.

40. Shroder, *Old Souls,* p. 81.

41. Shroder, *Old Souls,* p. 91.

42. Tucker, *Life before Life,* p. 9.

43. Tucker, *Life before Life,* p. 165.

44. Tucker, *Life before Life,* pp. 164–68.

45. Tucker, *Life before Life,* p. 2.

46. Tucker, *Life before Life,* p. 141.

47. Tucker, *Life before Life,* p. 142.

48. Tucker, *Life before Life,* p. 142.

49. Tucker, *Life before Life,* p. 30.

50. Tucker, *Life before Life,* p. 130.

51. Tucker, *Life before Life,* pp. 129–32 (for full account).

52. Tucker, *Life before Life,* pp. 52–53.

53. Kean, *Surviving Death,* pp. 54–79.

54. Kean, *Surviving Death,* p. 55.

55. Kean, *Surviving Death,* pp. 56–57, 70–72.

56. Kean, *Surviving Death,* pp. 75.

57. Kean, *Surviving Death,* pp. 57–58, 64, 73; Jim B. Tucker, "Reports of Past-Life Memories," in Presti, *Mind beyond Brain,* p. 60.

58. Kean, *Surviving Death,* pp. 56–57, 72–73.

59. Kean, *Surviving Death,* p. 61.

60. Kean, *Surviving Death,* p. 60.

61. Kean, *Surviving Death,* p. 61.

62. Kean, *Surviving Death,* p. 61.

63. Kean, *Surviving Death,* p. 69.

64. Kean, *Surviving Death,* p. 78.

65. Shroder, *Old Souls,* p. 93.

66. Shroder, *Old Souls,* p. 223.

67. Shroder, *Old Souls,* p. 120.

68. Kean, *Surviving Death,* pp. 75–76.

69. Kean, *Surviving Death,* p. 59.

70. Tucker, *Life before Life,* p. 94.

71. Shroder, *Old Souls,* p. 119.

72. Tucker, *Life before Life,* p. 120.

73. Tucker, *Life before Life,* p. 124.

74. Tucker, *Life before Life,* p. 123.

75. Tucker, *Life before Life,* p. 118.

76. Tucker, *Life before Life,* p. 39.

77. Tucker, *Life before Life,* p. 109.

78. Jung, "The Interpretation of Nature and Psyche."

79. Arthur Schopenhauer, quoted in Zabriskie, "Jung and Pauli: A Meeting of Rare Minds," p. 37.

80. Khatri, *136 Incredible Coincidences.*

81. Tucker, *Life before Life,* p. 32.

82. Tucker, *Life before Life,* p. 100.

83. Shroder, *Old Souls,* p. 72.

84. Tucker, *Life before Life,* p. 199.

85. Paul Edwards, quoted in Shroder, *Old Souls,* p. 36.

Chapter Three
Transdimensional Physics and Biology

1. Sacks, "Seeing God in the Third Millennium."

2. Reimann et al., "Cliques of Neurons Bound into Cavities Provide a Missing Link between Structure and Function."

3. Kripal, *Secret Body,* p. 232.

4. Kripal, *Authors of the Impossible,* p. 80.

5. Klimo, *Channeling,* pp. 61–62.

6. Jim B. Tucker, "Reports of Past-Life Memories," in Presti, *Mind beyond Brain,* pp. 50–51.

7. Kripal, *Secret Body,* p. 383.

8. Kean, *Surviving Death,* p. 50.

9. Stevenson, *Reincarnation and Biology.* This book comprises 2,200 pages in two volumes. Stevenson also wrote *When Reincarnation and Biology Intersect.*

10. Tucker, *Life before Life,* p. 68.

11. Upledger, *Cell Talk.*

12. Tucker, *Life before Life,* p. 72.

13. Jim B. Tucker, "Reports of Past-Life Memories," in Presti, *Mind beyond Brain,* p. 51.

14. Levine and van der Kolk, *Trauma and Memory.* See also Dias and Ressler, "Parental Olfactory Experience."

15. Ouspensky, *In Search of the Miraculous.*

16. Russell, *An Outline of Philosophy,* p. 171.

17. Dorn, *Recollections of Gran Apachería,* p. 16. See Grossinger, *The Night Sky,* pp. 291–96, for corresponding cosmogonies from Haiti, Japan, Finland, Tahiti, Africa, First Nations North America, and elsewhere.

18. Terrence W. Deacon, personal communication, email, 2015.

19. Deacon, "A Role for Relaxed Selection in the Evolution of the Language Capacity," pp. 742–43.

20. Deacon and Cashman, "Steps to a Metaphysics of Incompleteness," unpublished version.

21. Deacon, "Relaxed Selection and the Role of Epigenesis in the Evolution of Language," p. 731.

22. Deacon and Cashman, "Steps to a Metaphysics of Incompleteness," unpublished version.

23. Deacon, *Incomplete Nature,* p. 203.

24. Deacon and Cashman, "Teleology Versus Mechanism in Biology: Beyond Self-Organization."

Chapter Four
James Leininger or James Huston?

1. Leininger et al., *Soul Survivor,* pp. 3–5.

2. *The Telegraph,* "Is James Leininger Reincarnation of Second World War Fighter Pilot?"

3. Leininger et al., *Soul Survivor,* p. 55.

4. Leininger et al., *Soul Survivor,* p. 59.

5. Leininger et al., *Soul Survivor,* p. 16.

6. Leininger et al., *Soul Survivor,* pp. 110–11.

7. Leininger et al., *Soul Survivor,* pp. 33, 43.

8. Leininger et al., *Soul Survivor,* p. 105.

9. ABC *Primetime,* "Reincarnation: James Leininger."

10. ABC *Primetime,* "Reincarnation: James Leininger."

11. Leininger et al., *Soul Survivor,* p. 109.

12. Leininger et al., *Soul Survivor,* p. 106.

13. Leininger et al., *Soul Survivor,* pp. 68–70.

14. Leininger et al., *Soul Survivor,* p. 91.

15. Leininger et al., *Soul Survivor,* pp. 202–3.

16. Leininger et al., *Soul Survivor,* p. 214.

17. Leininger et al., *Soul Survivor,* p. 145.

18. Leininger et al., *Soul Survivor,* p. 146.

19. Leininger et al., *Soul Survivor,* p. 154.

20. Leininger et al., *Soul Survivor,* p. 170.

21. Tucker, *Life before Life,* p. 172.

22. Tucker, *Life before Life,* p. 173.

23. Tucker, *Life before Life,* p. 134.

24. Shroder, *Old Souls,* p. 17.

25. Leininger et al., *Soul Survivor,* p. 214.

26. Leininger et al., *Soul Survivor,* p. 217.

27. Leininger et al., *Soul Survivor,* p. 222.

28. Leininger et al., *Soul Survivor,* pp. 196–98.

29. Leininger et al., *Soul Survivor,* p. 249.

30. Leininger et al., *Soul Survivor,* p. 254.

31. Leininger et al., *Soul Survivor,* p. 255.

32. Leininger et al., *Soul Survivor,* pp. 225–26.

33. ABC *Primetime,* "Reincarnation: James Leininger."

34. ABC *Primetime,* "Reincarnation: James Leininger."

35. Daniel C. Dennett, quoted in Laszlo, Houston, and Dossey, *What Is Consciousness,* p. 52.

36. Larry Dossey, in Laszlo, Houston, and Dossey, *What Is Consciousness,* p. 74.

37. Eisenbud, *The World of Ted Serios;* Eisenbud, personal communication, 1972.

38. Eisenstein, "A State of Belief Is a State of Being," pp. 3–6

39. Carl Sagan, interview conducted by Richard Grossinger, *Earth Geography Booklet,* no. 3, p. 384.

40. Kripal, *Secret Body,* p. 360.

41. Eisenbud, interview conducted by Richard Grossinger, *Ecology and Consciousness,* p. 158.

42. Eisenbud, "Interview," *Ecology and Consciousness,* pp. 158–59.

43. Kripal, *Secret Body,* p. 379

44. Kripal, *Secret Body,* p. 388.

45. Kaufman, "A Religious Interpretation of Emergence," p. 919.

46. Betsy MacGregor, "Mom's Bird," unpublished story.

47. Betsy MacGregor, "Mom's Bird," unpublished story.

48. Betsy MacGregor, "Mom's Bird," unpublished story.

49. Tiso, *Rainbow Body and Resurrection,* p. 318.

50. Tucker, *Life before Life,* p. 211.

51. Shroder, *Old Souls,* p. 71.

52. Shroder, *Old Souls,* p. 253.

53. Roberts, *Adventures in Consciousness,* p. 117.

Chapter Five
Karma, Nonduality, and Meaning

I have drawn on John Friedlander's distinctions of duality and nonduality throughout this chapter. I am also grateful to reader Bhupendra Madhiwalla in Mumbai, who sent me his writings on karma in response to my earlier book *Dark Pool of Light.*

1. Suzuki, *Zen Mind,* p. 25.
2. I am grateful to Buddhist teacher Gary Buck for clarification on this concept.
3. Dustin DiPerna, *In Streams of Wisdom,* unpublished manuscript, 2013.
4. Camus, *Myth of Sisyphus and Other Essays,* p. 3.
5. Arthur Schopenhauer, "On Suicide," in *Works of Schopenhauer,* p. 437.
6. Roberts, *The "Unknown" Reality, Volume Two,* pp. 695-696.
7. This paragraph was reworded by me from several of John Friedlander's lectures.
8. Faulkner, *The Wild Palms,* p. 324.
9. Ferrante, *The Story of a New Name,* p. 289.
10. Friedlander, my edited transcription from a class, September 2011.
11. Friedlander, "beer hall" paragraph put together from three different classes, 2011–2014.
12. Friedlander, "The Big Picture: Joy, Meaning, and Luminosity Workshop."
13. Friedlander, unpublished CD of tele-class, *The Seven Planes of Consciousness,* August 15, 2007.
14. Friedlander, personal communication, 2013.
15. Friedlander, personal communication, 2013.
16. Friedlander, personal communication, 2013.
17. Friedlander, "mud run" material culled from five different classes, 2012–2015.
18. Friedlander, personal communication, 2013.

Chapter Six
The Universal Basis of Past-Life Memories

1. Cannon, *A Soul Remembers Hiroshima,* p. 43.
2. Cannon, *A Soul Remembers Hiroshima,* p. 43.
3. Cannon, *A Soul Remembers Hiroshima,* pp. 7–21.
4. Cannon, *A Soul Remembers Hiroshima,* p. 49.
5. Cannon, *A Soul Remembers Hiroshima,* p. 63.
6. Cannon, *A Soul Remembers Hiroshima,* p. 67.
7. Cannon, *A Soul Remembers Hiroshima,* p. 93.
8. Cannon, *A Soul Remembers Hiroshima,* p. 99.
9. Cannon, *A Soul Remembers Hiroshima,* p. 100.
10. Cannon, *A Soul Remembers Hiroshima,* p. 96.
11. Cannon, *A Soul Remembers Hiroshima,* p. 97.

12. Cannon, *A Soul Remembers Hiroshima*, p. 95.

13. Cannon, *A Soul Remembers Hiroshima*, p. 103.

14. Cannon, *A Soul Remembers Hiroshima*, p. 103.

15. Cannon, *A Soul Remembers Hiroshima*, p. 105.

16. Cannon, *A Soul Remembers Hiroshima*, pp. 105–6.

17. Cannon, *A Soul Remembers Hiroshima*, p. 106.

18. Roberts, *Adventures in Consciousness*, p. 90.

19. Cannon, *A Soul Remembers Hiroshima*, p. 107.

20. Cannon, *A Soul Remembers Hiroshima*, p. 56.

21. Cannon, *A Soul Remembers Hiroshima*, p. 107.

22. Cannon, *A Soul Remembers Hiroshima*, pp. 109, 112.

23. Cannon, *A Soul Remembers Hiroshima*, p. 119.

24. Cannon, *A Soul Remembers Hiroshima*, p. 111.

25. Cannon, *A Soul Remembers Hiroshima*, p. 117.

26. Cannon, *A Soul Remembers Hiroshima*, pp. 117–18.

27. Cannon, *A Soul Remembers Hiroshima*, p. 119.

28. Cannon, *A Soul Remembers Hiroshima*, p. 120.

29. Cannon, *A Soul Remembers Hiroshima*, p. 121.

30. Cannon, *A Soul Remembers Hiroshima*, pp. 122–23.

31. Cannon, *A Soul Remembers Hiroshima*, pp. 123–24.

32. Cannon, *A Soul Remembers Hiroshima*, pp. 124–25.

33. Cannon, *A Soul Remembers Hiroshima*, pp. 125–27.

34. Cannon, *A Soul Remembers Hiroshima*, pp. 128–29.

35. Cannon, *A Soul Remembers Hiroshima*, p. 45.

36. Cannon, *A Soul Remembers Hiroshima*, p. 47.

37. Cannon, *A Soul Remembers Hiroshima*, p. 130.

38. Roberts, *Adventures in Consciousness*, pp. 144, 127, 157.

39. Roberts, *The "Unknown" Reality, Volume Two*, p. 473.

40. Shroder, *Old Souls*, p. 239.

Chapter Seven
Cosmic Chicanery

1. Roberts, *Adventures in Consciousness*, p. 103.

2. Roberts, *Adventures in Consciousness*, p. 129.

3. Roberts, *Dreams, "Evolution," and Value Fulfillment, Volume One*, pp. 173, 169.

4. Poets House, Charles Stein, "Passwords: Gerrit Lansing."

5. John Visvader, personal communication.

6. See my earlier summary with references to the original discussions by Franz Boaz and Claude Lévi-Strauss in Grossinger, *Planet Medicine: Origins,* pp. 170–76.

7. Kripal, *Authors of the Impossible,* p. 52.

8. Kripal, *Authors of the Impossible,* p. 76.

9. Roberts, *Adventures in Consciousness,* p. 162.

10. Kagan, *The Afterlife of Billy Fingers.*

11. Kagan, *The Afterlife of Billy Fingers,* pp. 11–14.

12. Kagan, *The Afterlife of Billy Fingers,* p. 13.

13. Kagan, *The Afterlife of Billy Fingers,* pp. 150–52.

14. Kagan, *The Afterlife of Billy Fingers,* pp. 80–81.

15. Kagan, *The Afterlife of Billy Fingers,* pp. 168–69.

16. Kagan, *The Afterlife of Billy Fingers,* pp. 172–73.

17. Kagan, *The Afterlife of Billy Fingers,* pp. 175–77.

18. Kagan, *The Afterlife of Billy Fingers,* p. 179.

19. Kagan, *The Afterlife of Billy Fingers,* pp. 184–86.

20. Matthew McKay, *Jordan's Book of the Dead,* unpublished manuscript, 2019. Matt is a longtime colleague and friend, so I worked on his project as an editor, and some of that editing doubled into my text.

21. McKay, *Jordan's Book of the Dead.*

22. McKay, *Jordan's Book of the Dead.*

23. McKay, *Jordan's Book of the Dead.*

24. John Friedlander, transcription from a class, October 13, 2013.

25. Lonsdale, *Book of Theanna,* p. 24.

26. Lonsdale, *Book of Theanna,* p. 55.

27. Lonsdale, *Book of Theanna,* pp. 85–97.

28. Peter Ralston, spoken in a class, Cheng Hsin School of Internal Martial Arts and Ontology, Berkeley, Calif., 1993.

Chapter Eight
Trauma and Redemption

1. Light, *Angel of Auschwitz,* p. xi.

2. Light, *Angel of Auschwitz,* p. 24

3. Light, *Angel of Auschwitz,* pp. 27, 31

4. Light, *Angel of Auschwitz,* p. 28.

5. Light, *Angel of Auschwitz,* p. 29.

6. Light, *Angel of Auschwitz*, p. 125.

7. Light, *Angel of Auschwitz*, p. 48.

8. Light, *Angel of Auschwitz*, p. 73.

9. Light, *Angel of Auschwitz*, p. 56.

10. Light, *Angel of Auschwitz*, p. 56.

11. Light, *Angel of Auschwitz*, p. 55.

12. Light, *Angel of Auschwitz*, p. 102.

13. Light, *Angel of Auschwitz*, pp. 57, 69.

14. Light, *Angel of Auschwitz*, p. 57.

15. Light, *Angel of Auschwitz*, p. 120.

16. Light, *Angel of Auschwitz*, p. 91.

17. Light, *Angel of Auschwitz*, pp. 146–47.

18. Light, *Angel of Auschwitz*, p. 115.

19. Light, *Angel of Auschwitz*, p. 127.

20. Light, *Angel of Auschwitz*, p. 115.

21. Light, *Angel of Auschwitz*, p. 160.

22. Light, *Angel of Auschwitz*, p. 160.

23. Light, *Angel of Auschwitz*, p. 161.

24. Light, *Angel of Auschwitz*, pp. 168–69.

25. Light, *Angel of Auschwitz*, p. 170.

26. Light, *Angel of Auschwitz*, p. 171.

27. Light, *Angel of Auschwitz*, p. 164.

28. Light, *Angel of Auschwitz*, p. 175.

29. Winnicott, "Fear of Breakdown," pp. 103–7.

30. Manné, *Family Constellations*.

31. Reichard, *Navaho Religion*, p. xxxiv.

32. Eosastraios, "Theurgy, Theophany, and the Mundus Imaginalis."

33. Levine, *Healing Trauma*. I rearranged his spoken words from the audio of a talk he gave to keep with later conversations between the two of us.

34. Winnicott, "Fear of Breakdown," p. 103.

35. Roberts, *The "Unknown" Reality, Volume Two*, p. 366.

36. Tsoknyi Rinpoche, *Fearless Simplicity*, pp. 46–47.

37. Grossinger, *2013*, pp. 188–89.

38. Winnicott, "Fear of Breakdown," p. 103.

39. Winnicott, "Fear of Breakdown," p. 103.

40. Winnicott, "Fear of Breakdown," p. 104.

Chapter Nine
Worshipping the Algorithm

1. Deacon, *The Symbolic Species,* p. 460.
2. Larry Dossey, in Laszlo, Houston, and Dossey, *What Is Consciousness,* p. 53.
3. Sidney Schwab, Amherst Class of 1966 chatroom, Amherst College website, Amherst, Mass., 2016.
4. Sidney Schwab, Amherst Class of 1966 chatroom.
5. McKenna, *Dreaming Awake at the End of Time.*
6. Jeffrey Hoffman, personal conversation, 2017.
7. McKenna, *Dreaming Awake at the End of Time.*
8. Hedges, "A Message from the Dispossessed."
9. Charles Stein, journal note, June 6, 2016, posted on Facebook.
10. Morton, "Dawn of the Hyperobjects." See also Morton, *Hyperobjects.*
11. Morton, "Dawn of the Hyperobjects."
12. Morton, "Dawn of the Hyperobjects."

Chapter Ten
Personal Identity

1. Solomon, *The Noonday Demon,* p. 244.
2. Solomon, *The Noonday Demon,* p. 245.
3. Solomon, *The Noonday Demon,* pp. 245–46.
4. Roberts, *The Nature of Personal Reality,* pp. 14–15.
5. Wald, "Life and Mind in the Universe."
6. Vedral, "Living in a Quantum World," pp. 38–43; and Musser, "How Noise Can Help Quantum Entanglement."
7. Podgurski, *The Sacred Alignments & Dark Side of Sigils,* p. 36.
8. Roberts, *Dreams, "Evolution," and Value Fulfillment, Volume One,* pp. 127–29.
9. Roberts, *Adventures in Consciousness,* p. 122.
10. Roberts, *The "Unknown" Reality, Volume One,* p. 99.
11. Roberts, *Adventures in Consciousness,* p. 186.
12. John Friedlander, February 2015 workshop.
13. Kerouac, *Selected Letters,* vol. 2, pp. 7–8.
14. Koebler, "Elon Musk Says There's a 'One in Billions' Chance Reality Is Not a Simulation."
15. Loria, "Neil deGrasse Tyson Thinks There's a 'Very High' Chance the Universe Is Just a Simulation."

16. 2016 Isaac Asimov Memorial Debate. "Is the Universe a Simulation?" Remarks by Max Tegmark.

17. Andrew Lugg, quoted in Grossinger, *Embryos, Galaxies, and Sentient Beings,* p. 78.

18. Robert Butts, in Roberts, *The "Unknown" Reality, Volume Two,* p. 671.

19. Beckett, *Three Novels,* p. 219.

20. Gabbat, "Stephen Hawking Says Universe Not Created by God."

21. James Moore on Facebook, March 17, 2018.

22. Hawking, *The Universe in a Nutshell,* p. 57.

23. James Moore on Facebook, March 17, 2018.

24. Dyson, "Discussion on Metaphysics." The quote was transcribed and abridged by Will Cloughley.

25. Roberts, *The "Unknown" Reality, Volume Two,* p. 413.

26. Roberts, *Dreams, "Evolution," and Value Fulfillment, Volume One,* p. 171.

27. Lanza, "The Theory of Biocentrism."

28. Parmenides, Fragments 6 and 8, in Burnet, *Early Greek Philosophy,* pp. 261–62.

29. Kripal, *Secret Body,* pp. 200, 206. (italics mine)

30. Eiseley, *The Immense Journey,* p. 210.

31. Deacon, *The Symbolic Species,* p. 464.

32. McKay, *Jordan's Book of the Dead.*

33. Adi Da Samraj, *Crazy Wisdom,* apocryphal version of words cited in notes 34 and 35.

34. Adi Da Samraj, *Crazy Wisdom,* p. 17.

35. Adi Da Samraj, *Crazy Wisdom,* p. 17.

36. William Stranger, personal communication, September 2019.

37. Adi Da Samraj, *Crazy Wisdom,* p. 18.

38. Adi Da Samraj, *Crazy Wisdom,* pp. 18–19.

39. William Stranger, personal communication, September 2019.

40. Bubba Free John [Adi Da Samraj], *The Enlightenment of the Whole Body,* p. 564.

41. William Stranger, personal communication, September 2019.

Chapter Eleven
Multipersonhood

1. These paragraphs are from two classes of John Friedlander (2011 and 2014).

2. Roberts, *The "Unknown" Reality, Volume Two,* p. 472.

3. Roberts, *Adventures in Consciousness,* p. 119.

4. Roberts, *Adventures in Consciousness,* p. 95.

5. John Friedlander, workshop, February 14, 2014.

6. Roberts, *The "Unknown" Reality, Volume Two,* p. 530.

7. Roberts, *The "Unknown" Reality, Volume Two,* p. 480.

8. Roberts, *Adventures in Consciousness,* p. 118.

9. Roberts, *Adventures in Consciousness,* p. 95.

10. Roberts, *Adventures in Consciousness,* p. 120.

11. Roberts, *The "Unknown" Reality, Volume Two,* p. 358.

12. Roberts, *Adventures in Consciousness,* p. 124.

13. Roberts, *Adventures in Consciousness,* p. 186.

14. Roberts, *Adventures in Consciousness,* p. 117.

15. Roberts, *Adventures in Consciousness,* p. 136.

16. Harner, *Cave and Cosmos,* pp. 150–51.

17. John Friedlander, edited transcription from an undated class.

18. John Friedlander, edited transcription from an undated class.

19. John Friedlander, edited transcription from an undated class.

20. This section was edited by me from several of John Friedlander's undated classes.

21. John Friedlander, February 2015 workshop.

22. John Friedlander, Interconnected Ecological and Etheric Body workshop, 2012.

23. This section was reworded by me from several of John Friedlander's undated classes.

24. John Friedlander, Interconnected Ecological and Etheric Body workshop, 2012.

25. John Friedlander, Spring 2014 workshop.

Chapter Twelve
The Superconscious Source

1. Roberts, *The "Unknown" Reality, Volume Two,* p. 713.

2. Roberts, *The "Unknown" Reality, Volume Two,* p. 730.

3. Roberts, *The "Unknown" Reality, Volume Two,* p. 737.

4. Roberts, *The "Unknown" Reality, Volume Two,* p. 737.

5. Roberts, *The "Unknown" Reality, Volume Two,* p. 737.

6. John Friedlander, edited transcription from an undated class.

7. Roberts, *Adventures in Consciousness,* p. 103.

8. Roberts, *The "Unknown" Reality, Volume Two,* p. 727.

9. Roberts, *The "Unknown" Reality, Volume Two,* p. 715

10. Roberts, *Adventures in Consciousness,* p. 90.

11. Roberts, *The "Unknown" Reality, Volume Two,* p. 714.

12. Roberts, *Adventures in Consciousness,* 136.

13. Roberts, *Adventures in Consciousness,* pp.105–6.
14. Roberts, *The "Unknown" Reality, Volume Two,* pp. 648, 338.
15. Roberts, *The "Unknown" Reality, Volume Two,* p. 725.
16. Roberts, *Adventures in Consciousness,* p. 204.
17. Roberts, *The "Unknown" Reality, Volume Two,* p. 745.
18. Roberts, *The "Unknown" Reality, Volume Two,* p. 727.
19. John Friedlander, edited transcription from an undated class.
20. Roberts, *Adventures in Consciousness,* p. 64.
21. Roberts, *Adventures in Consciousness,* pp. 79–80.
22. Roberts, *The "Unknown" Reality, Volume Two,* p. 341; and Roberts, *Adventures in Consciousness,* pp. 200–203.

Chapter Thirteen
Undumbing the Universe

1. Roberts, *The "Unknown" Reality, Volume Two,* p. 344.
2. Roberts, *The "Unknown" Reality, Volume Two,* pp. 344–47.
3. See Gin, et al., "Challenger Crew Channeled," or watch the full press conference by FMBR, "Channeling the Challenger Astronauts."
4. Fernholz, "Jeff Bezos Explains How His Space Company Will Save Civilization."
5. John Friedlander, "etheric plane" insight taken from an undated class.
6. Szu-Whitney and Whitney, *Portals and Corridors,* p. 7.
7. Bob Frissell, personal communication, 1992. See also Frissell, *Nothing in This Book Is True, but It's Exactly How Things Are.*
8. Wolchover, "A Different Kind of Everything."
9. Wolchover, "A Different Kind of Everything."
10. Lanza, "The Theory of Biocentrism."
11. Henry, review of Robert Lanza, *Biocentrism.*
12. McIsaac, "Prominent Scientist Says Consciousness Is Key to a 'Theory of Everything.'"
13. Wald, "Life and Mind in the Universe."
14. Jeans, *The Mysterious Universe,* p. 137.
15. Planck, from a speech in Florence, Italy, "Das Wesen der Materie" (The Essence/Nature/Character of Matter), 1944.
16. Matloff, "Can Panpsychism Become an Observational Science?"
17. John Friedlander, Spring 2014 workshop.
18. Melville, *Moby Dick,* p. 302.

19. Roberts, *The "Unknown" Reality, Volume Two,* p. 798.

20. Roberts, *The "Unknown" Reality, Volume Two,* p. 665.

21. Roberts, *The "Unknown" Reality, Volume One,* p. 100.

22. Sartre, *The Reprieve,* p. 252.

23. John Friedlander, Spring 2014 workshop.

24. Presti, *Mind beyond Brain,* p. 145.

25. This insight is adapted from John Friedlander, undated class.

26. Roberts, *Adventures in Consciousness,* pp. 5, 7.

Bibliography

2016 Isaac Asimov Memorial Debate. "Is the Universe a Simulation?" April 5, 2016.

ABC *Primetime.* "Reincarnation: James Leininger." June 16, 2005. Posted by Unexplained Phenomena to YouTube on September 24, 2017.

Arnold, Matthew. "Dover Beach." In *Dover Beach and Other Poems.* Mineola, N.Y.: Dover Publications, 2012.

Beckett, Samuel. *Three Novels: Molloy, Malone Dies, The Unnamable.* New York: Grove/Atlantic, 2009.

Bernstein, Morey. *The Search for Bridey Murphy.* New York: Pocket Books, 1956.

Bowman, Carol. "Why Don't Most People Consciously Remember Past Lives?" Carol Bowman's Past Life Forum. Discussion started June 3, 2003.

Bubba Free John [Adi Da Samraj]. *The Enlightenment of the Whole Body.* Middletown, Calif.: The Dawn Horse Press, 1978.

Burnet, John. *Early Greek Philosophy.* London: A. and C. Black, 1908.

Camus, Albert. *Myth of Sisyphus and Other Essays.* Translated by Justin O'Brien. New York: Vintage International, 1991.

Cannon, Dolores. *A Soul Remembers Hiroshima.* Huntsville, Ark.: Ozark Mountain Publishers, 1993.

Cloughley, Will. Question asked in "Quantum Physics and the Hard Problem." Email posting, November, 13, 2018.

Darling, David. "Supposing Something Different: Reconciling Science and the Afterlife." *Omni* 17, no. 9 (1993).

Deacon, Terrence W. *Incomplete Nature: How Mind Emerged from Matter.* New York: W. W. Norton & Company, 2013.

———. "Relaxed Selection and the Role of Epigenesis in the Evolution of Language."

in *Oxford Handbook of Developmental Behavioral Neuroscience* edited by Mark Blumberg, John Freeman, and Scott Robinson. Oxford, England: Oxford University Press, 2011.

———. "A Role for Relaxed Selection in the Evolution of the Language Capacity" Paper delivered at colloquium titled "In the Light of Evolution IV: The Human Condition," December 10–12, 2009, Irvine, California. Proceedings of the National Academy of Sciences, direct submission, 2009, pp. 742–43.

———. *The Symbolic Species: The Co-evolution of Language and the Brain.* New York: W. W. Norton & Company, 1997.

Deacon, Terrence W., and Tyrone Cashman. "Steps to a Metaphysics of Incompleteness." Paper presented at Tucson Consciousness Conference and Center for Theology and Natural Science, Graduate Theological Unions, Berkeley, Calif., 2016, unpublished version.

———. "Teleology Versus Mechanism in Biology: Beyond Self-Organization." In *Beyond Mechanism: Putting Life Back into Biology,* edited by Brian G. Henning and Adam C. Scarfe. Lanham, Md.: Rowman & Littlefield, 2013.

Dennett, Daniel C. *Consciousness Explained.* Boston: Back Bay Books, 1992.

Dias, Brian G., and Kerry J. Ressler. "Parental Olfactory Experience Influences Behavior and Neural Structure in Subsequent Generations." *Nature Neuroscience* 17 (2014): 89–96.

Dorn, Edward. *Recollections of Gran Apachería.* Berkeley, Calif.: Turtle Island, 1974.

Dyson, Freeman. "3-Hour Discussion on Metaphysics (Sheldrake, Dennett, Dyson, Toulmin, Sacks, Gould, Kayzer)." Posted to YouTube on August 31, 2016, by What Do You Desire?

Eccles, John C. *The Human Psyche.* London: Routledge, 1992.

Eiseley, Loren. *The Immense Journey: An Imaginative Naturalist Explores the Mysteries of Man and Nature.* New York: Random House, 1959.

Eisenbud, Jule. Interview conducted by Richard Grossinger, January 8, 1972. Reprinted in *Ecology and Consciousness: Traditional Wisdom on the Environment,* edited by Richard Grossinger, Berkeley, Calif.: North Atlantic Books, 1992.

———. *The World of Ted Serios: Thoughtographic Studies of an Extraordinary Mind.* New York: William Morrow & Co., 1967.

Eisenstein, Charles. "A State of Belief Is a State of Being." *Network Review* 113 (Winter 2013).

Eosastraios, Fr. D. "Theurgy, Theophany, and the Mundus Imaginalis." Posted in the online blog *Spells of Art, Gnōsis, and Ritual,* September 30, 2012.

Faulkner, William. *The Wild Palms.* New York: Random House Vintage, 1964.

Fernholtz, Tim. "Jeff Bezos Explains How His Space Company Will Save Civilization." Quartz website, April 30, 2013.

Ferrante, Elena. *The Story of a New Name.* New York: Europa Editions, 2013.

FMBR. "Channeling the Challenger Astronauts." Posted by FMBRTV to YouTube on January 7, 2018.

Friedlander, John. "The Big Picture: Joy, Meaning, and Luminosity Workshop," 2012.

———. "Interconnected Ecological and Etheric Body Workshop," 2012.

Frissell, Bob. *Nothing in This Book Is True, but It's Exactly How Things Are.* Berkeley, Calif.: North Atlantic Books, 2019. First published 1994.

Gabbat, Adam. "Stephen Hawking Says Universe Not Created by God." *The Guardian* website, September 1, 2010.

Gin, Jerry, Mark Smith (ed.), and Ken Morley. "Challenger Crew Channeled." Challenger Crew Channeling website.

Grayson, Bruce. "Near-Death Experiences." In *Mind beyond Brain: Buddhism, Science, and the Paranormal,* edited by David E. Presti. New York: Columbia University Press, 2018.

Grossinger, Richard. *Dark Pool of Light: Reality and Consciousness.* Vol. 1. *The Neuroscience, Evolution, and Ontology of Consciousness.* Berkeley, Calif.: North Atlantic Books, 2012.

———. *Dark Pool of Light: Reality and Consciousness,* Vol. 2. *Consciousness in the Psychospiritual and Psychic Ranges.* Berkeley, Calif.: North Atlantic Books, 2012.

———. *Embryogenesis: Species, Gender, and Identity.* Berkeley, Calif.: North Atlantic Books, 2000.

———. *Embryos, Galaxies, and Sentient Beings: How the Universe Makes Life.* Berkeley, Calif.: North Atlantic Books, 2003.

———. *The Night Sky: Soul and Cosmos.* Berkeley, Calif.: North Atlantic Books, 2014.

———. *Planet Medicine: Origins.* Berkeley, Calif.: North Atlantic Books, 2005.

———. *2013: Raising the Earth to the Next Vibration.* Berkeley, Calif.: North Atlantic Books, 2010.

Harner, Michael. *Cave and Cosmos: Shamanic Encounters with Another Reality.* Berkeley, Calif.: North Atlantic Books, 2013.

Harris, Sam. "Opinionator." *New York Times,* September 7, 2014.

Hawking, Stephen. *The Universe in a Nutshell.* New York: Bantam Books, 2001.

Hedges, Chris. "A Message from the Dispossessed." Films for Action website, January 13, 2015.

Heisenberg, Werner. *Physics and Beyond.* Translated by A. J. Pomerans. New York: Harper & Row, 1971.

Henry, Richard Conn. Review of *Biocentrism: How Life and Consciousness are the Keys to Understand the True Nature of the Universe,* by Robert Lanza. Beyond Biocentrism website.

Jeans, Sir James. *The Mysterious Universe.* Cambridge, England: Cambridge University Press, 1930.

Jung, Carl G. "The Interpretation of Nature and Psyche." Translated from the German by R. F. C. Hull, edited by Violet S. de Laszlo. In *Psyche and Symbol.* Garden City, N.Y.: Doubleday, 1958.

Kagan, Annie. *The Afterlife of Billy Fingers: How My Bad-Boy Brother Proved to Me There's Life after Death.* Charlottesville, Va. Hampton Roads, 2013.

Kaufman, Gordon D. "A Religious Interpretation of Emergence: Creativity as God." *Zygon* 42 (2007).

Kean, Leslie. *Surviving Death: A Journalist Investigates Evidence for an Afterlife.* New York: Crown Archetype, 2017.

———. *UFOs: Generals, Pilots, and Government Officials Go on the Record.* New York: Random House, 2011.

Kerouac, Jack. *Selected Letters.* Vol. 2. *1957–1969.* New York: Penguin Books, 2000.

Khatri, Vikas. *136 Incredible Coincidences.* Delhi: Pustak Mahal, 2008.

Klimo, Jon. *Channeling: Investigations on Receiving Information from Paranormal Sources.* Berkeley, Calif.: North Atlantic Books, 1998.

Koebler, Jason. "Elon Musk Says There's a 'One in Billions' Chance Reality Is Not a Simulation: Elon Musk Firmly Believes Reality Is a Simulation Created by a Superintelligence." *Vice,* June 2, 2016.

Kripal, Jeffrey J. *Authors of the Impossible: The Paranormal and the Sacred.* Chicago: University of Chicago Press, 2010.

———. *Secret Body: Erotic and Esoteric Currents in the History of Religion.* Chicago: University of Chicago Press, 2017.

Lanza, Robert. "The Theory of Biocentrism." Science and Nonduality Conference, 2010.

Laszlo, Ervin, Jean Houston, and Larry Dossey. *What Is Consciousness: Three Sages Look behind the Veil.* New York: SelectBooks, 2016.

Leininger, Bruce, and Andrea Leninger, with Ken Gross. *Soul Survivor: The Reincarnation of a World War II Fighter Pilot.* Carlsbad, Calif.: Hay House, 2009.

Levine, Peter A. *Healing Trauma: Restoring the Wisdom of the Body* (audiobook). Louisville, Colo.: Sounds True, 2010.

Levine, Peter A., and Bessel A. van der Kolk. *Trauma and Memory: Brain and Body in a Search for the Living Past—A Practical Guide for Understanding and Working with Traumatic Memory*. Berkeley, Calif.: North Atlantic Books, 2015.

Light, Tarra. *Angel of Auschwitz*. Berkeley, Calif.: North Atlantic Books, 2009.

Lonsdale, Ellias and Theanna Lonsdale. *Book of Theanna: In the Lands that Follow Death*. Berkeley, Calif.: North Atlantic Books, 2011.

Loria, Kevin. "Neil deGrasse Tyson Thinks There's a 'Very High' Chance the Universe Is Just a Simulation." *Business Insider, December* 23, 2016.

Manné, Joy. *Family Constellations: A Practical Guide to Uncovering the Origins of Family Conflict*. Berkeley, Calif.: North Atlantic Books, 2009.

Matloff, Gregory L. "Can Panpsychism Become an Observational Science?" *Journal of Consciousness Exploration & Research* 7, no. 7 (2016).

McClure, Michael. "Wolf Net." edited by Richard Grossinger. In *Io 20, Biopoesis*, Plainfield, Vt., 1974.

McGinn, Colin. "Neuroscience and Philosophy: An Exchange." *The New York Review of Books* LX, no. 13 (August 15, 2013): 82–83.

McIsaac, Tara. "Prominent Scientist Says Consciousness Is Key to a 'Theory of Everything.'" *Epoch Times* website, July 27, 2015.

McKay, Matthew. *Jordan's Book of the Dead*. Berkeley, Calif.: North Atlantic Books, 2021. Publication plans, title, and date of publication are tentative.

McKenna, Terrence. *Dreaming Awake at the End of Time*. Lecture recorded by Sound Photosynthesis, San Francisco, December 13, 1998.

Melville, Herman. *Moby Dick*. New York: New American Library, 1961. First published 1851.

Moffitt, Phillip. *Awakening through the Nine Bodies: Explorations in Consciousness for Mindfulness Meditation and Yoga Practitioners*. Berkeley, Calif.: North Atlantic Books, 2017.

Morton, Timothy. "Dawn of the Hyperobjects." Posted to YouTube on June 16, 2011.

———. *Hyperobjects: Philosophy and Ecology after the End of the World*. Minneapolis: University of Minnesota Press, 2013.

Musser, George. "How Noise Can Help Quantum Entanglement," *Scientific American,* November 1, 2009.

Nagel, Thomas. Review of *From Bacteria to Bach and Back: The Evolution of Minds,* by Daniel C. Dennett. *The New York Review of Books,* March 9, 2017.

———. "Is Consciousness an Illusion?" *The New York Review of Books,* March 9, 2017.

Needleman, Jacob. *The Heart of Philosophy*. New York: Tarcher/Penguin, 1982.

Orr, H. Allen. Review of *Mind and Cosmos: Why the Materialist Neo-Darwininan Conception of Nature Is Almost Certainly False*, by Thomas Nagel. *The New York Review of Books*, vol. LX, no. 2 (February 7, 2013): 28.

Ouspensky, P. D. *In Search of the Miraculous*. Rev. ed. Boston: Mariner Books, Houghton-Mifflin, 2001.

Penfield, Wilder. *The Mystery of the Mind: A Critical Study of Consciousness and the Human Brain*. Princeton, N.J.: Princeton University Press, 1975.

Pinker, Steven. *How the Mind Works*. New York: W. W. Norton & Company, 1997.

Planck, Max. "Das Wesen der Materie" (The Essence/Nature/Character of Matter), 1944 speech in Florence, Italy.

Podgurski, Robert. *The Sacred Alignments & Dark Side of Sigils*. Louth, England: Mandrake Press, 2012.

Poets House. "Passwords: Gerrit Lansing," with Ruth Lepson, Kate Tarlow Morgan, Robert Podgurski, and Charles Stein. Poets House website, New York, March 16, 2019.

Presti, David E. *Mind beyond Brain: Buddhism, Science, and the Paranormal*. New York: Columbia University Press, 2018.

Prigogine, Ilya, and Isabelle Stengers. *The End of Certainty: Time, Chaos, and the New Laws of Nature*. New York: Free Press, 1997.

Reichard, Gladys. *Navaho Religion*. New York: Pantheon Books/Bollingen Foundation, 1950.

Reimann, Michael W., Max Nolte, Martina Scolamiero, Katharine Turner, Rodrigo Perin, Giuseppe Chindemi, Paweł Dłotko, Ran Levi, Kathleen Hess, and Henry Mankram, "Cliques of Neurons Bound into Cavities Provide a Missing Link between Structure and Function." *Frontiers in Computational Neuroscience*, June 12, 2017.

Roberts, Jane. *Adventures in Consciousness: An Introduction to Aspect Psychology*. Needham, Mass.: Moment Point Press, 1975.

———. *Dreams, "Evolution," and Value Fulfillment, Volume One*. San Rafael, Calif.: Amber-Allen Publications, 1997.

———. *The Nature of Personal Reality: Specific, Practical Techniques for Solving Everyday Problems and Enriching the Life You Know*. San Rafael, Calif.: Amber-Allen Publishing, 1994.

———. *The "Unknown" Reality, Volume One*. San Rafael, Calif.: Amber-Allen Publications, 1996.

———. *The "Unknown" Reality, Volume Two.* San Rafael, Calif.: Amber-Allen Publications, 1996.

Russell, Bertrand. *An Outline of Philosophy.* London: George Allen & Unwin, Ltd., 1927.

Sacks, Oliver. "Seeing God in the Third Millennium," *The Atlantic,* December 12, 2012.

Sagan, Carl. Interview conducted by Richard Grossinger. January 23, 1972, *Io,* no. 14 (*Earth Geography Booklet,* no. 3: Imago Mundi), Cape Elizabeth, Maine, 1972.

Samraj, Adi Da. *Crazy Wisdom* nos. 3, 8–9, August/September 1984 (special double issue).

Sartre, Jean-Paul. *The Reprieve.* New York: Bantam Books, 1960.

Schopenhauer, Arthur. "On Suicide." In *Works of Schopenhauer,* edited by Will Durant. New York: Simon & Schuster, 1931.

Shroder, Tom. *Old Souls: The Scientific Evidence for Past Lives.* New York: Simon & Schuster, 1999.

Shteyngart, Gary. *Absurdistan.* New York: Random House, 2007.

Solomon, Andrew. *The Noonday Demon: An Atlas of Depression.* New York: Scribner, 2001.

Staletovich, Jenny. "Outrage over Shark-Dragging Video Deepens as New Pictures Surface." *Miami Herald,* July 27, 2017.

Stevenson, Ian. *Reincarnation and Biology: A Contribution to the Etiology of Birthmarks and Birth Defects.* Westport, Conn.: Praeger, 1997.

———. *Twenty Cases Suggestive of Reincarnation.* New York: American Society for Psychical Research, 1966.

———. *When Reincarnation and Biology Intersect.* Westport, Conn.: Praeger, 1997.

Sullivan, J. W. N. "Interviews with Great Scientists VI: Max Planck." *The Observer,* January 25, 1931, 17.

Suzuki, Shunryu. *Zen Mind, Beginner's Mind: Informal Talks on Zen Meditation and Practice.* Trumble, Conn: Weatherhill, 1970.

Szu-Whitney, Monica, and Gary Whitney. *Portals and Corridors: A Visionary Guide to Hyperspace.* Berkeley, Calif.: Frog, Ltd., 1999.

Telegraph. "Is James Leininger Reincarnation of Second World War Fighter Pilot?" August 20, 2009.

Tiso, Francis V. *Rainbow Body and Resurrection: Spiritual Attainment, the Dissolution of the Material Body, and the Case of Khenpo A Chö.* Berkeley, Calif.: North Atlantic Books, 2016.

Torres, Justin. *We the Animals.* New York: Houghton-Mifflin/Mariner Books, 2012.

Tsoknyi Rinpoche and Ngawang Gyatso. *Fearless Simplicity: The Dzogchen Way of Living Freely in a Complex World*. Boudhanath, Hong Kong, Esby: Ranjung Yeshe Publications, 2003.

Tucker, Jim B. *Life before Life: A Scientific Investigation of Children's Memories of Previous Lives*. New York: St. Martin's Press, 2005.

Upledger, John. *Cell Talk: Transmitting Mind into DNA*. Berkeley, Calif.: North Atlantic Books, 2010.

Vedral, Vlatko. "Living in a Quantum World." *Scientific American* 304, no. 6 (2011), pp. 38–43.

Wald, George. "Life and Mind in the Universe." *International Journal of Quantum Chemistry,* March 12, 1984. Available on the Elijah Wald website, lecture delivered throughout the 1980s.

Whorf, Benjamin Lee. "The Punctual and Segmentative Aspects of Verbs in Hopi" and "An American Indian Model of the Universe." In *Language, Thought, and Reality*. Cambridge, Mass.: MIT Press, 1956.

Winnicott, D. W. "Fear of Breakdown," *The International Review of Psycho-Analysis* 1 (1974), pp. 103–7.

Wolchover, Natalie. "A Different Kind of Everything." *New Yorker* online, February 19, 2019.

Zabriskie, Beverley. "Jung and Pauli: A Meeting of Rare Minds." In *Atom and Archetype: The Pauli-Jung Letters, 1932–1958,* edited by C. G. Jung, Wolfgang Pauli, and C. A. Meier, and translated by David Roscoe. Princeton, N.J.: Princeton University Press, 2001.

Index

absence, organizational force of, 92–94
accessible DNA grid, 97
Adi Da, 227–31
Adi plane, 88
afterlife, messages from, 162–64
Akashic records, 90
Al-Danaf, Nazih, 54
algorithm, the
  and capitalism, 193–95
  as coming out of the algorithm, 187
  cult of, 187–91
  defined, 186
  dissemination of, 188
  distribution, 197
  God or Spirit and, 196
  marrying, to an international market, 195
  reinforcement of, 187–88
  science and, 186–87
  viscosity, 196–97
  worshipping, 186–98
animal consciousness, 25–27
animal totems, 118
Aristotle, 90–91, 92
Arkani-Hamed, Nima, 261
artificial intelligence (AI)
  as algorithmic intelligence, 187

all intelligence as, 20
  ethics and, 32–33
Astral plane, 85–86, 260
astrophysical subplanes, 260
Atmic plane, 87
autogene, 12–13, 97–98
awareness
  as mentation phase, 19
  nondual, 134
  of ourselves, 216

Barbanell, Maurice, 37
beingness, 25, 128, 130
Bernstein, Morey, 39–43, 45–47
Bezos, Jeff, 256–57
Big Bang
  characteristics of, 11
  defined, 10–11
  as false "shock and awe," 273
  inventory source, 220
  as random implosion, 223
  reality as beginning with, 156
  rescaling, 158
  in science explanation of universe, 1, 5–6
birthmark telekinesis, 80–81